ABORIGINAL VOICES
AND THE POLITICS
OF REPRESENTATION
IN CANADIAN
INTRODUCTORY
SOCIOLOGY
TEXTBOOKS

ABORIGINAL VOICES AND THE POLITICS OF REPRESENTATION IN CANADIAN INTRODUCTORY SOCIOLOGY TEXTBOOKS

JOHN STECKLEY

Canadian Scholars' Press Inc.

Toronto

Aboriginal Voices and the Politics of Representation in Canadian Introductory Sociology Textbooks
by John Steckley

First published in 2003 by
Canadian Scholars' Press Inc.
180 Bloor Street West, Suite 801
Toronto, Ontario
M5S 2V6

www.cspi.org

CSPI gratefully acknowledges financial support for our publishing activities from the Government of Canada through the Book Publishing Industry Development Program (BPIDP) and the Government of Ontario through the Ontario Book Publishers Tax Credit Program.

National Library of Canada Cataloguing in Publication Data

Steckley, John, 1949–
    Aboriginal voices and the politics of representation in Canadian introductory sociology textbooks / John Steckley.

Includes bibliographical references.
ISBN 1-55130-248-9

1. Indians of North America in textbooks—Canada. 2. Sociology—Textbooks. 3. Native peoples—Study and teaching (Higher)—Canada. I. Title.

HM578.C3S74 2003   305.897'071'0711   C2003-903701-0

Cover design by Susan Thomas/Digital Zone
Text design and layout by Susan Thomas/Digital Zone

03   04   05   06   07 08   7   6   5   4   3   2   1

Printed and bound in Canada by AGMV Marquis Imprimeur Inc.

ONTARIO ARTS COUNCIL
CONSEIL DES ARTS DE L'ONTARIO

THE CANADA COUNCIL | LE CONSEIL DES ARTS
FOR THE ARTS | DU CANADA
SINCE 1957 | DEPUIS 1957

Contents

Acknowledgments

THERE ARE MANY PEOPLE I would like to thank for helping me through this process. I begin with my thesis committee. First, Jamie-Lynn Magnusson took on the difficult task of supervising a stubborn person. I thank her for forcing me to read things I didn't want to read, for putting a lid on me when I would say things I shouldn't say, and for dealing, patiently, with my panic attacks. Secondly, I thank Linda Muzzin, whose detailed critical comments were incredibly useful in speeding this thesis on its way, and Laara Fitznor for her wise words about the use of words and for giving me the supreme compliment of saying I answered one question like an elder would. Berta Laden I especially thank for gently conveying an optimism that the process would be "completED." Nina Bascia met the challenge of dealing both with my thesis and my attitude. Finally, Jon Young saved my soul by joining the committee at a late date and helped the thesis process both with his kind words of praise and his astute questions.

I was fortunate to be in a program that is unique: the Community College Leadership program. It gives me many people to thank, including the "Cohortians," who helped me get through the initial stages. Roy Giroux and Mirella Cirfi Walton were invaluable help when I needed people in the program at Humber College. In the department, I would like to acknowledge Michael Skolnik and Charles Pascal (as well as Roy again) for developing a program that excited my interest.

The people I worked with at Canadian Scholars' Press are all to be thanked: Althea Prince for her early acceptance of the work and her enthusiasm for the project; Betsy Struthers for her detailed and diligent copy editing; and Rebecca Conolly for her patience with a Luddite.

Then there are my colleagues. First, I thank my writing partner, Bryan Cummins, whose editing made the thesis sharper, whose practice thesis questions in the Toby Jug gave me confidence, and whose support is always appreciated. Second, there are the "Humber doctors": Dr. Herman Suligoj, my long-time mentor, Dr. John Wilson, and Dr. Tom Olien, all of whom showed me that those who have walked the path before are the best guides. Then there are those colleagues who helped me keep my sanity: Mike Badyk and Robert Mills with their J.J. Muggs' meetings, the sociology cluster with their constant support, and my office mates, who put up with my ranting.

My sociology and anthropology students at Humber College were helpful as guinea pigs for trying out my ideas and are thanked for their concern about how I would do in my oral defence.

The members of my band I have to acknowledge for giving me an escape. Without them I don't know that I could have reached a stage in which "I will survive."

At home, there is my "pack." My dogs, Egwene and Cosmo, kept me close to the ground, even when it was only to pick something up. Finally, and most appreciated of all is my wife, Angelika Steckley, my biggest supporter.

CHAPTER ONE

Introduction

INTRODUCTION

Introductory sociology courses are taught in virtually all community colleges and universities in Ontario. These courses are usually presented either as one of the offerings in the general education package of electives from which students choose, or they are mandatory service courses in programs such as Nursing. While Aboriginal peoples are not always specifically mentioned in course outlines,[1] Aboriginal issues are usually included in some aspect of the course. Sociology textbooks in North America typically discuss Aboriginal peoples and Aboriginal issues at some point, usually in chapters dedicated to "race and ethnicity."[2] This includes all the textbooks researched for this study.

For community college introductory courses, the discussion of Aboriginal peoples in the classroom and in the material presented in textbooks are of particular importance because students rarely take other courses in sociology. The delivery of general education courses varies across the community colleges in Ontario, the system I know best. They differ as to the number of courses a student must take and what can be considered a "Gen-Ed" (or elective) course. It is important to recognize that college sociology courses are not progressive. To the best of my knowledge, there are no offerings of Sociology 100 and 200 in the Ontario community college system. Even though the sociology course is typically called "Introduction to Sociology," it is more accurate to state that it is a general survey of sociology, not a first step or introduction to be built upon later. I teach at Humber College, which has the most extensive general education package in this system, and we have no such progressive offerings. The same is true of service course sociology courses.

This increases the salience of the introductory sociology textbooks as a tool teaching about Aboriginal peoples, as it is extremely unlikely that an Ontario community college student will ever see another textbook that makes mention of Aboriginal peoples and Aboriginal issues. While some courses are offered in subjects such as "Contemporary Native Peoples," their frequency is considerably less than that of introductory sociology courses. In many cases, sociology courses provide the only opportunity in their academic career for community college students to grapple with controversial contemporary issues involving Aboriginal peoples. Experiences at the elementary school level are typically focussed on material aspects of traditional culture[3] more than issues per se, and secondary school classes in which issues could be taken up are few and far between. Look at the academic path taken in Ontario concerning what is termed "Native Studies." The following Ministry of Education document describes the common trail followed by Ontario students prior to Grade 9:

> In the elementary program, students compare cultures found within Canada, examine lifestyles from different geographic settings, and study the accomplishments of important people in Canada. The Grade 7 and 8 history and geography program emphasizes the partnerships and alliances between Aboriginal peoples within the Canadian nation during the final decades of the nineteenth century. (Ministry of Education, Ontario; 1999: 3)

From Grades 9 to 12, there are no mandatory courses in Native Studies in Ontario. The courses offered in the new curriculum (1999–2000) are the following. All are available to students who are taking courses that lead to community college:

> Grade 9: *Expressing Aboriginal Cultures*, a course providing "an overview of the various art forms used by Aboriginal peoples to communicate information about Aboriginal cultures."
> Grade 10: *Aboriginal Peoples in Canada*, which "highlights twentieth-century history and contemporary issues from an Aboriginal perspective."
> Grade 11: *Aboriginal Beliefs, Values, and Aspirations in Contemporary Society; Contemporary Aboriginal Authors; Current Aboriginal Issues in Canada.*
> Grade 12: *Aboriginal Governance—Emerging Directions; Aboriginal Issues in a Global Context.*
> (Ministry of Education, Ontario 1999)

While this seems to offer, in Grades 10 to 12, an opportunity for students bound for community college to take courses that relate to Aboriginal issues, it can safely be assumed that, in practice, relatively few such students have that opportunity. All these courses are optional, both for the student and for the school. The combination of reduced budgets and low local demand in most areas, as well as scarce teacher competence and comfort with teaching such a course, lowers the likelihood that students in most Ontario schools are able to take these courses.

This lack of coverage of Aboriginal peoples and issues prior to post-secondary education makes introductory sociology textbooks the main written sources for community college students concerning social issues related to Aboriginal peoples. This highlights the significance of the nature of how these books present information relating to Aboriginal peoples and issues.

THE STUDY
The Purpose of the Study

The purpose of this study is the development and application of a critical framework for the assessment of Aboriginal content in introductory sociology textbooks, one that can be used not only by sociology professors, textbook writers, and editors and publishers, but by college students as well—as engaging them in the framework involves important sociological lessons of problematizing texts. There is a strong need for such a framework, as, outside of Aboriginal scholars, writers, elders, and non-Aboriginal academics who specialize in "Native Studies," there is a tremendous ignorance of Aboriginal issues and Aboriginal peoples in the academy. It is often difficult for non-Aboriginal peoples to grasp the extent to which that ignorance exists. Years of experience as a "Native specialist" have taught me that hard lesson. The situation resembles in some ways the lack of awareness and information about women's history and issues, and the patriarchal framing of questions that existed prior to the feminist revolution of the 1960s and 1970s. I believe that the ignorance in this case is even greater.

The Corpus: 77 Canadian Introductory Sociology Textbooks

The texts to be analysed in this study are Canadian sociology textbooks used in community college and university introductory courses. Counting into the mix different editions of what I am calling individual "traditions," 77 books have been studied (see Appendix A). Most of the textbooks were generated with Canadian students as the target audience, while some are Canadian adaptations of American textbooks. I have excluded from my study American introductory sociology textbooks that have not been "Canadianized," regardless of their likelihood of adoption for Canadian courses.

In terms of format, some of these books are collections of readings often taken from other sources. Some have clearly defined chapters written by different authors; some are co-authored, and some have a single author. The books range in publication date from 1961 to 2002, with six coming from the 1960s, 14 from the 1970s, 28 from the 1980s, 24 from the 1990s, and five from the twenty-first century.

In terms of the writers and editors involved, the vast majority are both male and white. While up to the mid-1970s, a few contributors of articles (not chapters) were Aboriginal peoples, none of the writers of chapters or texts or the editors is Aboriginal.

The Three Issues Being Studied

The analysis of these textbooks concentrates on three issues: culturally determined Inuit elder suicide (CDIES), the potlatch, and the Oka confrontation of 1990 concerning Mohawk rights to land in Quebec. The reasons behind the choice of these three issues are as much personal as they are analytical. CDIES was chosen in part because I myself had reproduced the non-Aboriginal sociological/anthropological mistaken understanding on a number of occasions. It was only when I read a grossly exaggerated version of Inuit elder suicide (Henslin et al. 2001: 216) that I first asked myself, "How do I know that this story is true?" The discovery of the depth of this mistaken perception proved a great investigative adventure for me.

I have for a long time noticed the contradiction in sociological and Aboriginal stories about the potlatch, but this came to a head when I reread *Guests Never Leave Hungry: The Autobiography of James Sewid, A Kwakiutl Indian* (Spradley 1969), the book that introduced me to the potlatch as an undergraduate. I revisited this book as part of my research in writing about the potlatch for another work (Steckley and Cummins 2001). In so doing, I returned to a story that did not jibe well with what I was reading in introductory sociology textbooks. It was easy to see which version had the greatest validity.

The easiest to discuss is the Oka issue. As a writer of Huron history for the last 25 years, I am quite familiar with the history of the Mohawk. The two peoples have had a long history, sometimes conflicted, sometimes shared. A substantial number of Huron joined the Mohawk during the mid-1650s. I knew that, by not including Mohawk history, the writers of introductory sociology textbooks were missing key elements in the Oka story. In addition, exposure to Aboriginal sources of knowledge shortly after the Oka confrontation made me further aware of what was missing from the sociological version. Two years after the Oka confrontation of 1990, from 1992 to 1994, I had the privilege of having as a colleague, neighbour, and good friend, a Kahnawake Mohawk who taught me much about the oral tradition of the Great Law of Peace. Three years after Oka, I saw and started showing to my students an excellent video on the subject by Abenaki film-maker Alanis Obomsawin. From it, I learned a great deal about the contradictions between Aboriginal views and those of the mainstream media in their coverage of the Oka confrontation.

It should be pointed out that, not in a deliberate way, I have excluded topics that directly pertain to Métis and Non-status peoples. This is not to say that such topics are not of equal importance, nor that they are not also treated poorly by Canadian introductory sociology textbooks.[4] In the third chapter, I discuss the lack of input allowed to three important Métis writers (Howard Adams, Maria Campbell, and Emma Laroque). Silencing their voices means that Métis issues are not covered adequately in these texts.

TRADITIONAL TEXTBOOK ANALYSES CONCERNING ABORIGINAL PEOPLES

There are two ways in which textbooks have traditionally been analysed in terms of how well they discuss Aboriginal peoples and Aboriginal issues. One involves the presence or absence of "factual errors." In what follows, we will look at how such mistakes occur in terms of naming of peoples and their languages, and how those contribute to a negative stereotyping of Aboriginal peoples. Another way of analysing textbooks—and this resulted in the development of a sophisticated series of techniques—involves counting evaluative terms and assessing pictures.

"Factual" Accuracy

A common-sense notion of a critical approach to textbooks (one often included in the questions given to textbook reviewers by publishers) is the extent to which the works in question contain "factual errors." While, as will be argued below, there are severe limitations in such an approach (they only deal with obvious "sins of commission," not the subtler ones, nor with the equally perni-cious "sins of omission"), it is nonetheless important to point out that the textbooks studied often do present errors of a basic level that would not be excused in other areas of study. To a certain extent, this is because the writers and editors of Canadian intro-ductory sociology textbooks are, with one exception (Linda Gerber), not people who can be considered "Native experts." Their expertise is elsewhere. This seems to indicate that the same is true of the sociology teachers who review the manuscripts prior to publication of a new or revised textbook. It should also be noted that the books do not get more accurate with time. New textbooks are not much better than the old ones in this regard.

The basic level of the errors is indicative of the lack of expert-ise. Sometimes these mistakes are errors of naming. For instance, Brym (2001) states that "people who were defined by Europeans as Sarcee Indians for most of this century renamed themselves the Siksika nation" (Brym 2001: 217). Siksika (which means "Black Foot") is the name for the people known in English as Blackfoot, the neighbours and historic allies (in the Blackfoot Confederacy) of the Sarcee. The language of the Sarcee is unre-lated to Blackfoot. The people usually refer to themselves as Tsuu T'ina ("Earth People"; Steckley and Cummins 2001: 97).

In *Sociology: An Introduction: First Canadian Edition*, by Richard T. Schaefer, Robert P. Lamm, Penny Biles, and Susannah J. Wilson, it was written that: "The Northwest Territories—where there is a very large Innu population—have ten times the rate of sexually transmitted diseases of any province" (1996: 330). The Innu is a term meaning "people, men" in the Algonquian languages of the First Nations referred to in the early historical and anthropological literature (and still sometimes today) as the Montagnais and the Naskapi. Their communities are situated in Labrador and on the east coast of Quebec. The authors might have confused "Innu" with the visually similar but unrelated term "Inuit," a term meaning "men, people" in Inuktitut (the language of the Inuit). My students have often made this mistake.

Metta Spencer shows a similar lack of understanding of Inuktitut terms with her consistent use of the ungrammatical term "Inuits" (1981: 294; 1996: 378), also a mistake my students often make. Inuit is a plural term. The singular term is Inuk.

Similar to these naming errors are ones made in reference to the terms for Aboriginal languages and language families. This is an especially sensitive issue with me because I have worked for almost 30 years in this field; I twice taught the Aboriginal languages course in the Native Studies program at Laurentian University. Knowing the names of Aboriginal languages and language families is as basic to that course, and to student knowledge, as knowing who Durkheim is to students of introductory sociology. In Henslin and Nelson (1996), for example, we read that:

> [T]here are over 50 indigenous languages, which are generally grouped into a dozen linguistic families: Algonkian, Athapaskan, Beothukan, Chinookan, Haidan, Iroquoian, Kootenayan, Salishan, Siousan, Koluschan, Tsimshian, and Wakashan. Beothukan and Chinookan are now extinct. Of the rest, only Algonkian, Athapaskan, Salishan, Siousan, and Inuktitut have escaped being classified as "endangered"

that is, only they [i.e., they are only] are spoken by more
than 5,000 people. (Henslin and Nelson 1996: 334)

The errors here are several. For example, "Chinookan" is not
a language family. The "Chinook" language belongs to the
Penutian family, a living language family not found in Canada
but in the Western United States. The trade jargon "Chinook,"
used in the nineteenth century as a *lingua franca* for communications between Europeans and Aboriginal peoples who were
native speakers of a diversity of languages and made up of a
simplified Chinook base, with Nootka, French, and English
words added, is extinct. The language family misspelled as
"Siousan" is really "Siouan." I do not know where the term
"Koluschan" comes from. Judging from its position in the alpha-
betized list, I suspect that the authors were trying to refer to the
language isolate "Tlingit." Inuktitut, not included in the list, but
discussed in the sentence following the listing, belongs to the
Eskimo-Aleut language family.

Further, it is indicative of more serious problems with how
Aboriginal issues are presented in introductory sociology textbooks that "the sociological issue" about Aboriginal languages
is usually that they are becoming extinct, never that the people
have been developing innovative programs to fight that potential extinction.

More problematic than the citations above are errors that
paint a more negative picture of Aboriginal peoples than would
be represented by a more accurate statement. This is especially
true when the inaccurate statements support the notion that "the
Indians were warlike and were killing each other off anyway,"
an untenable notion that can and has been used to try to lessen
the impact of the interrogation of the colonialist/racist policies
of Canadian governments and settlers, past and present.
Certainly, I have often heard my students come up with statements that reflect this notion, (mis)informed by their elementary
and secondary school education.

Two examples of this type of error will illustrate my point. One consistently appears in two editions of Lundy and Warme's *Sociology: A Window on the World* (1986 and 1990) and repeated in the third edition, which they published in 1994 with a third editor, Elinor Malus. It is contained in the following quotation that reproduces the ill-founded opinion of a questionable source:

> By 1800 the Beothuk population of Newfoundland had reached a critical point. Increased settlement had upset the delicate balance of their nomadic way of life and they were being indiscriminately slaughtered by the whites and their Micmac fur-trade allies, who were encroaching on Beothuk territory. Evidence suggests that about this time three or four hundred Beothuk were herded onto a point of land near their favourite sealing-site and shot down like deer. (Such 1973: vii, as quoted in Lundy and Warme 1986: 174)

Here Lundy and Warme reproduce through novelist Peter Such two myths that have never been substantiated. One is the "Hant Harbour Massacre" (i.e., the killing of 300 to 400 Beothuk). Other than the fact that there is no evidence supporting this story, the alleged incident is supposed to have taken place at a time when it is now generally believed there were about 200 Beothuk left. And no community with a population of the 300 to 400 supposedly killed would have existed during the time of Beothuk/European contact. Beothuk culture could not have supported a population this large.

Potentially more destructive is the reproduction of the myth (known as the "Mi'kmaq Mercenary Myth") that the French hired the Mi'kmaq to kill off the Beothuk. I suspect that the popularity of this idea among English writers of the nineteenth century came from the fact that it passed the blame for the extinction of the Beothuk into the non-English hands of the French (who had fought the English during the seventeenth and eighteenth centuries in Newfoundland) and their Mi'kmaq allies. There is no evidence that directly supports the contention of an antagonistic relationship between the French and the Beothuk. The French made sporadic, but failed, attempts to trade with the Aboriginal peoples of the island of Newfoundland (see Marshall 1996: 53; and Howley 1974: 20), but limited as they were to the west coast and the extreme north of the island (west and east), they had little contact with the Beothuk, who lived inland and went to sea at that time by the east coast south of French-claimed territory. They had no "good" reason to want the Beothuk out of the way. The English-speaking settlers, whose territory on the east coast significantly intersected with that of the Beothuk, had much greater cause. Further, the Mi'kmaq were more independent players on the historical stage than they are credited for by these English writers (Steckley 1999: 102–03). They were far from being the hired guns or lackeys of the French as some early writers made them out to be.

The main danger of this misrepresentation is that it casts unwarranted aspersions on the Mi'kmaq of Newfoundland. The reproduction of this story in history textbooks, as well as in Lundy and Warme's works, may hinder the struggle that the Mi'kmaq have had (and still have) for recognition of their rights in that province.

Perhaps more damning in its implications for the present is the factually inaccurate statement made by Johnstone and Bauer (1998) concerning "genocide" and the fate of two Southern Ontario First Nations:

> There have been examples of genocide in North America. In Southern Ontario, at least two Indian nations, the Neutrals and the Tobacco Indians, were wiped out largely as a result of the military efforts of other Indian nations. And in the United States, many Indians were massacred in pursuit of the American policy of *manifest destiny*, the belief that white people were given dominion over North America as a result of divine intervention, and were thus justified in removing the Indian nations. (Johnstone and Bauer 1998: 75)

There is a great deal that is wrong about this passage. At the more subtle level, it discounts the role of the French and the English in escalating traditional small-scale warfare, and it promotes the dubious idea that "We" (white Canadians) were somehow kinder and gentler to, and more respectful of, "our Indians" than were the Americans. The obvious case of the extinction of the Beothuk does not support this view. More concretely, it is simply inaccurate. The Tobacco or Petun (with the Huron and some Neutral as well) became the people known historically and currently as the Wyandot. They still survive as "tribal" communities, both in Kansas and in Oklahoma.

This inaccurate statement about the extinction of the Tobacco and Neutral affects student knowledge concerning the people that it implicates (even though they are not directly mentioned): the Mohawk. It is a feature of the teaching of history in elementary school Canada that students are taught that in the 1640s and early 1650s, the Mohawk and the other member nations of the Iroquois Confederacy defeated the Petun, the Neutral, and their Huron neighbours. It is one of the most well-known (if that term can ever be used to talk about Aboriginal history in Canada) of any event in Canadian history. Less well-known is the fact that these three peoples were not killed off. Some joined the Mohawk and other Iroquois, and some led a future independent existence elsewhere, either as the Huron of Lorette in Quebec or as the Wyandot. The defeat of the three peoples has often been upgraded in the past, in textbook and classroom, to a total "genocide." Students coming into my classroom have often told me that that is what they learned in Grade 6. Grade 6 teachers in southern Ontario to whom I have spoken have told me that the textbooks they use often lead their students (and them) to believe in that notion. Already possessing that misinformation, and having it reinforced by a post-secondary textbook, contributes to a student believing in the essentialized Mohawk Warrior image that interferes with student understanding of the Oka situation.

Counting Evaluative Terms

More sophisticated techniques than merely looking for factual errors have been used in Canada since the 1960s to appraise textbooks that present information concerning Aboriginal peoples. A number of approaches were tried, but the method that came to dominate was that applied by David Pratt (Pratt 1971; Pratt and McDiarmid 1971). Pratt employed quantitative measures such as calculating the ratio of favourable to unfavourable evaluative terms and the number of times key characteristics are shown in pictures. His focus was on primary and secondary school textbooks. This approach, not unexpectedly, revealed that these textbooks did not do an equitable job of presenting Aboriginal peoples to students at these levels of education. In fact, the presentation was generally negative.

How useful is this approach when applied to introductory sociology textbooks? They do have a limited use. Some of these books do have unthinking, negative portrayals such as the following from Rodney Stark's *Sociology*, an American textbook published in 1987. Negative evaluative terms, such as Pratt picks out, are in italics. Not surprisingly, this passage also contains factually inaccurate statements, which are discussed in the notes:

> Let's return to 1862, to the western prairies of North America. Many Indian tribes still move across their ancestral hunting grounds in pursuit of the great buffalo herds. Each tribe is quite small, often having no more than 1,000 members.[5] Each small tribe holds *strongly negative*[6] beliefs about the other tribes, and *conflicts* among tribes are frequent. However, all of the Plains tribes reserve their greatest *contempt* and *hatred* for the Utes,[7] who live in the foothills of the Rockies. The Utes have darker skins than the other tribes, and they are universally *loathed* and described as *ugly*. Everyone thinks it natural to *kill* Utes whenever possible. Meanwhile, white settlers are moving onto the plains. They cannot tell one tribe from another,

and to them all Indians are *savages, thieves, drunkards,*
and *dangerous killers.*[8] In time they begin to say that the
only good Indian is a dead Indian. (Stark 1987: 276;
emphasis mine)

However, despite such extreme claims, which do appear from
time to time in the sociological literature I examined, I usually
found that sociology textbook writers were typically knowledgeable enough not to use such gross stereotypical portrayals.
A discussion of the harmful effects of stereotyping and the use
of negative evaluative terms is standard fare in an introductory
sociology textbook.[9] I argue that the negatively evaluative terms
and pictures have been reduced by a kind of "politically correct
tinkering" that does not fundamentally change what is wrong
with the textbooks. This tinkering "looks good" (or at least
better) in Pratt's type of analysis, but the basic flaws of introductory sociology textbooks are invisible to Pratt's quantitative
radar. So much of what is wrong with Canadian introductory
sociology textbooks in their discussion of Aboriginal peoples
involves what they don't say, the questions they don't ask, the
answers they never think of, the sources they don't cite, and the
voices they do not listen to or allow to speak.

Looking at Pictures

Pictures are a somewhat different matter than words. It is not
unusual to find pictures in introductory sociology textbooks that
portray negative images of Aboriginal peoples and in so doing
reinforce stereotypes. An illustrative example is provided by
pictures portraying life on a reserve. Karen Anderson, under the
caption, "Living conditions on a reserve in northern Manitoba.
Poverty has become the norm among many Native communities," shows a picture of two Aboriginal children in a crowded,
dirty room full of old mattresses and piled-up clothes (Anderson
1996: 424). The picture undermines Anderson's position and

unintentionally reinforces the government's assimilationist view as accurate, a view that Anderson intends to critique:

> Over the past 125 years, Canadian governments have remained strongly committed to a policy of assimilation and civilization. The prevalence of poverty has been considered central to Native problems, and only the elimination of poverty will alleviate the situation. To facilitate this, governments have encouraged Native people to move off the reserves, which they see as breeding grounds for violence, poverty, and apathy, and to get exposure to "modern" values, institutions, and culture. (Anderson 1996: 424)

The discussion that follows in her text (below), when coupled with the negative depiction in the picture, fails to adequately present an alternative portrayal of life in at least some reserves (which, as we will see in Chapter Three, is a general failing of introductory sociology textbooks). She assumes that Aboriginal peoples reject the government's assimilationist position, but she does not allow them to put concrete substance to an alternative view of reserves. A positive picture could have helped in that regard:

> But Native leaders vociferously reject their people being labelled as social problems and the easy solution of calling in "experts" to analyze the situation. Moreover, they reject the idea that Native cultures and values are an impediment to security and to a satisfying life. Native cultural values, they insist, must be retained because they provide valuable sources of identity as well as a basis for community renewal. (Anderson 1996: 425)

That Aboriginal peoples are "always protesting about something," a stereotype that a good number of my community college students have introduced into discussions and into written assignments, is reinforced by pictures found in some introductory sociology textbooks (see Schaefer et al. 1996: 174). Macionis and Gerber, for example, show Aboriginal peoples protesting. The caption reads:

> Canada's Native peoples have long been seeking self-determination, a struggle that has been more prominent in the media in recent years but, in fact, has been going on throughout Canada's history. A sign in this protest on Parliament Hill hints at the frustration over another failed attempt at resolution. (Macionis and Gerber 2002: 362)

The caption and the surrounding discussion fail to contextualize sociologically the impact of the media's (and the textbook's) use of such pictures.

The most significant example of this use of pictures to reinforce stereotypes occurs with respect to the use of photographs of Mohawk Warriors in the confrontation at Oka. (This will be discussed in Chapter Seven.) Again, no attempt is made by the authors using such pictures to talk about the impact of the image, both in the media and in the textbooks.

A discussion of the use of pictures in introductory sociology textbooks, although it can lead to insights, does not provide sufficient material for a thorough investigation of how Canadian introductory sociology textbooks fail in their presentation of Aboriginal peoples. Much more is required.

Beyond the Factual and the Evaluative

What I am proposing in this study goes beyond the search for factual errors and the quantification of negative evaluative terms and pictures that reinforce stereotypes, although these methods can be used, as we have seen above, to show some sense of the inadequacy of the texts in their representation of Aboriginal peoples. Sociology and its sister Western social science of anthropology have produced knowledge about Aboriginal peoples that is regularly reproduced in introductory sociology textbooks, books that teach the canon of sociology when it comes to Aboriginal peoples and Aboriginal issues. I will demonstrate that, in the standard process of producing and reproducing this canon, the writers and editors of these textbooks silence or marginalize Aboriginal voices, not allowing for Aboriginal epistemology—a "Native sociology"—to have an impact on the books and ultimately upon the students who take the introductory courses and read the introductory textbooks. In so doing, these writers and editors are missing vital elements of what should be told.

This is a project in the sociological treatment of the understanding of those who are "others" to the writers of introductory sociology textbooks. The overwhelmingly predominant social location of the writers of these books is White and male. This project is similar in some senses to those undertaken by feminist sociologists and sociologists of colour, both of whom are not generally involved in the production of these texts. Yet, it is important to realize that this study is also unique to the subject matter. The oppression of Aboriginal peoples has unique characteristics, and feminist sociologists and sociologists of colour have reached a critical mass of numbers and influence in the discipline of sociology that has no parallel among Aboriginal scholars.

PERSONAL LOCATION AND THIS RESEARCH PROJECT

With a research project of this type, the location of the researcher in terms of important social factors such as race, ethnicity, class, and gender is a significant consideration. My location in this project can be considered to be problematic on the surface. I am male, non-Aboriginal, and middle class, so I share to some extent some of the influences that negatively affect the majority of the writers of Canadian introductory sociology textbooks.

My academic background, too, is a relevant component of my location. As an undergraduate, I took several courses in sociology, and, as a college professor, I have taught introductory courses in sociology, off and on, for 15 years, so I have been strongly influenced by the discipline. My BA and MA are in anthropology, which is the main course that I teach at the college level.

I believe that it is important in looking at the location of a researcher not to see people merely in terms of binary oppositions, such as Aboriginal/non-Aboriginal. A number of Aboriginal writers have cautioned against the simple-minded application of this binary (Manuel and Posluns 1974: Chapter 4, "We Honour Our Grandfathers Who Kept Us Alive" and Chapter 5, "Scratching for a Start"). More recently, and extensively, Mohawk/Michel First Nation postmodernist writer and educator Sharilyn Calliou has dealt with the subject in her insightful article "Us/Them, Me/You: Who? (Re)thinking the Binary of First Nations and Non-First Nations" (Calliou 1998):

> I do know that the emphasis is often exclusively political, without attention to other aspects of interactions—including those who assisted the rightness of justicemaking. Representational text teaches much about the oppressors, generally, generically groups; but the role models (e.g., former Justice Berger, former Justice Alf Scow) who modeled and nurtured truthtelling and collaboration are lesser known. When we don't know our heroes we become impotent. (Calliou 1998: 15)

On this point, I refer to Henry Giroux's concept of "border pedagogy":

> [T]here is no single, predetermined relationship between a cultural code and the subject position that a student occupies. One's class, racial, gender or ethnic position may influence but does not irrevocably predetermine how one takes up a particular ideology, reads a particular text, or responds to particular forms of oppression. Border pedagogy recognizes

that teachers, students, and others often "read and write culture on multiple levels." (Giroux 1997: 150, quoting from Kaplan 1987: 87)

Essentialism is a flawed belief in "unchanging human characteristics that are uniform and stable within a certain category and impervious to social context or historical modification" (Fleras and Elliot 1999: 434). In other words, "All x are alike; they speak with one voice. When you see/hear one x, you have seen/heard them all."

To consider me as being "totally non-Aboriginal" or even a "typical non-Aboriginal" is to essentialize my identity so as to misread me intellectually. Aboriginal epistemology has had a profound effect on how I think, do research, and write. The primary component of that epistemology for me has been my exposure to, and work with, Aboriginal languages.

In the fall of 1971, I went to what was then called the Indian Friendship Centre to find someone to teach me the Ojibwe language. There, I met Ojibwa Elder Fred Wheatley, who was offering a course in the language once every week, for roughly a school year. He had intended his teaching to be for Ojibwa youth, but he ended up with a mixed group of non-Aboriginal students. Despite the original intent of his course, I always felt welcome in his circle of knowledge and teaching. He taught me a number of key lessons, among them that no matter how many words of English I knew, I would never be able to express much of what I thought without the Ojibwe language, a lesson I later transferred to my study of the Huron language. Every course I teach at Humber College reflects that idea. My students are exposed to different concepts through the medium of words in Ojibwe, as well as Huron and a number of other Aboriginal languages.

Wheatley also taught me the importance of Aboriginal languages to the people who speak them. Following his teachings, in 1974, I began studying the Huron language. Since that time, I have published more than 70 articles in which Aboriginal languages such as Huron, Ojibwe, Mi'kmaq, and Mohawk were vital knowledge production tools. I have also composed prayers and translated and composed names in Huron and Wyandot. Recently, I translated the culturally important Thanksgiving Address or The Words Before All Else into Huron from English and Mohawk.

Since my classes with Fred Wheatley, I have learned from a number of elders, both in listening to their teachings and reading what they have written. This has had an impact not only on what I write and teach, but also in how I live.

This being stated, there is still, of course, a tension in being a non-Aboriginal writing about Aboriginal peoples. I have seen a good number of my non-Aboriginal contemporaries leave the field, and one major reason for that is this tension. My location challenges me constantly to decide what I think is appropriate for me to write and where I might be appropriating voice. Being a non-Aboriginal in the field of Aboriginal studies demands no less. On the other hand, in my experience it seems to me that non-Aboriginal members of the academy are much more worried (or even disdainful) about what I do than Aboriginal peoples are. A classic example of this occurred with my first attempt to publish my book, *Beyond Their Years: Five Native Women's Stories*. A publisher, who eventually rejected my manuscript, said publication depended on government funding, a not unusual precondition. An Aboriginal woman reviewed the manuscript and was so positive that she stated that she looked forward to reading it published as a book. Her review was in stark contrast to the nasty comments that came from the other reviewers. Although they did not locate themselves, it was clear from their comments, and from their ignorance of things Aboriginal, that they were non-Aboriginal women. They were clearly affronted by a White man writing about Aboriginal women and could not get past that idea in their review.

When I was adopted by the Kansas Wyandot in 1999, I was given the name "Tehaondechoren," meaning "He splits the country in two." My adoptive mother explained to me that in her mind this name connoted that I stood in two countries, one Aboriginal, one non-Aboriginal, and that my role was to explain to those in the latter country what I knew about the former. I see that as being different work from that of Aboriginal academics, whose main task, it seems to me, is to strengthen the Aboriginal world with their scholarship and more secondarily to explain it to the outsiders.

Using the Term "Aboriginal"

At this point, it is necessary to say a few words about choosing the term "Aboriginal." No collective term for the first peoples of this country is without flaws; the best that can be achieved is adequacy. Aboriginal peoples themselves are not in total agreement as to what is the most appropriate term. Of course, the traditional "Indian," the term I, as a non-Aboriginal, grew up using, is now acknowledged to be a historical mistake, a misleading reference, and a term that does not deliver much respect. That being said, "in house," a good number of Aboriginal peoples use the term, rather like the African-American use of "nigger" as Mohawk writer/educator Patricia Monture-Angus explains:

> I am more comfortable with the word Indian than I am with the words Native or Aboriginal Peoples. Perhaps it is because it is the term I grew up with.... I know that others are more critical of the use of the word Indian, a word forced on our people because explorers got themselves lost.... I want to re-claim that word, Indian, once forced upon us and make it feel mine.... I have decided to set aside my concerns with the inappropriate labels that have been forced on Indian people. After all, this labelling is not the responsibility of those who carry the false names. (Monture-Angus 1995: 22–23)

There is another reason to sometimes use the term "Indian" and that is in the legal sense regarding "status Indian"; however, that does not justify using the term generically.

During the 1970s, I used the term "Amerindian," largely the function of reading a good number of French-Canadian historians and anthropologists, who employed the term "amérindien" as it contrasts neatly with "Euroamerican." In her discussion of the difficult of generic terminology, Métis scholar Olive Dickason, after talking about the inappropriateness of "Indian," stated that:

> Francophones have solved the problem by using "amérindien," which is specific to the Americas, or "autochtone," which translates as Aboriginal. Anglophones have not reached such an accord; in Canada, "Native" has come to be widely used, but it is not accepted in the United States on the grounds that anyone born in that country is a native, regardless of racial origin; their accepted form is "native American." In Canada, "Aboriginal" is becoming widely used by Indians as well as non-Indians. "Amerindian" has not received popular acceptance in English-language Canada and has even less in the United States. However, as it avoids the ambiguities of "Indian" and "Native," and is more specific than "Aboriginal," it is my term of preference. (Dickason 1997: xvi)

Still, because of its lack of popularity, and because I do not like using the word "Indian" even when it is embedded in a larger word, I will not use this word.

The term "First Nations" is useful in some context, because it makes two important points: that Aboriginal peoples were here first and that they were and are nations. Yet, there is a significant limitation put on this word. It is exclusionary, not being strictly applicable to Métis or Inuit. It is best applied to a band community. For that reason, I will not be using that term for generic reference either.

I have long used the terms "Natives" or "Native people." This is partially the function of my age, since, in the late 1960s and the 1970s, I was part of a movement to use these terms to replace "Indians." In addition, having taught in the Native Studies Department at Laurentian University from 1992 to 1994, I became used to such terms as "Native Studies Approach," etc. It also neatly parallels the term "Native American" used in the United States. Yet this term is, as Dickason notes, an ambiguous term, and one that generates some opposition from non-Aboriginal peoples who are "native" to Canada, as their ancestors and themselves were born here. It has recently been brought to my attention that some Native Studies departments have changed their designation to "Aboriginal Studies."

There are many good reasons to choose "Aboriginal." One is its connection with the 1982 constitutional amendments, in which "Aboriginal rights" and "Aboriginal" became legally recognized terms. The important Royal Commission on Aboriginal Peoples of the early to mid 1990s also bore the name. Sociologists are beginning to use the term more and more in Canadian introductory sociology textbooks (see Henslin and Nelson 1996; Kendall, Linden, and Murray 1998 and 2000; Macionis and Gerber 1999; and Schaefer et al. 1996), and Frideres used the term in the title for the fifth and sixth editions of his book (see discussion of this book's significance in Chapter Three). Most importantly, it seems to be a name that most Aboriginal peoples accept, although it should be pointed out that there is still some objection to it in some circles.[10]

SUMMARY

This introductory chapter began with a statement that Canadian introductory sociology textbooks are influential sources of information about Aboriginal peoples and Aboriginal issues for community college students. In the 77 Canadian introductory sociology textbooks analysed for this study, the primary investigative focus was placed on three issues: culturally determined Inuit elder suicide, the potlatch, and the Oka confrontation of 1990.

Key to this study is the notion that there are fundamental flaws in the information about Aboriginal peoples and Aboriginal issues being generated in the introductory sociology textbooks used in community colleges. The nature of these flaws is such that they are insufficiently detected by traditional techniques employed in looking for weaknesses and biases in textbooks (i.e., looking for factual errors, counting positive and negative evaluative terms, and assessing pictures).

Finally, as is necessary in a project of this sort, I have identified my social location, establishing the point, made by Aboriginal writers George Manuel and Sharilyn Calliou, that binaries of Aboriginal and non-Aboriginal can have a limited value in understanding the nature of the work of a scholar or social activist involved with Aboriginal peoples.

Notes

1   In the outlines of the two introductory sociology courses we have at Humber College—Sociology of Everyday Life" and "Sociology: An Introduction"—there is no specific mention of Aboriginal peoples as such. That has been the prevailing pattern in Humber College sociology outlines over the last 25 years or so. However, according to colleagues I consulted who teach these courses, Aboriginal issues regularly are a part of what they teach.

2   The exceptions are those that are collections of readings or analyses of "great sociologists" or "great sociological works." An example of such an exception is Bailey and Gayle 1993.

3   I often talk about Aboriginal peoples to Grade 6 classes in southern Ontario (e.g., Etobicoke, Bolton, and Bradford), and a common complaint of the good teachers I talk to is how the curriculum and teaching materials are restricted to the material culture (food, clothes, modes of transportation) and don't properly address Aboriginal issues.

4   For example, the 1885 "Riel Rebellion" is sometimes incorrectly framed more as a French-Canadian than a Métis struggle (see Spencer 1996: 273).

5   This figure is inaccurate, underestimating the population of most groups that were in the Plains. To mention only groups that live in what is now Canada, in 1823, it was estimated that there were 4,200 Siksika or Blackfoot, 2,800 Kainai or Blood, and 4,200 Peigan. The Plains Cree were estimated at being about 12,500 in number in 1860.

6   There were at all times series of alliances between different nations. It was rare that any one nation would stand alone. This portrayal appears to assume Thomas Hobbes's hypothesized "state of nature" (which Hobbes himself applied to Aboriginal peoples) rather than being based on exposure to well-researched Aboriginal history.

7   This is, at the very least, an exaggeration. I am not knowledgeable enough about the

specifics to comment, but I know that a good number of peoples of the Prairies would have had little or no contact with the Ute, making such hypothesized hatred highly unlikely. This seems to be a crude attempt by the author to have "the facts" conform to his notion of the nature of "intergroup conflict."

8   Again this is an exaggeration. There was a significant amount of positive interaction between Aboriginal and non-Aboriginal peoples in the Plains. The early development of the Métis as a mixed Cree/French nation testifies to that.

9   For example, see Schaefer, Lamm, Biles, and Wilson 1996: 37, especially the insert entitled "Stereotypes Hurt Black Students": 49, Box 2-2.

10   I recently received a call from an editor of a major textbook publisher asking me what term they could use instead of "Aboriginal" as they had received some complaints from Aboriginal academics in Saskatchewan about it. I recommended that they use the term "Indigenous" instead.

Analytical Framework and Methodology

In the following chapters, I will look at three case studies in which the writers of Canadian introductory sociology textbooks present a narrow view of Aboriginal peoples and Aboriginal issues that is destructive to a more complete understanding of the situations described. In this chapter, I will establish the analytical framework that will be used in each of the case studies. This framework will help the reader to understand how the narrow view was developed in each case and what interests such a narrow view serves. It also outlines how to find alternatives to the knowledge-creating processes employed, alternatives that contribute to the creation of a broader perspective, one more likely to create understanding of Aboriginal peoples in Canada and to have Aboriginal peoples benefit from that understanding.

In establishing this analytical framework, I will convey a general sense of the methodology employed in both analysing the sociological view and developing the alternative views.

A number of critical thinkers have been invaluable in developing this analytical framework. These include Michel Foucault, Jean Baudrillard, Dorothy Smith, Sylvia Hale, and Linda Tuhiwai Smith. It should be noted that, while the terminology taken from these writers has proven valuable, the writers themselves did not develop their theories in order to try to understand Aboriginal issues, as their work did not involve Aboriginal studies. I have had to adapt their work to fit into an Aboriginal context. Each thinker will have her or his relevant ideas discussed on its own, with connections made when relevant both to what they might entail in the methodology of this study and to how what they say is supported by statements made by Aboriginal writers.

MICHEL FOUCAULT
Totalitarian Theories or Discourses

In his seminal article, "Two Lectures" (1980), Michel Foucault talked about the misleading nature of what he termed "totalitarian" (but what other postmodernist writers might call "global," "universalizing," or "totalizing") theories or discourses. These theories make up part of a Grand or Master Narrative that makes claims to being a "distanced objective" or "scientific" telling of "truth," but which in fact makes up part of a discourse of power that subjugates other forms of knowledge.

Discourse is a key term here. A good working definition of discourse is:

> A conceptual framework with its own internal logic and underlying assumptions that may be readily recognizable to the audience. A discourse involves a distinct way of speaking about some aspect of reality. [Use of the term] also suggests that the item under discussion is not a natural attribute of reality but socially constructed and defined. (Fleras and Elliot 1999: 433)

Delimiting a Specific Discourse: Undertaking Archaeology of Knowledge

In his work *The Archaeology of Knowledge* (1994; originally in French, 1969, and in English 1972), Foucault spoke of the importance of delimiting (or doing the archaeology of) the extent of a particular discourse in understanding its nature. He described the process of undertaking this archaeology of knowledge as follows:

> [W]e must grasp the statement in the exact specificity of its occurrence; determine its conditions of existence, fix at least its limits, establish its correlations with other statements that may be connected with it, and show what other forms of statements it excludes...; we must show why it could not be other than it was, in what respect it is exclusive or any other, how it assumes, in the midst of others and in relation to them, a place that no other could occupy. The question proper to such an analysis might be formulated in this way: what is this specific existence that emerges from what is said and nowhere else. (Foucault 1994: 28)

In this study, I have engaged in just such an "archaeological" analysis of the discourse in Canadian introductory sociology textbooks about Aboriginal peoples. In each of the three cases under discussion—culturally determined Inuit elder suicide (CDIES), the potlatch, and the Oka situation—there is a sociological discourse to be analysed. The archaeology of each is approached somewhat differently. With CDIES, I will dig up the history of sociology, uncovering the discursive connection of CDIES with such early sociological concepts as Emile Durkheim's "altruistic suicide," William Sumner's "mores," and the idea that deviance is culturally determined. A key methodological step in the archaeological process here is to discover the secondary sources that the introductory sociology textbooks drew upon, secondary sources such as Cavan (1965; originally 1928), Hoebel (1941 and 1965), and Weyer (1962; originally 1932), which contain discussions of Inuit suicide and references to primary sources. With the potlatch, the trowel work will find a similar connection with the cultural relativism of Ruth Benedict (1934). For the Oka situation, a more recent event (1990), the discourse analysis will not involve the same depth of time.

Buried and Disqualified Knowledges

Foucault spoke of two different kinds of knowledge that are "subjugated" by mainstream discourse. One he termed "buried knowledges of erudition" (Foucault 1980: 82), which he describes as "the products of meticulous, erudite, exact historical knowledge" that have been buried or disguised to serve the purposes of mainstream discourse. These purposes were defined by Foucault as "functionalist" or "systematising."

How does one find such buried knowledges? How does one know where to dig? Each of the three case studies differs, but some general statements can be made. About each group discussed—the Inuit, the Kwakiutl (and other Northwest Coast peoples), and the Mohawk—as about all Aboriginal groups, there are the early works of what can be called "travellers," explorers, government agents, missionaries, traders, and upper-class adventurers who visited the country of the First Nations and reported back to the non-Aboriginal mainstream population in North America and Europe. While the biases of these sources restrict their capacity to be employed to develop and support a framing of Aboriginal issues that provides an alternative to that in introductory sociology textbooks, they are still primary sources of buried knowledges. I assumed, and this was borne out in the analysis, that the writers of the textbooks did not engage in reading this early literature when researching their works. Anyone trying to apply the framework developed here to other Aboriginal issues would be well advised to consult this travel literature.

The absence of published Inuit voices during the critical period discussed here makes this form of evidence more important in considering CDIES than in the other two case studies. Inuit country travel literature from the 1800s and early 1900s[1] proved most useful, as it clearly shows that the elders were greatly respected, and it demonstrates the extreme rarity of any instances of elder abandonment or other forms of CDIES. This message and this demonstration are both glaringly absent from the sociology textbooks.

A second source of buried knowledges about Aboriginal peoples comes from non-Aboriginal journalists. They are generally a suspect source, as they typically spend too short a time with Aboriginal peoples to develop an alternative perspective to that of the mainstream. However, some journalists do stay beyond a daily or weekly deadline. As we shall see in the Oka situation, most journalists created and/or sustained a government-friendly, biased angle on the events. However, Geoffrey York and Loreen Pindera (1991) and Rick Hornung (1991) published interviews with Aboriginal peoples, interviews that provide a much different perspective.

A third source comes from anthropological literature, which, while containing biases similar to those of the writers of introductory sociology textbooks, produces knowledge that is useful in alternative framing. This is particularly the case in those works that follow the tradition of the edited Aboriginal autobiography, especially concerning the potlatch. It has often been remarked that the Kwakiutl are "the most anthropologized people in the world" (Webster 1993). Fortunately, the result is some good autobiographies, in which the Aboriginal source is more than just an informant and the anthropologist exercises a light editorial hand.

For CDIES, this source has an uneven utility. Some anthropological writers identify cultural respect for elders and problematize elder abandonment, while others, notably Guemple (1969, 1974, and 1980), have participated in the creation of CDIES. No writing by any anthropologist proved useful in presenting an alternative perspective on Oka.

The fourth source of buried knowledges concerning Aboriginal peoples and Aboriginal issues, and the one most capable of producing an alternative framing, is Aboriginal peoples themselves. Unfortunately, in terms of Foucault's analysis, they are doubly damned. They provide a source of knowledge that is both buried and disqualified. Foucault referred to "disqualified knowledges" as involving "a whole set of knowledges that have been disqualified as inadequate to their task or insufficiently elaborated; naive knowledges located down on the hierarchy, beneath the required cognition of scientificity" (Foucault 1980: 82). I would add to this that those who speak with this knowledge are themselves disqualified as producers of knowledge.

The type of disqualified knowledges considered in this study can generically be termed "indigenous knowledges." Dei et al. define this type of knowledge in the following instructive way:

> By Indigenous knowledges, we refer to the common-sense ideas and cultural knowledges of local peoples concerning the everyday realities of living. Those knowledges are part of the cultural heritage and histories of peoples ...We refer, specifically, to the epistemic salience of cultural traditions, values, belief systems, and world views that are imparted to the younger generation by community elders. Such knowledge constitutes an "Indigenous informed epistemology." It is a worldview that shapes the community's relationship with its environments. It is the product of the direct experience of nature and its relationship with the social world. It is knowledge that is crucial for the survival of society. It is knowledge that is based on cognitive understandings and interpretations of the social and physical/spiritual worlds. It includes concepts, beliefs and perceptions and experiences of local peoples and their natural and human-built environments. (Dei et al. 2000: 49–50)

Drawing upon indigenous knowledges provided a varying degree of success in each case. The Inuit, unfortunately, were given little opportunity to speak about their elders from the 1800s through most of the 1900s, so the more filtered media of the travel literature and the anthropological literature have had to speak for them. Anthropological autobiographies have been the main route through which indigenous knowledge about the potlatch has travelled. The exception has been the writing of Gloria Webster (1993 and 1996), particularly as it pertains to the treatment of the confiscated sacred Kwakiutl potlatch items. Indigenous knowledge proved most useful in the Oka situation. Given their long period of close contact with urban Canada in southern Ontario and Quebec, the Mohawk have made writing one of their important resistance strategies. Both the Akwesasne and Kahnawake communities have produced journals— *Akwesasne Notes* and *The Eastern Door* respectively—which are respected by Aboriginal peoples and by non-Aboriginal scholars who are exposed to them. Contemporary Mohawk educators and writers such as Gerald Alfred (1995) and Patricia Monture-Angus (1995) have produced best-selling and often-quoted books that are essential in understanding the lives of the Mohawk today.

Generally speaking, anyone writing about Aboriginal issues today must consult the growing number of Aboriginal media— newspaper/magazines such as *Windspeaker* (see it and others at www.ammsa.com) and on-line Aboriginal news services, such as NatNews-owner@yahoogroups.com—which provide alternative framings of every Aboriginal issue in Canada.

The Intellectual Model of the Sexual Confession

One of the main means of disqualifying indigenous knowledges is the intellectual model that was problematized by Foucault in his discussion of the "sexual confession" in the first volume of *The History of Sexuality* (Foucault 1978). According to this model, the subject being studied (and marginalized in knowledge production) provides information that comes from his or her subjective experience, but this does not become authenticated knowledge until it is interpreted by an "objective" outsider/expert who is in the inherently privileged position of "pronouncing truth" by virtue of being an expert. The subject being studied in this way is not allowed to have a voice that is heard without translation from the outsider/expert.

A number of Aboriginal writers have commented on the negative effects of outsider-pronounced truth automatically overriding the insights of Aboriginal insiders. In his scathing but humourous look at anthropologists in the chapter "Anthropologists and Other Friends" in *Custer Died for Your Sins: An Indian Manifesto*, first published in 1969, Sioux intellectual Vine Deloria Jr. spoke, among other things, of how anthropologists usurp authority concerning knowledge of Aboriginal ways:

> Over the years anthropologists have succeeded in burying Indian communities so completely beneath the mass of irrelevant information that the total impact of the scholarly community on Indian people has become one of simple authority. Many Indians have come to parrot the ideas of anthropologists because it appears that the anthropologists know everything about Indian communities. Thus many ideas that pass for Indian thinking are in reality theories originally advanced by anthropologists and echoed by Indian people in an attempt to communicate the real situation. (Deloria 1969: 82)

A similar point was made by Shuswap politician and writer George Manuel when he wrote that:

> There were those [anthropologists] who stood in our kitchens and our Long Houses and said that we were not drying the fish, or cooking the corn soup, or doing the dances according to the reference books with which they had prepared themselves for this expedition. Sometimes they even offered to show us how it was done. (Manuel and Posluns 1974: 158)

JEAN BAUDRILLARD AND SIMULACRA

In an excellent piece, not dated by the fact that it is almost 30 years old, Chippewa/Cree anthropologist D'arcy McNickle wrote about the negative consequences that result when an oral people are written about by outsiders who have a written tradition. He highlighted the potential danger of the anthropological concept of "culture areas" when grouping together diverse Aboriginal peoples, a concept that informs primary and secondary students[2] as well as writers and readers of introductory sociology textbooks:

> A later consequence of the non-literate Indian condition was a concentration of studies which described Indian life as fixed in time and in culture content. Tribes were seen as components of "culture areas," frozen in ecological domains and social systems. Such studies recorded impressively long lists of behavioral practices, technologies, and material artifacts which seemed to describe a tribe exhaustively, and yet said nothing about it at all. Usually it was not clear whether the traits described were still practiced or were long defunct. In instances where it was clearly shown that the traits were nonexistent, the tribe was pronounced dead or dying. At the other extreme, tribes that had disappeared as living societies were described in the literature as possessing the attributes of a contemporary community. The traits themselves—their origins, their diffusion through time and space, their cognate forms in neighboring areas—became so central to the exercise that association with a tribal name was noted almost as an afterthought. (McNickle 1972: 33)

McNickle anticipates Jean Baudrillard's (1983) criticism of ethnology as producing "simulacra," intellectual commodities that are codified and readily reproduced in media, including textbooks. These simulacra are "hyperreal," in that they are considered "more real" than what actually may be existing or have existed. In Baudrillard's terminology, there is a "precession" of the image or model over the "reality" or "fact." The simulacrum takes precedence in terms of the respect given to it in knowledge production and reproduction. To use an analogy that Baudrillard himself uses to good effect in illustrating the nature of simulacra, it is like the map being given precedence over the territory. If a place exists on the map and not in the territory, that place exists. If a place does not exist on the map, regardless of its presence in the territory, it is not considered to exist.

As we can see in the quotes from Deloria, Manuel and Posluns, and McNickle above, simulacra about Aboriginal peoples relate primarily to the past, a time often put forward as an era of pristine purity of culture (see Kulchyski, McCaskill, and Newhouse 1999: xiii) that lives on in textbooks and can be used as a point of criticism of the lack of such cultural purity and "reality" in what Aboriginal peoples say and do today. In this way, they resemble the simulacrum described by Edward Said in his ground-breaking study of "Orientalism" (1978) of the Western imperialist development of its own notions of the Middle East. In the following quotation, one could replace Said's word "Orient" with the words "Aboriginal world," "Oriental" with the word "Aboriginal," and "Orientalist" with "Aboriginal expert" and come up with a statement that has some applicability to how Aboriginal peoples have been presented in Canadian introductory textbooks:

> Faced with the obvious decrepitude and political impotence of the modern Oriental, the European Orientalist found it his duty to rescue some portion of a lost, past classical Oriental grandeur in order to "facilitate ameliorations" in the present Orient. What the European took from the classical Oriental past was a vision (and thousands of facts and artifacts) which only he could employ to the best advantage; to the modern Oriental he gave facilitation and

amelioration—and, too, the benefit of his judgment as to what was best for the modern Orient. (Said 1978: 79)

Aboriginal epistemology opposes this fixation on the purity of the past with a strong sense that Aboriginal core values have persisted through time and that these values have not "evolved away" through an inevitable assimilation. They are considered to be in some ways superior to the values of Western society, particularly when dealing with ecological and social problems. Wendat scholar and educator Georges Sioui expresses these concepts well in the following:

> An examination of the Amerindian philosophical tradition will show the persistence, vivacity, and universality of the essential values proper to America. Using this tool for increasing non-Native awareness, we shall be able to show that if history is to be sensitive to society's needs, it must also study and reveal to the dominant society what is salutary, instead of continuing to talk about "primitive" cultures that are dead or dying. Such history is socially irresponsible, pointless, and misleading. History written in this way is like a shell without its animal content: its subject is matter, not thought. (Sioui 1992: 22)

These Aboriginal core values are best epitomized by the elders. A standard feature of Native Studies departments is the presence in some significant capacity of an elder or elders, typically either through an elder-in-residence or a visiting elder program. The "teachings" of the elders, in the stories they tell, the advice they give, or the examples they set, are key aspects of Aboriginal epistemology. They are considered experts who must stand as authorities at least on a par with professors, both Aboriginal and non-Aboriginal. Ojibwa educator James Dumont makes this point in the following way:

Because Native Studies implies a uniquely different philosophy and world view, it will become important to involve those Native people who best express this approach—namely the Native elders and spiritual leaders. This means that these people will have to become accepted, without reservations, as a necessary aspect of the teaching of Native Studies. The professor, then, may become one who assures that these people are available in the teaching situation, rather than simply the one who is charged with the total responsibility of teaching the course him/herself. It may also require that these elders and spiritual leaders be recognized as having equivalence in terms of degree qualifications necessary to teach in the University. (Dumont 1981: 181)

This is not to say that elders as sources of contemporary Aboriginal epistemology are any more unproblematic than those Aboriginal peoples who have Western educational credentials and whom Maori writer Linda Tuhiwai Smith (and others) term "native intellectuals" (see Tuhiwai Smith 1999: 69–72). She identifies the following problem involving Maori elders during the 1980s:

In New Zealand one struggle over the value of Western education was played out in the 1980s through a process of reprivileging of "elders" and a reification of elders as the holders of all traditional knowledge and a parallel deprivileging of the younger, frequently much better educated members (in a Western sense) of an *iwi* (tribe). (Tuhiwai Smith 1999: 71–72; emphasized in original)

In 1987, Beatrice Medicine, a leading Lakota educator, addressed some of the basic problems encountered in the first stages when elders become involved with formal education. She was concerned that, although First Nations wanted elders involved, they were not sure how to address concrete issues such as who was an elder and who wasn't, and what an elder should do. Early in the process, not surprisingly, mistakes were made. The following comment, made to her by Roderick Mark, is a telling one:

> [W]e have misused the role of elder through our ignorance and failure to see that not all elders are teachers, not all elders are spiritual leaders and not all old people are elders. (Medicine 1987: 147)

That caveat being acknowledged, the insights of Aboriginal elders still should inform what is said about Aboriginal peoples in introductory textbooks. Unfortunately, they do not, any more than do the insights of the Western-educated "Aboriginal intellectuals." Instead of the culture-informed words of the elders we have simulacra taking precedence. This will be discussed in more detail in Chapter Four.

DOROTHY SMITH

This study is also informed by Dorothy Smith's critique of sociology, as contained in her important work, *The Conceptual Practices of Power: A Feminist Sociology of Knowledge* (1990). First, I found useful Smith's stress on the need to have subjects who, drawing from their life experiences, are agents in sociological texts, producers of the knowledge recorded in these works, not mere objects of study. The subjects that she speaks of are, of course, women, but her analysis is equally applicable to Aboriginal peoples. Often, in reading her work, I found I could substitute the term "Aboriginal peoples" for "women" with no loss of intellectual validity. The following is a case in point:

> It is not enough to supplement an established sociology by addressing ourselves to what has been left out or overlooked, or my making women's issues into sociological issues. That does not change the standpoint built into existing sociological procedures, but merely makes the sociology

of women an addendum to the body of knowledge. (Smith 1990: 12–14)

This problem—having the issues of the intellectually marginalized merely added to a list rather than they themselves being included in the development of theory—has also been identified by Michael Apple and Linda Christian-Smith in their important work, *The Politics of the Textbook* (1991). They refer to the "addendum" process as "mentioning":

> As disenfranchised groups have fought to have their knowledge take center stage in the debates over cultural legitimacy, one trend has dominated in text production. In essence, very little tends to be dropped from textbooks. Major ideological frameworks do not get markedly changed. Textbook publishers are under considerable and constant pressure to include *more* in their books. Progressive *items* are perhaps mentioned, then, but not developed in depth. Dominance is partly maintained here through compromise and the process of "mentioning." (Apple and Christian-Smith 1991: 10)

In the chapters that follow, I will demonstrate how Aboriginal issues constitute just such an addendum to introductory sociology textbooks, being mentioned but not developed in a way that might challenge the theoretical approach being taken. As we have seen in the last chapter, after the mid 1970s, Aboriginal peoples as subjects are not seen, the Aboriginal voice is not heard, and Aboriginal standpoints are not represented nor developed.

A particularly powerful part of Smith's criticism concerning the lack of theoretical production from a woman's standpoint is the fact that "worlds that are traditionally women's and still are predominantly women's—the worlds of household, children and neighborhood—" are represented from the standpoint of men and not women. Much is obviously lost in that process. As we will see in the next chapter, there is a ready parallel with non-Aboriginal sociologists producing knowledge that supposedly represents the world of the Aboriginal reserve.

Smith's second major criticism of sociology, one that is shared in part with Foucault, is her problematizing of the way that ideologically produced knowledge is presented as if it were "objective," rather than acknowledged as reproducing a particular standpoint, one that generally denies the presence of subjects as agents. In her words, "Objective knowledge, as we engage with it, subdues, discounts, and disqualifies our various interests, perspectives, angles, and experience, and what we might have to say speaking from them" (Smith 1990: 80).

Of great significance to this book is how Smith connects this denial with "relations of ruling":

> Suspending the presence of particular subjects is the accomplishment of organized practices in and of the everyday world. It is not peculiar to the domain of scientific discourse. The objectification of knowledge is a general feature of contemporary relations of ruling. (Smith 1990: 67)

As the discipline of sociology developed in Canada, the "organized practices" of the writers and editors of introductory sociology textbooks suspended the presence of Aboriginal peoples as "particular subjects" (see discussion in Chapter Three). Of special salience to the analysis used here is that, in so doing, sociological writers are maintaining the "relations of ruling" of governments and their agencies in Canada. In Smith's words, "The governing of our kind of society is done in abstract concepts and symbols and sociology helps create them by transposing the actualities of people's lives and experience into the conceptual currency with which they can be governed" (Smith 1990: 14).

More concretely important to my analysis, in discussing the specific example of how "domestic violence" is represented in one sociological work, Smith points out that when neither the governing nor the governed are identified as subjective agents, but are objectified, we can be blinded to acts of oppression: "the representatives of the state, do not do violence: police, national guard, military—their forms of physical coercion are not identified" (Smith 1990: 55). This resonates with my analysis of how the Oka situation is represented in introductory sociology textbooks, where the Sûreté du Quebec is overly objectified as merely a police force with no ethnicity of its own nor history of conflict with the Mohawk.

Drawing on Smith's notion that sociology serves the "relations of ruling," I will show that the way in which the writers and editors of Canadian introductory sociology textbooks present the key issues well serve federal and provincial governments and their agencies. In the case of the potlatch, we will see how their framing of that ceremony as destructively competitive blinds the readers to the ethnocentrism of the federal government in banning the ceremonies for more than 60 years, a fact never mentioned in these books. In the case of CDIES, I look at how the simulacrum of the Inuit abandoning their elders blinded readers of sociology textbooks to the ill-conceived and sometimes disastrous relocation projects that took place during the twentieth century, as well as to the government's neglect of Inuit citizens that resulted in the premature death of a significant number of people.

SYLVIA HALE

Sylvia Hale's "Facticity and Dogma in Introductory Sociology Texts: The Need for Alternative Methods" (1992), draws heavily upon Dorothy Smith's work, with equal reliance on the works of the philosopher of science Paul Feyerabend (1970 and 1975) and the American sociologist Ben Agger (1989). Concerning the former, Hale writes:

Feyerabend advocates developing a plurality of theories, and the more radically they differ in basic assumptions from the dominant paradigm, the better. Feyerabend's central argument is that there exist facts that cannot be unearthed except with the help of alternative theories. The ideal is to strive for theories that are so totally different from the prevailing theory that the background conceptualization of what constitutes factual knowledge itself comes into question. (Hale 1992: 138)

The main significance of Hale's article for this study lies in her critique of introductory sociology textbooks. Based on her reading of Smith and Feyerabend, Hale feels that there is a "need for radical change in the format of introductory textbooks to present sociology as a body of theories that are used to conceptualize, or to factualize, evidence, rather than a body of facts about which we theorize" (Hale 1992: 136). Speaking more concretely in her critique of these textbooks, she follows Agger's lead (1989) in two primary ways. First, she interrogates the standard textbook approach of canonizing three schools of thought—structural functionalism, conflict, and symbolic interactionism—at the cost of any other theoretical approach, thus imposing a problematic theoretical closure. Second, she questions whether the latter two approaches (and potentially radical alternative feminisms) are presented as true alternatives; instead, she suggests, they are collapsed in a conservative-biased functionalist paradigm:

An important problem that he [Agger] identifies with this approach is that the supposedly diverse theories are quickly collapsed into each other in an effort to maintain synthesis. Symbolic interactionism is not a theory at all, he suggests, but a research strategy in microsociology. Textbook Marxism loses all its critical political edge to become a safe, respectable variant of functionalist conflict theory. In this "Boy Scout Marxism" conflict is an unavoidable fact of social and economic life that must be dealt with piecemeal by the capitalist welfare state. Girl

Scout feminism, on the other hand, is domesticated in the gender, family and sex role chapter(s). It too becomes a variant of mainstream conflict theory, with women urged to work "with men" to sort out their mutual problems. The potential for Marxism or feminism as radical critiques of conventional theoretical wisdom is lost. (Hale 1992: 143)

Having symbolic interactionism serve a functionalist master and pulling the critical teeth of the conflict approach with "Boy Scout Marxism" neutralizes the effectiveness of writers of introductory sociology textbooks. Most important for this study, such theoretical closure shuts out any Aboriginal epistemological contribution. I will put special emphasis of the effects of this in the discussion of the Oka situation.

Linda Tuhiwai Smith

Missing so far from the theories reviewed are specific mention of the impact of colonialism on knowledge production and of the need for decolonization to address the negative aspects of that impact. One of the leading writers in this area, particularly as she makes explicit what decolonization entails, is Maori academic and writer Linda Tuhiwai Smith. In her ground-breaking work, *Decolonizing Methodologies: Research and Indigenous Peoples* (1999), she speaks of her own and her people's discontent with what outsider researchers have done in making Maori "objects" of study that exist primarily as outsider-defined "problems" (Tuhiwai Smith 1999: 60–61). She moves from a mere articulation of the discontent to develop an alternative, Maori-defined approach to researching themselves. This approach provides a good framework for identifying what the writers and editors of Canadian introductory sociology textbooks are missing by not including Aboriginal voice in their works.

For the purposes of this book, the most useful aspect of her framing of indigenous research is contained in the chapter entitled

"Twenty-Five Indigenous Projects." Of course, the agendas of indigenous researchers and of writers of introductory sociology textbooks are, and should be, quite different. As such, this list of 25 different purposes of research projects should not be thought of as a checklist for an indigenizing scavenger hunt for sociologists. However, I have identified five projects on the list as readily applicable to sociology textbooks: celebrating survival, remembering, reading, reframing, and democratizing.

Celebrating survival refers to balancing the outsider researcher preoccupation with the ills of indigenous cultures with a more positive approach that celebrates or honours the ways in which the people have successfully coped with the impact of colonialism (Tuhiwai Smith 1999: 145). Aboriginal writers are loud in their criticism of this outsider researcher preoccupation, and are equally vocal in calling for a more balanced approach. Robinson and Quinney, for example, state that:

> Many books have been written on the plight of Indian people. So many that the spirit and vitality of our people is often suffocated by them. We have been probed, prodded and analysed as if an autopsy were being performed on dead people. Few people are willing to look behind the devastating statistics of our poverty, unemployment, high suicide, alcoholism, cancer and mortality rates, poor housing, inadequate education, high proportion of prison inmates, etc, etc, etc. Few people see the life which has kept us going despite these deplorable effects of colonialism. (Robinson and Quinney 1985: 2)

Wilson and Wilson refer to these alternative indigenous approaches as "relational accountability" (1998). They use the term to define the difficulty experienced by Aboriginal graduate students who study conditions in Aboriginal communities other than their own, but for which they still feel responsibility for or accountability to. In the words of one such graduate student:

I readily reacted to the state of powerlessness, helplessness, and apathy that was visible in the transcripts, by being remorseful. I could not present this information as it was too negative. In my heart I believed in the people's will. There was much to learn from these people, only it was not yet within my grasp.... I was not prepared to present a thesis that cast a negative frame onto any First Nations community ... thus my personal journey began. I placed the manuscript aside for a time while I began this learning trek. (Wilson and Wilson 1998)

Two years later, "Only when she was able to present her material in a context that honored all those involved was she able to proceed with her thesis defence" (Wilson and Wilson 1998).[3]

Remembering entails the written recording of the people's memories of a "painful past" and of their responses to that pain (Tuhiwai Smith 1999: 146). It incorporates what William Tierney refers to as encouraging "dangerous memory":

Encouraging "dangerous memory" involves creating conditions so that the Other is able to speak from his or her personal and intellectual experience. "Dangerous memories," to use Sharon Welch's (1990) term, are those stories and experiences that have been silenced by the power of the term [of dominant knowledge production] ... The purpose in telling these stories is not to find one true narrative tale to which we may all subscribe, but rather, as Sharon Welch points out, to "call upon those of us who are, often unknowingly, complicit in structures of control to join in resistance and transformation" (1990, p 139). (Tierney 1994: 146–47)

A key component is the time factor: the deeper in time, the less "dangerous" (or challenging and instructive) the memory. Contemporary responsibility can be sloughed off, complicity denied. But the dangerous memories chosen for this study are relatively recent, roughly within the time frame of the sociology textbooks themselves. Shuswap writer George Manuel stressed the importance of recognizing that some of the worst times are recent, rather than some period safely tucked into the pockets of the past. In the early 1970s, he wrote the following:

> "WHAT WAS THE low point of Indian history in the interior of British Columbia? Economically?" The question was posed by a journalist to a friend of mine who is a scholar of native history.
>
> My friend, looking at his calendar watch, hesitated before speaking. "It may be 1972," he said. "The grandfathers of the present generation were often in a better economic relationship with the surrounding culture than their grandchildren have now." He explained "...The economic situation of the Indian people sixty, seventy years ago has to be called better than it is today. Maybe we haven't reached the low point yet." (Manuel and Posluns 1974: 33; capital letters in original)

Also of relevance to this study is that the dangerous memories are more dangerous if they are Canadian. A dangerous memory that is American serves the often-repeated, comfortable, contrasting stereotype that I have heard a good number of my students articulate: "the Americans treated 'their' Natives with much more cruelty than 'we' did 'ours.'" The three featured substantive areas of analysis in this book—CDIES, the potlatch, and Oka—all relate to Canada, and all involve dangerous memories that at some level are out of the frame of the portrayal of these issues in Canadian introductory sociology textbooks.[4]

The indigenous project of reading (Tuhiwai Smith 1999: 149) involves a critical reading of how Western history involving indigenous peoples has been written. As Canadian introductory sociology textbooks draw from these written sources in talking about Aboriginal peoples, such a critical reading is vital to the presentation of Aboriginal issues. In all three of the chosen focus areas, this kind of reading has not taken place.

Reframing is central both to Tuhiwai Smith's arguments (in a way encapsulating the others) and my own, so her statement will be quoted at some length:

> Reframing is about taking much greater control over the ways in which indigenous issues and social problems are discussed and handled. One of the reasons why so many of the social problems which beset indigenous communities are never solved is that the issues have been framed in a particular way. For example, governments and social agencies have failed to see many indigenous social problems as being related to any sort of history. They have framed an "indigenous problem" basket, to be handled in the usual cynical and paternalistic manner. The framing of an issue is about making decisions about its parameters, about what is in the foreground, what is in the background, and what shadings or complexities exist within the frame. The project of reframing is related to defining the problem or issue and determining how best to solve that problem. Many indigenous activists have argued that such things as mental illness, alcoholism and suicide, for example, are not about psychological and individualized failure but about colonization or lack of collective self-determination. Many community health initiatives address the whole community, its history and its wider context as part of the problem and part of the solution. (Tuhiwai Smith 1999: 153)

Finally, democratizing involves research directed toward returning to indigenous forms of democracy the political structures set up by the colonial powers. As I hope to establish in the Oka chapters, this has long been one of the major goals of the Mohawk people (among others), a goal that the government and its agencies have been blocking. And yet, this democratizing process is not discussed (other than under the bland, explain-nothing term "self-government") in Canadian introductory sociology textbooks.

SUMMARY

In this chapter, I have discussed, through the theorizing of five critical thinkers, two different ways of framing information presented about Aboriginal peoples. One reflects the practices of the writers of Canadian introductory sociology textbooks. The second involves a discussion of alternative ways of framing this information, based fundamentally on Aboriginal-produced knowledge. Concerning the first, following Foucault, I have suggested that the writers of these textbooks have produced a totalitarian discourse on Aboriginal peoples and Aboriginal issues that needs to be investigated through undertaking an archaeology of that discourse. Methodologically, what this latter has entailed is performing an archaeology of the sociological presentation of each case at different depths. In the Inuit and potlatch study, both involving subjects that have long been written about by non-Aboriginal social scientists, I uncover key early concepts in the development of sociology that have influenced the discourse on the Aboriginal issue involved, as well as identifying the secondary sources that that have framed the concepts and the issues as interconnected. In the case of Oka, a more recent event, the analysis of the discourse is limited to 1990s sources. Connected with this, and pursuing the thinking of Dorothy Smith, I have investigated how this discourse serves what she terms the "relations of ruling." This has involved documenting government practices (and inaction) that have had a negative impact on the Inuit, Kwakiutl, and Mohawk during the time period covered by the discourse.

By its nature, this discourse excludes information produced by alternative means. Reflecting one privileged standpoint, it has buried and disqualified others. Following Baudrillard, I have referred to the exclusionary nature of the discourse as making each discourse a simulacrum, an outsider-produced piece of knowledge that disallows insider-produced knowledge by setting the standard for what is "real." Therefore, it is necessary to seek out that which has been disallowed, that which can produce alternative frames for delivering information involving Aboriginal peoples and Aboriginal issues. Toward that end, I have identified and discussed the availability of four different sources of information: early travel writers or visitors to Aboriginal country, journalists, anthropologists, and Aboriginal writers. The purposes that these alternative frames can usefully serve have been linked to Maori writer Linda Tuhiwai Smith's decolonizing methodologies of attending to "indigenous research projects."

NOTES

1 My research in this literature was conducted at Trent University's Bata Library and Anthropology Department Library from late April to the end of June, 2001. As that university has the oldest Native Studies Department (1969) in Canada, and as it has a strong anthropology department, the libraries provided an incredibly extensive collection of early material. It was extremely rare that I would read about an early Inuit source and not be able to find that source at Trent.

2 I have been made aware of McNickle's concern on a number of occasions when speaking to classes from Grades 6 to 8. Recently, when I asked students in a Grade 7 class who were the Aboriginal peoples who had lived closest to our town (Bolton—about 15 kilometres north of Toronto), they all answered "Huron" because that was what was on the map they had studied in their textbook. The answer I wanted was Ojibwa, who for more than 300 years have had the closest communities. The Huron were driven out of the area about 350 years ago.

3 I have some small sense of what this person was going through. When I was writing the chapter on "Child Welfare" in my recent book (Steckley and Cummins 2001), I knew that I could not complete the chapter until I could find a way to honour the people who were finding ways to overcome the effects on their children of past oppression. I was greatly relieved when I found what I knew was there, but had not previously discovered in written form.

4 There are, of course, many other Canadian dangerous memories that have been framed badly by introductory sociology textbooks (e.g., residential schools and the "Sixties Scoop" in which thousands of Aboriginal children were taken from their homes, families, communities, province, and, sometimes, their country to be adopted by White families) that could have been chosen for my analysis, but that would have made for an unnecessarily large and cumbersome work.

	Disciplining
	Sociology
CHAPTER THREE	Textbooks

Aboriginal voice is almost completely absent from contemporary Canadian introductory sociology textbooks. I believe that one of the main reasons for this absence is the "disciplining" of those textbooks, the narrowing of perspective to fit more neatly into the discipline of sociology.

Sociology was slow to develop in Canada, relative to the initiation and growth of the discipline in the United States and Britain. The first sociology department in Canada was established at McGill University by Carl Addington Dawson (formerly of the University of Chicago) in 1922. He also wrote the first "Canadian" or, more accurately, "Canadianized" introductory sociology textbook in 1948 (Dawson and Getty 1948), the earliest version of which I have seen in the library at Trent University.[1] In 1958, there were fewer than 20 sociology professors in Canada, teaching at nine Canadian universities (Clark 1976: 120). Sociology did not become a significant area of study and teaching in Canada until the 1960s and 1970s, as baby-boomers entered university and, after 1967 in Ontario, community colleges.

Related to this slow development are two significant influences on how information was presented concerning Aboriginal peoples in early Canadian introductory sociology textbooks. One of these is the powerful influence of non-Canadians up until well into the 1970s. As with many other disciplines in Canada, when large-scale hirings became necessary to teach the baby-boomers in post-secondary education, Canadian universities and colleges had to dig deep into the United States and Britain to get staff. Of all those with doctorates teaching in sociology and anthropology in Canada in 1967, 72 percent received their PhDs in the United States, 10 percent in Britain, and only 6 percent in Canada (Gallagher and Lambert 1971: vii). In 1973–74, 45 percent of full-time faculty teaching sociology in Canada were non-Canadians (Hofley 1992: 106). This should not be too surprising, as between 1924 and 1967, only 22 doctorates in sociology were conferred in Canadian universities (Gallagher and Lambert 1971: vi). This had an impact on my early sociological education. Of the four sociology courses that I took as an undergraduate at Lakehead University in Thunder Bay and York University in Toronto, not one was taught by a native-born Canadian.[2]

Of course this meant that textbooks chosen tended to be influenced by the country of origin and the country of doctorate of the writers and editors. John Hofley, writing in 1992 a retrospective entitled "Canadianization: A Journey Completed?," stated that when he was hired to teach sociology at Carleton University in 1966, he "found very little about Canada in the sociology texts that were available" (Hofley 1992: 104). The introductory sociology textbook I learned from in my first year sociology course was a collection of readings published in the United States. Not one of the articles referred to Canada.

At the college where I teach, the first time a Canadian textbook was assigned as recommended or required reading was in the academic year 1983–84, when Nick Mansfield's book (1982) was used. From that year to the present, we have used only Canadian sociology textbooks. Two American books that were used in sociology courses prior to that time are illustrative. *Why Study Sociology* by Elliot Krause (1980) was used in the academic year 1982–83. The only reference (Krause 1980: 120) in the entire book to anything Canadian is to *Crestwood Heights: A Study of the Culture of Suburban Life*, by John Seeley, R.A. Sim, and E.W. Loosely (1963), a study of Forest Hill in Toronto. Interestingly, while Horton and Hunt (1976) was recommended and required reading for sociology students several times during the late 1970s at the college and similarly lacking in Canadian content, there is one quotation taken from a work written by William Wuttunee, a Cree living in Alberta (Horton and Hunt 1976: 353–54). He is not located as to his nation or his country of origin.

In Canada, the discipline of sociology and the sub-discipline of social (the British term) or cultural (the American term) anthropology have had close connections. Historically, it was not uncommon for the two fields of study to share one department.[3] Such sharing still exists today (although there is a Canadian Sociology and Anthropology Association vote this year—2002—concerning whether the two should be divided). In writing the foreword for the first sociology textbook written specifically for Canadian students (a collection of readings edited by leading sociologists Bernard Blishen, Frank Jones, Kaspar Naegele, and John Porter, first published in 1961), Carl Dawson stated that the book was "designed particularly for Canadian students in the specific fields of sociology and anthropology" (Dawson 1961: v). As we will see, the contributors to the text came from both fields.

One reason for the link between the two disciplines was the reliance of the writers of these early textbooks on anthropologists for information concerning Aboriginal peoples in Canada. This reliance was explicitly acknowledged in a number of these works. Blishen et al. stated clearly in their preface that "Our indigenous ethnic groups, the Indians and the Eskimos, have been studied extensively by social anthropologists" (Blishen et al. 1961: viii) and the articles about Aboriginal peoples in that book were written by anthropologists. In apologizing for the lack of Aboriginal content in their early (1971) textbook, Gallagher and Lambert wrote:

> We acknowledge a striking omission, both in the contents of this chapter and in the activities of professional sociologists. We have included no articles bearing on the Indians, Eskimos, and Metis of Canada... Most analyses of Canada's native peoples have been provided by anthropologists, not by sociologists. (Gallagher and Lambert 1971: 453)

This last sentence is something of an understatement. It would have been more accurate at that time to have said, "Almost every analysis of Canada's native peoples has been provided by anthropologists, not by sociologists."

Two strategies concerning the presentation of information about Aboriginal peoples were taken. First, little or nothing was written about Aboriginal peoples, placing them as marginal to the purview of sociology. This strategy was employed by Daniel Rossides, in his 1968 textbook, which almost completely omitted Aboriginal peoples from its pages. Rossides stated emphatically in his introduction that he felt his book (and Canadian sociology) should focus on what he termed "Industrial Society," something in which he felt Aboriginal peoples had a negligible part to play. It is clear that he had the social Darwinist notion that Aboriginal peoples were static, "primitive" peoples who would be swept away by modern, industrial society:

> There is no better way of illustrating the need to employ the concept of culture in economic analysis than to contrast the way in which the native Indian inhabitants of North America utilized the Canadian natural environment with the way it was utilized by early Europeans. For 10,000 years the Canadian Indian made use of his native natural environment in terms of a static hunting and farming economy. Europeans with the same human nature and with the same natural

environment developed, first a systematic exploitation of timber, fish and fur resources and then in the relatively short expanse of two or three centuries, they developed an economy which could actively identify, extract, use and transform a host of natural resources (coals, minerals, oil, etc). In so doing, Canada's settlers have created a material standard of living which would be incomprehensible to Canada's original inhabitants. The vital variable which explains this difference is the complex socio-cultural system of Europe (her imperial appetites, her luxury economy, her mathematics, her missionary zeal, her technology, her bourgeois values, her Protestantism, etc) which European settlers brought with them to Canada. (Rossides 1968: 188)

To their credit, the writers who edited collections of readings included articles with an exclusively Aboriginal content written by "outsiders" to the discipline. This meant not only articles authored by anthropologists, as with all the Aboriginal-themed articles in the four editions of Blishen et al. (1961, 1964, 1968, and 1971) and with the one Aboriginal-themed article in W.E. Mann's *Canada: A Sociological Profile* (1968a), but also articles written by Aboriginal peoples themselves.

During the 1960s and 1970s, articles written by Aboriginal peoples appear in five collections of such readings. In Richard Laskin's *Social Problems: A Canadian Perspective*, there is an insightful article entitled "What does it mean to be an Eskimo?" (Okpik 1964: 129–31), written by Abraham Okpik, an important Inuit leader of the late 1950s and the 1960s (see Tester and Kulchyski 1994: 343ff). With words that would be echoed by contemporary Aboriginal writers, Okpik cogently argues the importance of maintaining the language and culture of the people as key to successfully facing the future. Unfortunately, a great deal of the impact of this article is lost because it is buried in a poorly selected and uncritically edited collection of material about Aboriginal peoples. This collection ranges from the merely paternalistic and assimilationist—"Canada's Indians Yesterday: What of Today?" by the influential anthropologist Diamond Jenness; "The Plight of the Indian in Canada" by William Morris; and "Cultural Assimilation between Indians and Non-Indians in Southern Alberta" by Henry Zentner—to the outright racist— "Lo, the Poor, Irresponsible, Lazy Indian" by yellow journalist John Schmidt, which concludes with: "the Indian has been given a chance. But it seems that he can't or won't pull himself into an improved status in today's Canada. The fault is no one's but his own" (Schmidt 1964: 111). No attempt is made by the editor to direct the student reader to a critical reading of the articles. Schmidt's racist rant is given equal authoritative weight to Okpik's knowledgeable presentation.

Of course, a good sociology professor with an anti-racist or anti-colonialist perspective can contextualize such readings and encourage a critical reading (in Tuhiwai Smith's sense) of the material. However, one cannot count on such teaching; the textbook itself should be pedagogically sound.

In Stewart Crysdale and Christopher Beattie's *Sociology Canada: Readings* (1974), there are two articles written by anthropologists: Lee Guemple's "The Dilemma of the Aging Eskimo" and an excerpt from James Van Stone's book on the Snowdrift Chipewyan. Along with that is an excellent article entitled "A Good Blanket Has Four Corners: A Comparison of Aboriginal Administration in Canada and the United States" by Aboriginal writer Don Whiteside, then a research director for the National Indian Brotherhood. It is one of the most informative, readable, and useful articles I have ever read on the differences between Canada and the United States in historic Aboriginal policies.

Mann and Wheatcroft's *Canada: A Sociological Profile* (1976) contains several articles about Aboriginal peoples: Ojibwa writer Wilfred Pelletier's thought-provoking "Childhood in an Indian Village," Frank G. Vallee's "The Emerging Northern Mosaic," and Trevor Denton's "Canadian Indian Migrants and Impression Management of Ethnic Stigma."

In Boydell, Grindstaff, and Whitehead's *Critical Issues in Canadian Society* (1971), there is an excerpt from Cree leader Harold Cardinal's best-selling *The Unjust Society* (1969: 254–69). The other Aboriginal-themed article in the collection is anthropologist Frank G. Vallee's often reproduced "Kabloona and Eskimo: Social Control" (for example, it appears in the last three editions of Blishen et al.), excerpted from his influential *Kabloona and Eskimo* (1962). In Haas and Shaffir's *Shaping Identity in Canadian Society* (1978), another selection from Cardinal's book is used.

In total, then, in the introductory sociology textbooks published from 1960 until 1976, there are only five articles written by Aboriginal peoples. After 1976, we have none. What happened?

JAMES S. FRIDERES

During the 1970s, sociologists in Canada began researching Aboriginal peoples. Foremost among them in terms of his impact on Canadian sociology textbooks, and arguably on Canadian sociologists and sociology classes, was James S. Frideres of the sociology department of the University of Calgary. Frideres's primary work, initially titled *Canada's Indians: Contemporary Conflicts*, has gone through six editions over more than a quarter century (i.e., from 1974 to 2001). It has consistently maintained its position as the most influential book on Aboriginal peoples in Canada. Other writers of Canadian introductory sociology textbook reference this work far more than any other study of Aboriginal peoples (Fry 1984; Hagedorn 1980; Henslin and Nelson 1996; Hiller 1976, Himelfarb and Richardson 1979; Kendall et al. 1998 and 2000; Macionis and Gerber 1999 and 2002; Schaefer et al. 1996; Spencer 1981; Teevan 1987 and 1988; Tepperman and Curtis 1987; Tepperman and Rosenberg 1998).

The history of this book reflects, and is reflected by, the way that introductory sociology textbooks represent Aboriginal peoples. In the initial edition of his work, Frideres included the aforementioned Ojibwa writer Wilfred Pelletier, who contributed a chapter (Frideres 1974: 101–10), excerpted from his *For Every North American Indian that Begins to Disappear I Also Begin to Disappear*. Although Frideres wrote most of the chapters for his book himself, he also included another Aboriginal-written article, Walter Stewart's "Red Power" (Frideres 1974: 191–98) and two articles written by anthropologists: R.W. Dunning (Frideres 1974: 59–86), who also contributed to Blishen et al, and Phil Drucker (Frideres 1974: 133–56). Both these chapters were significantly longer than the Aboriginal-written chapters.

These articles/chapters did not make a repeat appearance in the subsequent five editions of Frideres's book. The approach employed in editions two to six is one that stresses statistics and political/legal definitions/distinctions and their implications and that pays very little attention to Aboriginal culture. While the theoretic bent of the book in its various incarnations is generally pro-Aboriginal, there is virtually no Aboriginal voice.

A look at the preface of the sixth edition,[4] entitled *Aboriginal Peoples in Canada: Contemporary Conflicts* (Frideres and Gadacz 2001) is instructive in this regard. There are no references to Aboriginal peoples writing about themselves from their standpoint. Instead, there is a "We" (non-Aboriginal Canadians) and "Them" (Aboriginal peoples) approach. Also, note how, paradoxically, although Frideres rightfully urges the reader to be aware that the "dominant group" has written much of what we read about Aboriginal peoples, he tries to claim a neutral "outsider" status between dominant and minorities Aboriginal peoples:

> Novelists, academics, and politicians have been inspired for years to write about their observations of Aboriginal people. While many Canadians (10–15 percent)[5] have little knowledge or conception about Aboriginal people, most of *us* have few encounters with Aboriginal people directly. Yet, at a more abstract level, *we* speak about *their* plight

and treatment... Our goal is to write a book that provides critical interpretation of the events that have shaped Aboriginal-White relations. As we note in the text, many of the original works on Aboriginal people were written from the point of view of the dominant group. The material offered in this book tries to present ethnic relation [sic] from the position of "outsider," identifying both the majority and minority perspectives. (Frideres and Gadacz 2001: x; emphasis mine)

Aboriginal voice is rarely heard in *Aboriginal Peoples in Canada*. In the most recent edition, over 420 pages, I found only seven quotations from Aboriginal peoples (Frideres and Gadacz 2001: 107, 140, 176, 181, 217, 337, and 334), some of them not identified as such. Citing Aboriginal sources is almost as rare. It should further be noted that, although he allowed two co-writers to contribute to various editions of the book, neither of them was Aboriginal.

URBANIZATION STUDIES

Sociologists Vic Satzewich and Terry Wotherspoon, in the introduction to their *First Nations: Race, Class and Gender Relations* (1993), comment on how, while other social science disciplines have maintained a constant study of Aboriginal peoples over the years, sociologists studied urbanization of Aboriginal peoples in the 1970s in several prominent studies and then fundamentally backed away:

Somewhat ironically, Canadian sociologists have not kept pace with these other disciplines in the study of aboriginal peoples. While there was a flurry of sociological and anthropological studies of aboriginal peoples in the early 1970s, particularly in the context of Indian urbanization (see Dosman, 1972; Nagler, 1971 [1970]; Brody, 1971;

Ryan, 1978; Stymeist,[6] 1975; Braroe, 1975), the issue of aboriginal/non-aboriginal relations has been placed on the so-called "backburner" by sociologists. (Satzewich and Wotherspoon 1993: xii)

Of the works cited, four have had an impact on Canadian introductory sociology textbooks: Brody (quoted and cited in Mansfield 1982; Ramu and Johnson 1976; and in Zeitlin and Brym 1991), Dosman (quoted and cited in Himelfarb and Richardson 1979; Ramu and Johnson 1976; Teevan 1982a, 1982b, 1987, and 1988; and in Tepperman and Curtis 1987), Nagler (quoted and cited in Crysdale and Beattie 1977; and Himelfarb and Richardson 1979), and Stymeist (quoted and cited in Lundy and Warme 1986 and 1990; in Stebbins 1987; and excerpted in Himelfarb and Richardson 1984: 505–19). All four are referred to by Frideres: Dosman and Nagler in all six editions, Stymeist from the second to the sixth edition, and Brody from the third to the sixth edition. Brody, Dosman, and Nagler are also cited in Peter McGahan's *Urban Sociology in Canada* (1995), which is currently a course reading at Humber College (winter 2003).

It is important to note that all take as their fundamental frame that Aboriginal peoples are a "social problem"[7] much in the way that Tuhiwai Smith anticipated, and that Métis writer Emma Laroque "problematizes" in her article "Three Conventional Approaches to Native People in Society and in Literature":

> Viewing/treating Native people as a social problem distorts reality. For while it is true that a substantial number of Native people do face some very serious socioeconomic problems, that is not all there is to the Native scene. There is much, much more. There are healthy Native communities and individuals. There are thousands of Native individuals who contribute more than their share to Canadian society. And what concerns me so very much about the social problems view of Native people is that it is so prevalent, so

profound in Canadian society that editorials, radio, television and even academic works seem to see nothing but social problems in regards to Native peoples. (Laroque 1993: 212)

Connected with this is the denial of Aboriginal voice that can clearly be seen in Dosman, Nagler, and Stymeist's books. As such, like Frideres, they both reflect and are reflected in the practice of sociology as it was developing in the 1970s in Canada. Dosman studied Aboriginal peoples in the city of Saskatoon in 1968 and 1969 (20 years before the publication of the introductory sociology textbooks that valorize his work as a source of knowledge). He rarely used Aboriginal voice at all, and when he did, he was likely to be critical of the individual quoted. His constant use of the expression "the subject" depersonalizes and objectifies the people about whom he is writing. He overstresses the significance of class over the unifying experience of race among urban Aboriginal peoples, referring to groups with the somewhat patronizing and misleading labels of "aristocracy," "bourgeoisie," and "welfare and anomic." In so doing, he disqualified the leaders in the urban Aboriginal community from legitimately articulating a position worthy of sociological consideration. He specifically attacks two significant western Aboriginal leaders of the time: Métis academic and writer Howard Adams and Cree politician Harold Cardinal (see discussion below, p. 63), whose important publications date from the same period (Adams 1975; Cardinal 1969 and 1977). In a chapter entitled "Leaders Without Followers: The Dilemma of Urban Indian Organizations," he writes, "Dr. Adams's prose is too flowery and intellectual for the native people; it is geared to the young students who crowd his meetings" (Dosman 1972: 162). This seems to be purely speculation on Dosman's part, developed without asking Aboriginal peoples of all "classes" what they might think of Adams (a long-respected figure in Aboriginal circles). He later quotes Cardinal, but dismisses Cardinal's words with the terse remark, "What, however, does that mean in the real world?" (Dosman 1972: 183). Clearly, he was not prepared to respect the standpoint Cardinal brought to the discussion.

Nagler studied 150 Aboriginal peoples in Toronto from May 1964 to September 1966, again work done much earlier than the period in which he is cited by introductory sociology textbooks. Like Dosman, he too stresses the overriding importance of class over race, using traditional sociological distinctions such as "white-collar workers" and "blue-collar workers." This is similar to the way in which male neo-Marxists of the 1960s and 1970s were class reductionists at the cost of gender, and early White feminists were gender reductionists at the cost of race. While Nagler incorporates more Aboriginal voice in his work than Dosman did, he too emphasizes the disconnection between the leaders of Aboriginal organizations and the rest of the urban Aboriginal population (see Nagler 1970: 76). In this way, as with Dosman, Nagler disqualifies Aboriginal leaders from being knowledge producers, rather than mere objects of study.

Stymeist did his research over 16 months in 1971 and 1972 in Kenora in northwestern Ontario. His book, entitled *Ethnics and Indians: Social Relations in a Northwestern Ontario Town*, reflects much more the voice and views of the "Ethnics" than the "Indians." Only three times does he present a quotation from an Aboriginal person (Stymeist 1975: 65, 74, and 78), while he allows local non-Aboriginal peoples many opportunities to articulate their views (Stymeist 1975: 7, 11, 26, 29, 30, 35, 53, 55, 56, 62, 63, 71, 72, and 76).

When Stymeist's book is quoted or cited at length in introductory sociology textbooks, racism is discussed and portrayed, but the discussion and portrayal creates a scenario of victimology. Aboriginal peoples are victims of racism, *and* they are powerless, without agency. They are not presented as having any significant capacity to resist or overcome the racism they encounter. Both Lundy and Warme (1986 and 1990) and Himelfarb and Richardson (1979: 117 and 1991: 193) use Stymeist in this way, quoting and referring to a specific passage about how Aboriginal peoples and non-Aboriginal peoples are treated differently after drinking in the largest tavern in Kenora:

> Most arrests in Crow Lake are for public intoxication. Ontario Provincial Police cars park outside the entrance to the Crow Lake Hotel, the town's largest central pub, for an hour or so before and after the pub closes. The waiters will ask a drunk white man, who is perhaps a relative, friend or steady customer, if he wants to call a cab. The cab will arrive at the back door of the hotel and the man in question will leave unseen. Many Indians, however, are arrested as they leave the pub, and some have been arrested for public drunkenness as they were climbing the stairs to their rooms in the hotel. (Stymeist 1975: 75)

Himelfarb and Richardson present Stymeist as follows:

> [P]art of the reason that the powerless groups are more likely to be arrested can be found in the actions of the ordinary citizen. An excellent example is provided by David Stymeist (1975) in his study of "Crow Lake," the fictitious town in Northern Ontario. In Crow Lake, as elsewhere in Canada, native people are frequently arrested and almost always for public drunkenness.... Stymeist describes how the police routinely park outside of the Crow Lake Hotel, the town's largest tavern, around closing time, waiting for "arrests." The patron, who may be a friend or a steady customer, is asked if he wishes them (the police) to call a cab. The white customers are often picked up at the rear entrance and driven home unseen by the police.[8] Native people are not accorded this kind of treatment and must leave by the front entrance where they are often picked up by the police. (Himelfarb and Richardson 1991: 193)

The Aboriginal peoples are "powerless" and the "ordinary citizen" (someone who is not Aboriginal) is the only one who can take action. This is repeated in Lundy and Warme. After an extended excerpt from the quotation referred to and paraphrased by Himelfarb and Richardson, Lundy and Warme talk about what the non-Aboriginal peoples involved (e.g., police and hotel staff) could do differently to remedy the situation. Absent is mention of how Aboriginal peoples, individually and collectively, could combat this form of discrimination (e.g., through Aboriginal police, Aboriginal designated drivers, or Aboriginal watchdog groups to monitor what goes on in such situations). Sympathy for the Aboriginal peoples' "plight" is allowed, but seemingly not their agency.

HAROLD CARDINAL: THE SOCIOLOGISTS' DESIGNATED INDIAN

The Aboriginal writer cited most often in introductory sociology textbooks is Harold Cardinal, a Cree born in 1945 in High Prairie, Alberta. After working for the Canadian Union of Students and the Canadian Indian Youth Council, he was elected president of the Indian Association of Alberta (IAA), with accompanying membership on the board of the National Indian Brotherhood. After reaching national prominence in the 1970s as the president of the IAA, as an author, and generally as the most vocal Aboriginal critic of federal policy, he fell into disrepute after a funding scandal within the IAA and left the national stage. He has remained active as a scholar, recently being Indigenous Scholar in Residence at the University of Alberta Law School, and is completing his doctorate in law at the University of British Columbia. In 2001, he received a National Aboriginal Achievement Award in the lifetime achievement category.

Cardinal's first book, *The Unjust Society, The Tragedy of Canadian Indians* (1969), was referenced in introductory sociology textbooks from 1976 to 1990 (Curtis and Tepperman

1990; Hagedorn 1980 and 1983; Hiller 1976; Holmes 1988; Ramu and Johnson 1976; Stebbins 1987; Tepperman and Curtis 1987),[9] even though much of what he said was a direct response to the federal government's "White Paper" of the late 1960s and, thus, had lost relevance in later years. It also has been cited (although not quoted) in every edition of Frideres. As noted above, excerpts also appeared in Boydell, Grindstaff, and Whitehead's *Critical Issues in Canadian Society* (1971: 254–69) and in Haas and Shaffir's *Shaping Identity in Canadian Society* (1978: 150–56). It is telling that the most frequently referenced Aboriginal work was written in the 1960s and was still appearing in textbooks in the 1980s.

Why has Cardinal's work been quoted so often, when most of his contemporaries, such as Howard Adams, Maria Campbell, Emma LaRoque, and George Manuel, were denied the same admittedly small, sociological platform from which to speak? Several reasons can be suggested. First, having studied sociology for two years at St. Patrick's College in Ottawa, he has been accorded some credibility as someone to be quoted and referenced in an introductory sociology textbook. This can be inferred from the following statement by Hiller:

> Cardinal's education in sociology (St. Patrick's College, Ottawa) has equipped him for leadership in the Indian-White conflict: He knows how to confront the white man on the white man's terms. He had participated successfully in white society; yet because he is an Indian and chooses to retain that identity, his status cannot fully crystallize in the white society. (Hiller 1976: 119–20)

Second, he fit neatly into a sociological package: the modern-day warrior. The Red Power movement in the United States was making headlines with the rise of the American Indian Movement (AIM), the high-profile Aboriginal occupation of Alcatraz, and the symbolic standoff at Wounded Knee. He was non-violent and his battles were verbal and highly quotable, so he did not pose a major threat. He was a youthful radical at a time when mainstream youthful radicals were considered important. As will be discussed in the chapters on Inuit elders, Aboriginal elders were not allowed a similar voice, as "Aboriginal elder" as a concept has proved elusive to the writers and editors of introductory sociology textbooks.

Further, Cardinal's work put him well into the "segregation versus assimilation" dichotomy that a number of sociologists then favoured in their portrayal of Aboriginal peoples. Take the following statements made in 1976 by S.D. Clark (about whom Lorne Tepperman would say in the Preface to a collection of Clark's works, "No Canadian scholar has made a larger or more varied contribution to the sociological study of Canadian society..." Clark 1976: vii). In *Canadian Society in Historical Perspective*, Clark wrote about the binary distinction of leader-invoked separation versus inevitable assimilation. Like Dosman and Nagler, he writes in a way that takes authority from these leaders:

> Thus the advocates of red power, though some of them may boast university degrees as distinguished as the Ph.D., would have their fellow Canadian Indians throw off the ways of the white man and return to the simple life of their native past;[10] a form of garb, unmistakably Indian in cut and material, is made to serve as a symbol of the Indian's distinctive culture. (Clark 1976: 47)

> Likewise, the effort of Canadian Indians leaders to preserve the isolation of their people within the larger society can be seen to serve their interests as Indian leaders and makes understandable their bitter opposition to the government white paper on Indian policy, but the consequences, if the effort succeeds, may be costly to the Indian people. (Clark 1976: 50)

The binary was personified by Hiller in a quotation debate that pitted Harold Cardinal against William Wuttunee (Hiller 1976: 119–20). Wuttunee, like Cardinal a Cree from western Canada, graduated in law from the University of Saskatchewan in 1952. His was an assimilationist approach, reflecting his own career working for the Saskatchewan and Alberta governments. His book, *Ruffled Feathers: Indians in Canadian Society*, was "a rebuttal to Harold Cardinal's *Unjust Society*" (Wuttunee 1971: v). Significantly, in his "Acknowledgments," he thanked Dean Frease of the Department of Sociology, University of Calgary "for his constructive suggestions."

When Harold Cardinal faded from the big screen of federal Aboriginal politics, no Aboriginal writer of the 1980s or 1990s was permitted to take his place in introductory sociology textbooks. This is not because they haven't been writing. For example, Ovide Mercredi, a fairly well-known media figure in the 1990s as the National Chief of the Assembly of First Nations, wrote a book published in 1993 (Mercredi and Turpel 1993) that is not referred to or quoted in any Canadian introductory sociology textbook.

SOCIOLOGY TEXTBOOKS AFTER 1976

After 1976, collections of articles or readings in Canadian introductory sociology usually had no articles exclusively devoted to Aboriginal themes (Forcese and Richer 1982 and 1988; Grayson 1983; Hagedorn 1980 and 1983; Holmes 1988; Richardson and Tepperman 1987; Teevan 1982, 1986, 1988, 1992). This is in keeping with monographs, which never contain a single chapter dedicated solely to Aboriginal peoples.

The five exceptions among the introductory sociology readers are B. Singh Bolaria's *Social Issues and Contradictions in Canadian Society* (1995); John A. Fry's *Contradictions in Canadian Society: Readings in Introductory Sociology*, (1984); A. Himelfarb and C. James Richardson's *Sociology for*

Canadians: A Reader (1984); Lorne Tepperman and James Curtis's *Readings in Sociology: An Introduction* (1987); and James Curtis and Lorne Tepperman's *Images of Canada: The Sociological Tradition* (1990). Of the five articles in these books, four are written by sociologists and reflect standard sociological research methodology (e.g., privileging statistics and a social problems approach): Paul D. Brady's "Contradictions and Consequences: The Social and Health Status of Canada's Registered Indian Population" in Fry (1984); Rita Bienvenue's "The Colonial Status of Canadian Indians" in Tepperman and Curtis (1987); J. Rick Ponting's "Canadians' Responses to Native Peoples" in Curtis and Tepperman (1990); and James Frideres's "From the Bottom Up: Institutional Structures and the Native People" in Bolaria (1995). The fifth is the excerpted Stymeist piece in Himelfarb and Richardson (1984).

EXCLUDING ABORIGINAL WRITERS
Howard Adams

One of the most important Aboriginal voices in Canada from the 1970s to the 1990s (with books published in 1975, 1993, 1995, and 1999) is Métis writer, scholar, and educator Dr. Howard Adams, winner of the 2000 National Aboriginal Achievement Award in the education category. After a long affiliation with the University of Saskatchewan, and just before his death in 2001, he was professor emeritus at the University of California (the university from which he received his PhD). In 1975, he published an important book, *Prison of Grass: Canada from the Native Point of View*, which was reprinted in 1989. This work is often cited by Aboriginal authors (e.g., Alfred 1999; Dickason 2002; and Monture-Angus 1995). His is a voice that should have been included, but was almost completely ignored, by writers of introductory sociology textbooks. The one reference is to his 1979 article (an excerpted adaptation from his book), "Canada from the Native Point of View," in J.L.

Elliot's *Two Nations: Many Cultures,* which is cited in Lundy and Warme (1986).

Why has Adams been so excluded? We have seen that one influential sociological work on Aboriginal peoples (Dosman) attacked him; that had an impact on his reputation. Secondly, much more than Cardinal, he presents an ongoing alternative authority for the generation of knowledge. His *Prison of Grass* contains a strong interrogation of the putative objectivity of mainstream sources, from a Marxist and an Aboriginal perspective:

> Although we are taught that history is true and objective when based on primary sources, the observers' interpretations are bound to reflect the specific emphasis of the period and its unique circumstances. Furthermore, these capitalist historical writings represent only the forces contending for power and their power relationships. Consequently, the experiences and relationships of the "common" people are largely omitted from historical writing, because in capitalism the masses are not a ruling force. (Adams 1975: 14)

He argues for and demonstrates the value of Aboriginal-produced knowledge, drawing both from his own experiences in ways that are quite like those of the similarly excluded and just as important female Aboriginal writers Maria Campbell and Emma Laroque and seeking out other examples of Aboriginal voice, as can be seen in the following:

> The historical interpretation contained in this book takes the following into account: objective conditions and consequences of historical colonialization, the present circumstances of Indians and Métis, discussion with senior native people, primary documents, and secondary sources. One study I have used extensively is *L'Histoire de la Nation Métisse dans l'Ouest Canadien,* by a H. de Trémaudan, a

book based on documents and statements collected from
the Métis people in the Red River and Batoche areas
between 1910 and 1925. A historical committee organized
by Ambrose Lépine accumulated "a mass of writings,
letters and official documents and conducted minute inves-
tigations among the people actually involved in the revolt."
(Adams 1975: xi)

Adams, whose arguments follow lines similar to those of
Maori writer Linda Tuhiwai Smith, has consistently argued the
case for what he terms "cultural decolonization." In an article
published in 1993, he defines this term as referring to "a new
focus on the understanding and awareness of Indian/Métis
culture and history from an authentic Aboriginal perspective and
sensitivity" (Adams 1993: 251). In his thinking, cultural decolonization bears three main characteristics: 1) that knowledge is
perceived "in terms of a specific place and time as a principle of
intellectual inquiry" (Adams 1993: 251); 2) that the major aim
or concern of Aboriginal writing should be to speak to the
Aboriginal audience first; and 3) that Aboriginal writers work
to attain an "Aboriginal counter-consciousness," which involves
"a spirit of devotion to the cause of self-determination, justice
and equality." (Adams 1993: 253)

George Manuel

Similarly marginalized by sociology, and arguably equally as
important as *Prison of Grass*, is *The Fourth World: An Indian
Reality*, co-authored by George Manuel and Michael Posluns
(1974). Shuswap politician George Manuel was a major figure
in the development of Aboriginal politics in Canada on a
national scale. He was president of the National Indian
Brotherhood from 1970 to 1976, was awarded the Order of
Canada, and was three times nominated for the Nobel Peace
Prize. His book was cited only once, by Holmes (1988). In that

one citation, none of his words are quoted, and his book is not one of those suggested for further reading.

Marginalizing as "Literary"

Why, generally, are works such as those by Adams and Manuel not included as important sources of sociological knowledge about Aboriginal peoples? One answer to that question can be found in the Preface to the third edition of *Unequal Relations: An Introduction to Race, Ethnic, and Aboriginal Dynamics* written by sociologists Augie Fleras and Jean Leonard Elliott. They write:

> There are several things this book is not.... It does not provide a literary platform for minority "voices" or "stories" by minority authors...With several notable exceptions, our preference rests with the theme of group interaction within unequal contexts. Micromodels of individual behaviour that focus on attitudes or beliefs are not dismissed outright. They simply are postponed as secondary in importance to a focus on institutions, social conditions, and structural level as explanatory variables. (Fleras and Elliott 1999: xii)

These two sociologists have had a major impact; their views are illustrative of the sociological mainstream in Canada. Elliott's *Native Peoples* (1971) was cited in Gallagher and Lambert (1971) and in Spencer (1981). Fleras and Elliott's *Multiculturalism in Canada* (1992) was cited in Kendall et al. (1998 and 2000), and an earlier edition of *Unequal Relations* is cited in Henslin and Nelson (1996) and Schaefer et al. (1996).

When sociologists such as Fleras and Elliott marginalize Aboriginal voices as merely "literary" and postpone (a word Aboriginal peoples are used to in promises from governments) as of "secondary ... importance" works that focus on the "attitudes and beliefs" of such voices, they replicate the "unequal contexts" they purport to combat with their non-Aboriginal sociological knowledge.

Three Times Marginalized: Female Aboriginal Literary Writers

The role of "literary," as opposed to more purely disciplined sociological, writing as culturally empowering resistance for Canadian Aboriginal peoples has been important since the 1970s. During that period, two Métis women (triply disenfranchised as sociological sources of knowledge for being Aboriginal peoples, women, and non-sociologists) wrote autobiographical books that have inspired and empowered Aboriginal women across Canada to tell their stories: Maria Campbell's *Halfbreed* (1973) and Emma LaRoque's[11] *Defeathering the Indian* (1975). These works bear the three fundamental characteristics of Adams's "cultural decolonization." In the words of Janice Acoose, a grateful Aboriginal writer of the next generation, Campbell's work "refuses to let Canada erase what has been done to her people" and Laroque "insists that Indigenous peoples were not rendered voiceless, despite very deliberate institutionally sanctioned attempts to silence [them]" (Acoose 1995: 101 and 111).

The exclusion of Emma Laroque's work is both predictable and unfortunate, as she adds an instructive combination of a decolonizing and feminist perspective (see Laroque 1975, 1988, 1990, and 1996), as can be seen in the following, which, although directed more at non-Aboriginal historians and literary writers, is equally true of the writers and editors of Canadian introductory sociology textbooks:

> Native scholars, particularly those of us who are decolonized and/or feminist, have been accused of "speaking in our own voices," which is taken as "being biased" or doing something less than "substantive" or "pure" research. Not only are such accusations glaringly ironic given the degree

of bias, inflammatory language, and barely concealed racism evident in much of early Canadian historical and literary writing on Native peoples, but they are also adversarial. Native scholars' contribution of contemporary scholarship is significant, for, in a sense, we bring "the other half" of Canada into light. Not only do we offer new ways of seeing and saying things, but we also provide new directions and fresh methodologies to cross-cultural research; we broaden the empirical and theoretical bases of numerous disciplines, and we pose new questions to old and tired traditions. (Laroque 1996: 12)

During the 1980s and 1990s, two women writers made an impact on Aboriginal Canada: Lee Maracle and Jeannette Armstrong. Lee Maracle is a Métis/Coast Salish writer born in Vancouver in 1950. She was a member of the Red Power movement in the 1960s and 1970s and is a long-time activist and public speaker on behalf of Aboriginal issues. On the back jacket cover of her novel, *Sundogs*, she is referred to as the most published Canadian Aboriginal writer. She published a number of books in the 1990s with the two British Columbia publishers that focus on Aboriginal issues, Theytus and Press Gang, including books of short stories, poetry, novels, and the autobiographical work *I Am Woman: A Native Perspective on Sociology and Feminism* (1996). Her work, fiction and nonfiction, is often anthologized, as she has been the editor and co-editor of a number of anthologies. She has been a Visiting Professor in both Women's Studies at the University of Toronto and Canadian Studies at the University of Waterloo; currently she is Distinguished Visiting Professor in Canadian Culture at Western Washington University in Bellingham, WA. Her work is a critique of how sociology discusses her people. In *Sundogs* (1992), which, set in 1990, concerns an Aboriginal family in British Columbia coming to terms with events such as Meech Lake and the Oka situation, the heroine is studying sociology, but comments critically of the discipline. The following quotation is illustrative, as it questions the value of the sociological staple, statistics. It also illustrates the principle of celebrating survival (as discussed here in Chapter One):

> It shames me some to hear the statistics about us in class.
> The shame burns holes in whatever sympathy I may have
> for Indians, not my mom though. (Maracle 1992: 3)

Her work offers a good example of an Aboriginal voice that could readily be included in an introductory sociology textbook. But she is ignored.

Jeannette Armstrong was born on an Okanagan reserve in British Columbia. She is referred to as the first Aboriginal Canadian woman novelist; her novel *Slash* (1985) has often been written about by academics studying Canadian literature (for example, Fee 1990). It has sociological relevance in that it discusses through the life of the hero, a young Okanagan male, the nature of the Red Power movement of the 1960s and 1970s. She has also published books for children (1982 and 1984) and a collection of poems (1991), edited a work of First Nations literary analysis (1993) and co-edited an anthology of Aboriginal poetry in Canada (2001), and has written a number of powerful essays (1998); her work is often anthologized (see King 1990 and Jaine and Hayden Taylor 1992). After receiving her Bachelor of Fine Arts in 1978, she began working at the Okanagan-run En'owkin Centre, eventually becoming a co-founder and director of the En'owkin School of International Writing, which is affiliated with the University of Victoria and is the first credit-awarding writing program in Canada that is managed and operated exclusively by and for Aboriginal peoples. She was awarded an honorary doctorate from St. Thomas University in 2000. It would be hard to exaggerate her impact as a writer, role model, and teacher. Yet, her voice is silent in introductory sociology texts.

It seems, then, that as sociology developed as a discipline in Canada, it became more rigid in what was allowed to be an authoritative voice on Aboriginal subjects in introductory textbooks, protecting its professional, disciplinary boundaries in the process: only sociologists need apply. This produced a virtual silencing of Aboriginal voice in these works, their alternative framing of issues disallowed.

Marginalizing the Exceptions

There are two exceptions to the exclusion of Aboriginal voice in the later texts. One comes from Ojibwa writer Wilfred Pelletier, who, as we have seen, was one of the Aboriginal voices in introductory sociology textbooks (and Frideres) in the early 1970s. Lundy and Warme (1986: 59–60 and again in 1990) permit a rather extended quotation from his "For Every North American Indian that Begins to Disappear I Also Begin to Disappear" (1971). Not only is he not located as to nation and experience, but there are marginalizing constraints put on his work that downplay him as an authoritative voice. His work is not listed either in the "Recommended Readings" at the end of the chapter (no Aboriginal work is ever included in the recommended readings of a Canadian introductory sociology textbook), nor is it listed in the References; it appears only in the credits. Finally, his name is not listed in the Name Index at the back of the book.

Similarly marginalized is a short piece included in Teevan (1989: 190–91) entitled "Life Among the Qallunaat (The White People): An Inuit Perspective" by Minnie Aodia Freeman, a series of excerpts from her book of the same name (1978). As with Pelletier's work, her book is not listed in the References in the back, or in the Suggested Readings at the end of the chapter, and her name is not given in the Name Index. Further, Teevan does not refer to the quotation in the body of the text, nor does he use it to make any point. It just hangs there, disconnected.

PRIVILEGING VOICES
Shkilnyk and Grassy Narrows: Talking about Reserves

A source of some significance to introductory sociology text-books written in the 1990s and the early twenty-first century is Anastasia M. Shkilnyk's poignant work, *A Poison Stronger than Love: The Destruction of an Ojibwa Community* (1985). It is quoted in three series of introductory sociology textbooks (Kendall et al. 1998 and 2000; Macionis and Gerber 1999 and 2002; Zeitlin and Brym 1991).

The community discussed is Grassy Narrows, 90 kilometres north of Kenora (the subject of Dosman's study) in northwest Ontario. This Ojibwa community suffered a double blow of outsider-imposed oppression: relocation and methyl mercury poisoning. In 1963, the community was forced to relocate to another site on their reserve by the federal Department of Indian Affairs and Northern Development (DIAND). DIAND's reasoning came at least as much for outside private interests—the extension of a logging road and the desire of the Hudson's Bay Company store to relocate—as for any government thought of improving services to the community. Certainly the people were in no sense consulted.

The second blow was at least equally devastating. After purchasing a pulp and paper mill in Dryden (170 kilometres upstream from Grassy Narrows), Reed Paper Company, a British-owned multinational, began dumping large amounts of mercury— about 20,000 pounds between 1962 and 1970—into the English-Wabigoon River system (Hutchison and Wallace 1977: 56). In 1970, significantly high amounts of mercury were noticed in the fish; two years later came the first human casualty: Tom Strong, a 42-year-old fishing guide.

The band council anxiously investigated the cause of Strong's death, which was officially listed as a heart attack. Fishing was important to the community, both as a source of food and income. One hundred and twenty-five people from Grassy Narrows and the neighbouring Ojibwa community of White

Dog (50 miles away) worked annually as guides at the 17 commercial fishing lodges in the area (Hutchison and Wallace 1977: 8). The provincial coroner's inquest downplayed the role of mercury poisoning, so the council persisted in exploring the effects of mercury on their fish and on their people. In 1973, they spoke eloquently of the problems of their community to a task force sent to inquire about mercury in the area:

> Our people have been relocated within the past decade and we are still suffering the effects of this social upheaval.... Our housing is extremely inadequate; there have been ten house fires in the past year and on the average they have burnt to the ground within a half hour. The dislocation in our lives has resulted in an excessive number of tragic deaths, violence, alcohol abuse, broken families, school drop-outs.
>
> All these are symptoms of our way of life now which is very much disrupted. In addition to the above situations, we also lost our commercial fishing and nearby guiding livelihoods owing to the mercury pollution. We have undergone many tests on the effects of mercury on our health and we are still in the dark as to what to do about the mercury problem.... (Hutchison and Wallace 1977: 81)

The provincial government, through the ministries of natural resources and health, was hesitant to act or even to declare that there was a problem. Much of the government's hesitancy came from the fact that it had significant financial interests at stake. Pulp and paper was a major employer in northwestern Ontario, as was the tourist business. The government had been giving Anglo-Canadian (the name of the Reed Paper subsidiary at that time) tax rebates on equipment under their pollution-control incentive program (Hutchison and Wallace 1977: 85). More directly, the government had heavily invested in Minaki Lodge, just 45 kilometres west of Grassy Narrows. It had a scheme to make the lodge "a jewel in the necklace of tourist facilities that threads throughout Ontario" (as quoted in Hutchison and Wallace 1977: 85). In January 1977, it was revealed that the government had sunk about $7.5 million into the acquisition and renovation of the then-vacant lodge (Hutchison and Wallace 1977: 97).

In 1974, young Ojibwa radicals (including 25-year-old Tom Keesick, for a short term chief at Grassy Narrows) occupied Anicinabe Park, a municipal park in Kenora, for 39 days to protest Ojibwa oppression at the hands of the justice system. While the chief was impeached by the people for his actions, the demonstration raised local Aboriginal consciousness of the need for collective action. In the words of Louis Cameron, a leader in the protest:

> I think the absolute thing that happened was that native people for the first time since maybe a hundred years back had taken up armed struggle to liberate themselves and direct confrontation to solve their problems and to meet the situation head-on. (Burke 1976: 387)

The newly elected and more conservative chief, Andy Keewatin, and band council continued to try to change the desperate situation with which they were confronted. In 1975, they contacted the people of Minamata, Japan, a fishing community whose name is now associated with Minamata disease, the motor and nervous disorder resulting from mercury poisoning. Experts from Japan came to assess the situation in Ontario. In December 1975, the chiefs and councillors of Grassy Narrows and Whitedog tried further to draw attention to their problem by threatening to begin regular deliveries of poisoned fish to the homes of the provincial premier, the minister of natural resources, the minister of health, the attorney general, the leaders of the opposition parties, and the president of Reed. They sent each of these people a six-page letter discussing their situation:

We know that the fish are poisonous. We know that eating the fish can destroy the mind and health and take the life of Indians and whites. This cannot fail to be known by anybody who, for five long years, has watched the growing violence, the deteriorating health and the declining morale of our people...

Unless you act to close these polluted rivers, our people are doomed....

For five years, we have fought the bias, indifference and hostility of your minister of natural resources.

It is long enough. Enough people have died. Enough of our people have been destroyed. Enough lack of understanding. Enough pro-polluter bias. Enough indifference. (Hutchison and Wallace 1977: 140)

This discussion is drawn largely from *Grassy Narrows* (1977), by journalists George Hutchison and Dick Wallace, who won the Michener Award for meritorious public service in 1975 in recognition of the coverage given by them in articles in the *London Free Press* to the mercury crisis in Lake St. Clair in southwestern Ontario and Grassy Narrows in northwestern Ontario. They incorporated a fair amount of Aboriginal voice in their work, especially that of chiefs Andy Keewatin and Bill Fobister and his family, clearly demonstrated the existence of Aboriginal agency, and assigned a significant amount of blame on the provincial government and Reed Paper. These features can also be seen in the short section that Métis scholar and writer Olive Dickason dedicates in her general history of First Nations in Canada (2002) to the story of Grassy Narrows. In this passage, Dickason discusses both Grassy Narrows and the neighbouring White Dog reserve:

The contamination forced the reserves to close their commercial fisheries; still, government reaction was slow even in the face of growing health problems in the two communities. Eventually, the Ojibwa took matters into their own hands and invited Japanese specialists from Minamata, Japan, where a similar situation had occurred, to assess what was happening. They confirmed the presence of "Minamata disease".... When Reed announced plans for a new mill in 1974, the people had to prepare their own case on land use and forest management. In the midst of the public scandal, an agreement for the new mill, containing some provision for environmental protection, was signed in 1976....

An out of court settlement for $8.7 million, reached in 1985, has paved the way for the reserves to develop a program encouraging environmentally friendly industries. (Dickason 2002: 394)

Shkilnyk's work differed significantly. In 1976, she was hired by DIAND to study the community and took a leave of absence from her doctoral program in urban and regional planning to do so. While her study is insightful in showing the negative effects of forced relocation, it fails to interrogate seriously the destructive role of the multinational company then fighting the community in the courts and the weak response by the federal (the people who hired her to do the study) and provincial governments. Further, Shkilnyk fails to show any agency on the part of the people. In her work, the people neither understand their situation nor mount any resistance. Hers is a study in victimology, in which Aboriginal peoples are unknowing, helpless people without the knowledge or will to help themselves. This victimology frame is clearly seen in the introduction by sociologist Kai Erikson:

Shkilnyk shows movingly, the Ojibwa of Grassy Narrows are a truly broken people. They neglect themselves out of an inability to believe that they matter, and though it may be difficult for those of us who live in secure comfort to understand, they not only neglect but abuse their own children.

> They live a life of sullen pain, blurred for days at a time by joyless bouts of drinking. And they die suddenly. Among these deaths are some that any coroner would feel compelled to call suicide, but there are others, impossible to document accurately, that come as the result of people destroying themselves out of a simple failure to care. (Shkilnyk 1985: xv-xvii)

Significantly, and with no surprise, there is very little Aboriginal voice in this book. The tone of one-sided knowledge production is set in the first chapter, in which Shkilnyk quotes extensively from the observations she made in her own journal and almost as extensively from non-Aboriginal teachers on the reserve.

The only hint that the people might be doing anything to help themselves resist the effects of oppression comes in one of the final paragraphs, in several sentences that say little to oppose the tone of the entire book. Significantly, no mention is made of their fight in the courts nor their work with the people from Minamata:

> Since the data on social pathology was first collected in 1977–78, the Grassy Narrows people have made valiant efforts to cope with their problems. They organized an Alcoholics Anonymous group. Some families formed a small subdivision within the reserve where drinking is forbidden. Young people have set up a night patrol to look after abandoned children. And there is a crisis intervention centre, whose volunteers try to prevent attempted suicide, vandalism, and family violence. When I returned to Grassy Narrows in the summer of 1981 and again in 1983, I was impressed by the remarkable strength of a few individuals in the face of awesome pressures. Yet there were other disturbing indications that the battle against further unravelling of the communal fabric was far from won. (Shkilnyk 1985: 232)

The way that the study is used in introductory sociology textbooks compounds its flaws. The most extreme example is found in Zeitlin and Brym (1991: 162–64), where extended reference is made to Shkilnyk's work. It begins with the following, a dazzling display of statistical (or what I would like to call "statistified") horror:

> Imagine a village of 490 souls in which three out of four deaths can be attributed to alcohol- or drug-related acts of violence. In a single year, over a third of all children between the ages of five and fourteen are removed from the community by a welfare agency because they are physically abused or severely neglected. Over the same twelve months, nearly a fifth of all children between the ages of eleven and nineteen try to commit suicide. Two-thirds of the population between the ages of sixteen and 64 are heavy or very heavy consumers of alcohol. In Grassy Narrows these and other similarly appalling statistics summarize the conditions of social existence circa 1978. (Zeitlin and Brym 1991: 162)

There is no attempt to balance this portrayal of what might arguably be one of the worst reserves in Canada with the depiction of a strong reserve, of which there are many. It would be like characterizing Canadian cities by speaking only of poor working-class and welfare housing areas such as Regent Park or Jane and Finch in Toronto. The only attempt to qualify this as being anything but typical is the following half-hearted statement: "The social crisis in Grassy Narrows is undoubtedly more severe than in most aboriginal communities" (Zeitlin and Brym 1991: 163). It does not state or even hint that there are good reserves, just ones that may be less horrible.

In Kendall et al. (2000), under the subheading of "Health Problems Among Aboriginal Peoples in Canada," we see the people of Grassy Narrows again portrayed as victims, again theirs the only reserve represented. Even though some of the ultimate causes of the problems are rightly identified (the province is let off of the hook), the impression is left that life on a reserve equals a horror story:

Finally, the legacy of colonialism still affects Aboriginal people's health problems. Anastasia Shkilnyk (1985), who studied the Ojibwa community of Grassy Narrows in northwestern Ontario, attributes the high rates of suicide and violent death and health problems on the reserve to colonial actions such as the destruction of Aboriginal language and religion, the family breakdown caused by enforced attendance at residential schools, and the forced relocation of the community by the Department of Indian Affairs. Environmental destruction by local industries that dumped methyl mercury into the lakes and rivers around the reserve was another contributor. This toxic substance had a direct impact on the health of Grassy Narrows residents and also had an indirect impact by destroying the traditional fishery that was the foundation of the community's way of life. (Kendall et al. 2000: 588)

Macionis and Gerber (1999: 443; 2002: 465) use Shkilnyk's study to make a brief reference to the community as an example of the seemingly (to the writers and readers of the book) inevitable breakup of the Aboriginal family, owing to the negative effects of missionaries and their residential schools. They add, "In addition, resettlement programs broke up whole communities and diminished family ties even further" (Shkilnyk 1985). Not only do they dismiss the possibility that Aboriginal families can be strong (as they often are), but they make it sound, with their use of the plural, as if "resettlement programs" were the norm and not just a deadly minority.[12]

One final criticism of the use by introductory sociology textbooks of Shkilnyk's study of Grassy Narrows is that they freeze the community in the 1970s. They do not show how the people's fight helped them to win $8.7 million dollars in an out-of-court settlement from Reed Paper in 1985 (the year Shkilnyk's book came out). And they do not talk about the community's current fight (since 1993) against the environmental impact of the logging practices of Abitibi Consolidated Corporation (see www.envirowatch.org/gndvst.htm).

It should be pointed out that the "only reserve is a bad reserve" storyline is also replicated in the way in which recent introductory sociology textbooks present the only other reserve that gets special attention: Davis Inlet, Labrador, another example of the minority case of forced relocation. For instance:

> The reserve system is an effective means of segregation that has created a huge gap in the living standards of Native and non-Native Canadians. Inadequate housing, overcrowded living conditions, poverty and unemployment, poor health care, substance abuse, and violence characterize the lives of too many Native Canadians. The devastating effects of such oppressive conditions have been reported in media coverage of adolescent suicide in communities such as Davis Inlet. Such reports indelibly impress the failure of existing policy to meet Aboriginal needs. (Schaefer et al. 1996: 193)

Kendall et al., in "Health, Health Care and Disability," also use the example of Davis Inlet:

> Rates of adolescent suicide are particularly high; the images of gasoline-sniffing young Innu from Davis Inlet in Labrador seen by most of us on television were a vivid and haunting illustration of this problem. (2000: 587)

Absent from these works are two key elements. One is the specificity of oppression that created the situation, such as is described by Dickason:

> [T]he process started in 1948 when the Newfoundland government decided that the caribou-hunting Innu would be better off as fishermen and woodcutters at a location 240

kilometres distant from their traditional territory. The deaths
of 70 of the Innu over the next two years led the community's survivors to take matters into their own hands, and
they walked back to their own homeland. Again, they were
not allowed to stay; less than 20 years later, in 1967, they
were moved again, this time from their mainland site to an
island in Davis Inlet. Once more, it was a move that made it
impossible for them to continue their traditional caribou-
hunting way of life. The government's expressed reason: the
new location was better suited for building housing and
sewage systems. For the Innu, the sense of powerlessness at
being once more involuntarily cut off from their customary
pursuits led to a spiral of welfare dependency, alcoholism,
gasoline sniffing, and suicide. (Dickason 1997: 398)

The second element missing is any attempt to balance the
reference to Davis Inlet with a look at other, more habitable
reserves. I have found that non-Aboriginal students often ask
the question "Why do Aboriginal peoples live on reserves?" It
is a predictable question given the way the media and introductory sociology textbooks frame reserves as problems, as ghettos-
in-the-bush. Here there is a great need for the textbooks to
understand an Aboriginal framing of reserves as homeland.[13] A
work that is strong in doing this, but to which no reference is
made, comes from Brian Maracle, a Mohawk writer who left
his home reserve when he was five years old but returned as an
adult keen on rebuilding his life. His excellent book, *Back on
the Rez: Finding the Way Back Home* (Maracle 1996), describes
the first year of his return to the Six Nations reserve near
Brantford, Ontario. This reserve is very different in some
respects from the more troubled reserves such as Davis Inlet and
Grassy Narrows that have suffered from relocation. Its people
have lived there for over 200 years, when it was given to them
as a reward for siding with the British during the American
Revolution. The fact that it includes good farmland and that the

Six Nations of the Iroquois were horticultural farmers prior to contact with Europeans helps contribute to the homeland feel of this particular reserve. It has been, and is, a cultural heartland for the people, even during the years when the federal government and the church had a more oppressive presence than they do now (see Chapter Six).

In the introduction, Maracle discusses the importance of the reserve to the people. He links the homeland feel to connection with the land and stresses the important point that reserves can be homelands because they function as refuges from non-Aboriginal society. In his terms, reserves are "free from oppressive anonymity and anonymous oppression." He goes on to describe his reserve:

> The reserves mean many things to the Onkwehonwe.[14] On one level, these postage-stamp remnants of our original territories are nagging reminders of the echoing vastness of what we have lost. On another, they are the legacy and bastion of our being. They are a refuge, a prison, a madhouse, a fortress, a birthplace, a Mecca, a resting-place, Home-Sweet-Home, Fatherland and Motherland rolled into one. (Maracle 1996: 3)

He speaks of the importance of the reserve as the home of the elders, who interpret and adapt the traditional to the present, thus stressing that the home of Aboriginal culture is the reserve. This same point is made by Mi'kmaq writer Noah Augustine, in an editorial piece for the *Toronto Star*, appropriately entitled "Indian Reserve a Haven from Racism." After moving to non-Aboriginal Ontario, and experiencing racism, he writes:

> I returned to the comfort and security of my home on the reserve. Others wonder why aboriginal people wish to stay on the reserves. It is no wonder to me. It was here where I began to seek out a purpose in life. It is here where I was

opened to the teachings of my elders, the power of the
sweat lodge and the pride of my people. It is here where I
found strength. Canadian society educated me in the ways
of the world; the sweat lodge taught me now to live respect-
fully within it. (Augustine 2000)

Linda Gerber: Distance Research

Sociologist Linda Gerber and her work play a major role in how
Aboriginal peoples are portrayed in introductory sociology textbooks. She co-authored the Canadian editions of the popular
Macionis series[15] (1994, 1999, 2002). Further, she wrote four articles and one paper that are cited in introductory sociology textbooks. The paper, "Community Characteristics and Out-migration
from Indian Communities: Regional Trends" (1977) is cited by
Frideres (1988, 1993, 1998, 2001) and in her own textbooks. Her
1979 paper, "The Development of Canadian Indian Communities:
a Two-Dimensional Typology Reflecting Strategies of Adaptation
of the Modern World" is cited in Frideres (1988, 1993, 1998,
2001), Richardson and Tepperman (1987), and Macionis and
Gerber (1999 and 2002). Her 1984 paper, her most cited work,
entitled "Community Characteristics and Outmigration from
Canadian Indian Reserves: Path Analyses," was cited in Frideres
(1988, 1993, 1998, 2001), Teevan (1987 and 1988), Tepperman
and Curtis (1988), Tepperman and Rosenberg (1998), and, of
course, her own textbooks. Her 1990 piece, "Multiple Jeopardy:
A Social-Economic Comparison of Men and Women among the
Indian, Métis and Inuit Peoples of Canada" is cited in Frideres
(1993, 1998, 2001), Henslin and Nelson (1996), and her own
works. As well, a 1995 adaptation of this piece is cited in her own
works. This means that during the late 1980s, 1990s, and early
twenty-first century, her work has been cited in nine different textbooks plus four editions of Frideres.

How did Gerber generate the information she used in her articles? How did she produce knowledge about Aboriginal peoples?

Her unpublished PhD thesis at the University of Toronto was entitled "Minority Survival: Community Characteristics and Out-Migration from Indian Communities across Canada" (1976). It is cited in her textbooks, and it forms the basis for the articles she wrote that have been used by the writers and editors of the textbooks. It is highly statistical in nature, which means that she did not need to go to a reserve or listen to the people.

The 1979 work investigated two features, "institutional completeness" and "personal resources," with numbers generated mainly from "a 1969 survey of socioeconomic conditions on all reserves across Canada," compiled by DIAND, with some updated census data. Institutional completeness was measured by the presence or absence of 11 variables: on-reserve employment; full-time on-reserve employment; Indian-owned enterprises; a band council; a school committee; self-government under Section 69 of the Indian Act; band administrators; farming; residents employed in professional, managerial, and technical positions; a federal school; and residents involved in adult educational programs. Personal resources was defined for statistical purposes as "experience with mainstream institutions."

Obviously, Aboriginal voice was almost completely silent in the production of this knowledge. The only Aboriginal reference is to a three-page bulletin issued by the Grand Council Treaty Number Nine (1977). The 1984 work, which is similar in methodology and whose main purpose was "to explain variation in off-reserve residence levels in terms of the aggregate characteristics of Canadian Indian bands (or communities)" (Gerber 1984: 145), establishing two "path models" concerning levels of complexity, had no Aboriginal reference.

What alternative frames could Aboriginal peoples establish? Take Gerber's use of employment statistics for example. Are they an accurate reflection of the economics of life where fishing, trapping, hunting, and gathering are still important activities generating food, identity, and other necessities? Just as significantly, do they set as goals that which Aboriginal peoples aspire to? This latter point has been raised by Mohawk/Michel First Nation scholar Sharilyn Calliou:

> If full employment is a desirable cultural, political, spiritual, or other goal for a First Nations sovereign cultural-community, then rather than a comparative standard, a within-community standard and justification must evolve as an act of self-determination with complementary respect for Original Instructions, or Teachings present from time immemorial. Simply to work because "Canadians" are working is not a completely adequate self-justification for further socioeconomic development, especially if there is a failure to discuss the spiritual, environmental, social, and other problems of capitalist-based economics, which can tempt any individual to be a member of the camp that [Ojibwa Elder Art] Solomon ... identifies as Greed and Avarice.
>
>   Justifications that progress as a compare-contrast journey, with an I-wonder-how-the-Joneses-are-doing? ideology, may clog self-governing capacity to see the falsity of claims, promises, and proposals of late 20th century capitalism, which is ideologically not a system of economic distributive justice or a system of environmental respect. (Calliou 1998: 17)

Ponting and Gibbins: The Irrelevance of Aboriginal Voice

Another important source for knowledge concerning Aboriginal peoples in later introductory sociology textbooks is J. Rick Ponting and Roger Gibbins's *Out of Irrelevance: A Socio-Political Introduction to Indian Affairs in Canada* (1980). It appears as a source for four sets of sociology textbooks during the 1980s: Mansfield (1982), Stebbins (1987), Teevan (1982, 1987, and 1988), and Tepperman and Curtis (1988 and 1990). The primary way in which knowledge was generated for this work can be readily seen in the authors' comments in the Preface:

> The book originated in the intent to make available, in readily readable form, and to a broad audience, the findings of a national survey which Gibbins and Ponting conducted in 1976. (Ponting and Gibbins 1980: i)

For the survey, they polled 1,832 non-Aboriginal Canadians to discover, as the chapter that deals most directly with the survey states, "Canadians' Perceptions of Indians." In Curtis and Tepperman's book, Ponting and Gibbins are excerpted as "Canadians' Responses to Native Peoples" (1990: 292–301). Clearly, in their book, Aboriginal voice plays a very small role in knowledge production.[16]

SUMMARY

Aboriginal voice, while initially included to a certain limited extent in early Canadian introductory sociology textbooks, was excluded or marginalized after the mid-1970s as the discipline of sociology developed in Canada. Harold Cardinal's book of 1971 is the most often cited and earliest quoted Aboriginal work; he was not replaced by such later important Aboriginal writers as Howard Adams, George Manuel, Maria Campbell, Emma Laroque, Jeannette Armstrong, or Lee Maracle who did not fit the discipline neatly. Instead, as "Aboriginal experts," sociologists and anthropologists cited by sociologists controlled the production of knowledge, especially with urbanization studies of the late 1960s and early 1970s (e.g., Dosman, Nagler, and Stymeist).

The weaknesses of this exclusionary form of knowledge production can be seen in particular in the way in which *the reserve* is framed, with Shkilnyk's study in victimology of Grassy Narrows (1985) and references to another tragic reserve, Davis Inlet, dominating the canvas of the portrait of the reserve, accompanied by statistical studies that are either horror shows of life on the reserve or bland distance learning, such as Gerber's, which compare the "success" of reserves by outsider standards.

No attempt has been made to balance the picture or to address the important Aboriginal-framed questions of why Aboriginal peoples choose to live on a reserve or what Aboriginal peoples would like to have on their reserves.

NOTES

1   In those odd little coincidences of research, this had been the private copy of Bernard Blishen, who edited the first truly Canadian introductory sociology textbook.

2   The same is true of my undergraduate anthropology professors, split roughly equally between British and Americans. In 1973–74, 60 percent of all full-time faculty teaching anthropology were non-Canadians (Hofley 1992: 106). The only Canadian instructors I remember as an undergraduate taught Canadian history and Canadian political science.

3   My own early academic career mirrored that development. I was a sociology major at York University in my second year, the year I first took an anthropology course from that department. The next year I became an anthropology major, and, in 1973, was one of the first anthropologists to graduate from that university.

4   It should be noted here that I read and reviewed the manuscript prior to its publication and am cited in the acknowledgments. I suggested some factual corrections for language and language family names, but these were not made.

5   There is no indication of how this statistic is derived. Frideres's books often carry statistics that present no history of derivation.

6   Technically speaking, Brody and Stymeist are anthropologists. However, as their work is used by sociologists, they are part of the sociological discourse on the subject.

7   Laroque specifically identified Brody, Dosman, and Nagler as providing examples of this "Indians as social problems" framing.

8   As can be seen in the quotation from Stymeist, he has the cab drivers, not the police, driving the non-Aboriginal peoples away.

9   Tepperman and Curtis also make reference to Cardinal's second book, *The Rebirth of Canada's Indians* (1977), as did Frideres in the second edition of his work.

10 This is a misread of what the Red Power advocates were saying.

11 It should be noted that her name is sometimes spelled as "Larocque."

12 For an excellent study of these programs among the Inuit (who were forced to relocate more often and more distantly than other First Nations people), see Tester and Kulchyski 1994.

13 Of course, in making this point about reserve as homeland, I am not denying that some Aboriginal peoples have been made to feel unwelcome in reserves when they were given status following the passage of Bill C-31. Nor does it deny that it can be easier for Aboriginal men than women to wax poetic about the reserve, as reserves have been sites of oppression for Aboriginal women because of the power of men to sweep abuse under the carpet because of their dominance in band councils (see McGillivray and Comasky 1999).

14 "Onkehonwe" is a Mohawk version of a general Iroquoian word that, in Maracle's interpretation, is translated as "real/first/original people." It is used as the equivalent of "Indian" or "native/aboriginal person" (Maracle 1996: x).

15 It has been used for the last few years at Humber College.

[16] Cardinal's work is cited a number of times, and there are a few references to work by Leroy Little Bear, George Manuel, and William Wuttunee, but they are fundamentally irrelevant to the main thrust of the Ponting and Gibbins book.

Elders on Ice:
Culturally Determined
Inuit Elder Suicide

Two recent events tell a story of the power of a simulacrum. In the October 2000 edition of the *Journal of the American Medical Association*, a medical student published an article in which he spoke of witnessing a 97-year-old Yup'ik Inuit kill himself by "vanishing into the early morning fog." The August 31, 2001 edition of the Nunavut paper *Nunatsiaq News* reported that the student had made up the story. In spring 2001, in Rick Mercer's television special "Talking with Americans" (a lampoon of the ignorance of Americans concerning Canada such as sending congratulations to the new Canadian prime minister "Jean Poutine" and signing petitions to end the seal hunt in Calgary), the interviewees were asked to sign a petition to end the Canadian practice of leaving their elders on ice floes. In this way, a typically Canadian (but shared with American) simulacrum was reproduced, the image of the Inuit abandoning their elders, a form of culturally approved suicide. In their insightful look at suicide among the Inuit, Kirmayer, Fletcher, and Boothroyd noted that:

> Suicide has become one of the emblematic cultural traits of
> the "Eskimo." Nearly every popular film with Inuit content

contains a scene in which a dutiful and wise elder ends his or her own existence for the good of the group, usually with remarkable equanimity. This "altruistic" suicide [see discussion on Durkheim below] is viewed as a distinctively Inuit practice, albeit one that demonstrates the harsh exigencies of life in the Arctic. (Kirmayer, Fletcher, and Boothroyd 1998: 194)

Charles Hughes, in writing about what he felt was the stereotypical image of the "Eskimo," says that it depicts:

a people living (presumably year round) in snow houses..., eating fish, swallowing raw meat, rubbing noses, swapping wives, *leaving old people out on the ice to die*, being childishly delighted with white man's tools, having no "government" (and hence according to some no social order), always wandering. (Hughes 1965: 12–13; emphasis mine)[1]

Sociology in general, and introductory sociology textbooks in particular, have ably assisted in the development of this image. This can be clearly seen in the following quotation taken from a recent textbook entitled *Sociology: A Down-to-Earth Approach* (Canadian Edition), edited by James Henslin, Dan Glenday, Ann Duffy, and Norene Pupo:

Shantu and Wishta fondly kissed their children and grandchildren farewell. Then sadly, but with resignation at the sacrifice they knew they had to make for their family, they slowly climbed onto the ice floe. The goodbyes were painfully made as the large slab of ice inched into the ocean currents. Shantu and Wishta would now starve. But they were old, and their death was necessary, for it reduced the demand on the small group's scarce food supply.

As the younger relatives watched Shantu and Wishta recede into the distance, each knew that their turn to make this sacrifice would come. Each hoped that they would face it as courageously.[2]

To grow old in traditional Inuit society meant a "voluntary" death. Survival in their harsh environment was so precarious that all except very young children, had to pull their own weight. The food supply was so limited that nothing was left over to give to anyone who could not participate in the closely integrated tasks required for survival. (Henslin et al. 2001: 216)

IDENTIFYING THE SIMULACRUM

It is necessary at this point to identify the main features of the simulacrum, or intellectual commodity, and to give it a name. I will refer to it as culturally determined Inuit elder suicide or CDIES. CDIES posits that Inuit families or communities abandon their elders to certain death, or that elders commit suicide, possibly with the assistance of others, but by their own culturally trained choice. The practice is assumed to be frequent and familiar.

Further, CDIES involves only two kinds of causation. The primary cause, either mentioned directly or implied, is environmental. CDIES is the "natural" result of living in the tough Arctic environment, where there is a "naturally occurring" periodic absence of the resources required to sustain the lives of everyone in an Inuit family or community. The secondary cause is cultural. This is more vaguely articulated, or merely implied by the absence of other notions of causation. The people kill too many caribou or seal, or they simply lack the cultural knowledge or practices necessary to insure survival every year of the oldest and the youngest (the latter resulting in female infanticide). In his article "Suicidal Behavior among the Netsilik[3] Eskimos" in the first Canadian-focussed introductory sociology textbook (Blishen et al. 1961: 575–87), Asen Balikci is unusual in rejecting what he refers to as "the well-known ecological factor." However, Balikci's thesis fits the CDIES pattern well in that he attributed the cause of 50 cases of suicide of young and old over the previous 50 years to "the framework of such a poorly integrated society, further weakened by in-group tensions and various anxieties" (Balikci 1961: 582).[4]

As a simulacrum, CDIES takes on an intellectual force that magnifies its presence, makes it "more real" (i.e., hyperreal) than the practice was in actuality. That does not mean that the practice did not take place, that it was not "real" in some sense. On some dark occasions in the Inuit past, healthy elders were abandoned and deathly ill elders were assisted in some way to die with dignity. I accept this, but, unlike the introductory sociology textbooks, I problematize key aspects of the simulacrum.

CHALLENGING THE FREQUENCY AND ASSUMED EASE OF CDIES

Key to my analysis is the fact that I challenge the reported or assumed frequency of the practice. It was probably no more a common practice among the different Inuit peoples than family murder-suicide is in contemporary southern Ontario. Both are over-reported. I challenge that acts of abandonment, on those infrequent occasions when they occurred, were generally intended to be "permanent." Primary sources talk about the hope that food would be found so that the elders would not have to die (see Rasmussen 1929: 160). For example, based on research undertaken in Alaska in the 1950s, Robert Spencer wrote:

> If a relative had to be abandoned, it was "very sad," "a hard decision," but the group might be saved at the expense of one life. The most recent case that anyone could recall took place in 1939, when an old shaman and his wife were left inland to starve. The family head, a son of the old man, was obliged to leave his father and stepmother and go on by team to get food. *He was unable to return in time to save his parents.* (Spencer 1959: 92; emphasis mine)

Government anthropologist Diamond Jenness wrote about his work with the "Copper Eskimos" during 1913–16:

> Under ordinary conditions the aged and infirm are never abandoned, as Hanbury says.[5] Haviron, who died in the spring of 1915, received a regular dole of food from all his kinsmen throughout the winter, though he was confined to his hut during the whole period and could do nothing to help himself. Whenever the Eskimos migrated to another sealing-ground he was carried on one of the sleds, usually, but not always, his son's. In Victoria Island he once left Tusayok's old wife all alone for several days with her tent and clothing and a stock of drying meat, because she was unable to maintain the constant travelling. She had an ample supply of food, and was perfectly happy and content, for she knew that her husband and son would rejoin her as soon as they were able. (Jenness 1922: 236)

Related to this is the problematic construction found in introductory sociology (and anthropology) textbooks, the sense of assumed ease with which people abandoned elders in such circumstances. Spencer's assessment is instructive in this regard:

> [A]ny case of abandonment was hard. Only in the direst of circumstances would it have taken place. There is the impression that the individual upbraided himself for leaving those dependent on him. (Spencer 1959: 93)

Knud Rasmussen, an anthropologist of mixed Danish-Inuit heritage, led a scientific enterprise known as the Fifth Thule Expedition across the Inuit Arctic from Greenland to Alaska, an enterprise that produced the important and relatively popular and reprinted works of Kaj Birket-Smith, Peter Freuchen, and Therkel Mathiassen (as well as Rasmussen's own volumes). In his often-cited *Across Arctic America: Intellectual Culture of the*

Iglulik Eskimos (1929), he spoke of how, in the traditional stories or mythology of the Iglulik, tales were told of the abandoned experiencing "some miraculous form of rescue ... with a cruel and ignominious death for those who abandoned them" (Rasmussen 1929: 160). This to me points to the people's sense that abandoning was wrong and not an accepted cultural norm.

Enhancing the central focus of CDIES in discussing Inuit in the introductory sociology textbooks is the decentering or marginalization of the respect given to elders by the people, although this is discussed much more frequently in the primary sources. Take, for example, the following passage from Dr. Samuel K. Hutton's *Among the Eskimos of Labrador: A Record of Five Years' Close Intercourse with the Eskimo Tribes of Labrador* (1912), a book that is readily available in university libraries, yet to which no reference is made by introductory sociology textbook editors and writers, or by the secondary sources that compile the information used by some of those writers. Hutton presents a fact that does not fit comfortably into the CDIES package:

> In my visits to the Eskimo households I could not fail to be struck by the patience and devotion with which the people care for their aged ones. The old man or woman, feeble and past work, is sure of a home with a married son or daughter or other relative, and if the poor old body has no relations, there is enough hospitality in the hearts of the poorest of the people to make them open their homes to the needy. (Hutton 1912: 111)

CHALLENGING CAUSALITY

I also challenge the notion of causality that goes along with CDIES. Colonialist contact has to be considered as a, if not *the*, major cause of elder abandonment. The negative effects of colonial contact on Inuit is discussed in sociological literature (see Brody 1991: 35), including textbooks (see, for example,

Crysdale and Beattie 1973: 34; and Ferguson in Mann 1970: 30). Yet, it is not once connected with CDIES. The cultures reported were not pristine, not even in the early years. The writers of all the primary sources were visiting Inuit, who had had intense and often lethal contact with Europeans. European and North American whalers had four centuries of impact on the people. During much of the twentieth century, the Hudson's Bay Company (HBC) created a literally deadly Inuit dependency on Arctic fox trapping, with its attendant debt creation, reliance on inferior foods and clothing, and fluctuating prices, to mention just a few factors that threatened their society. The following two quotations provide good examples of the types of commentary made by people in the field during the 1920s and 1930, one by a visiting medical specialist (Frederick G. Banting), the other by anthropologist Diamond Jenness:

> The gravest danger which faces the Eskimo is his transfer from a race-long hunter to a dependent trapper. When the Eskimo becomes a trapper, he becomes, to a large extent, dependent on the white man for food and clothing. Instead of wearing warm, light clothing which time has taught him is most suitable for the climate, he is given cheap woollen and cotton, which the white man would not wear himself under the same conditions. His native food is seal, walrus, whale, fish, clams, bear, caribou, rabbit, eggs, duck, geese and ptarmigan. His only vegetable is the occasional sea weed. In exchange for his furs he is given white flour or sea biscuits, tea and tobacco, which do not provide sufficient fuel to keep his body warm and nourished. (Banting, cited in Tester and Kulchyski 1994: 108)

> Very few Eskimo now hunt intensively during the winter months; instead they trap foxes, which are useless to them for either food or clothing. In order to maintain their families during that season they buy European food from the

fur-traders, largely flour, sugar, and tea. Now a diet of straight seal-meat will keep a hunter or a trapper in good health, but a diet that consists mainly of bannock and tea is practically starvation, so, over large parts of the Arctic and sub-Arctic the Eskimo are now worse clad, and more ill-nourished than in the days of their isolation. (Jenness 1932: 421–22)

Of course, to be added to the list of colonialist contact is federal government neglect and ill-conceived relocation plans, so well-documented and described by Tester and Kulchyski (1994) for the time period from the late 1930s to the early 1960s, the time when CDIES was developing as a premise and being replicated. While I do not think that there is necessarily a deliberate or intended connection between the creation and dissemination of CDIES and government practices that can be seen as creating or at least not acting effectively to stop several instances of multiple Inuit deaths by starvation (see Tester and Kulchyski 1994), I do say that the former served the latter well. Returning to the words of Linda Tuhiwai Smith, concerning research that has equal application for presentation of the results of that research in textbooks:

[I]t is surely difficult to discuss *research methodology* and *indigenous peoples* together, in the same breath, without having an analysis of imperialism, without understanding the complex ways in which the pursuit of knowledge is deeply embedded in the multiple layers of imperial and colonial practices. (Tuhiwai Smith 1999: 2)

CDIES teaches that the Inuit are a people to be saved, a notion that assisted governments and the HBC in their various imperialist policies. This quote from an influential work by Ruth Cavan illustrates how the two go hand-in-hand:

Missionaries redefined some of the Eskimo's ways of reducing life tensions as sinful, and police and other government officials defined the same acts as illegal or criminal. These acts, functioned in the Eskimo way of life, but strongly disapproved in the white culture, included the various forms of killing: infanticide, killing of the helpless old.... As various forms of cash relief were developed in the United States and Canada and extended to the Eskimos, some of the old ways of eliminating problems did become useless. In fact, when old people and children began to receive financial aid, their status was reversed. From a burden in the past they now became an important source of income. (Cavan 1968: 33)

One small, somewhat ironic, point should be made here. The Canadian Old Age Pension Act was passed in 1927. Despite the fact that a 1939 Supreme Court decision made the federal government officially responsible for the Inuit in the Canadian Arctic (no government had been so before), it was not until April 1, 1949, that an Inuk first received a pension cheque (Tester and Kulchyski 1994: 94). The Canadian government had abandoned the Inuit elders for more than 20 years.

Even when government colonialist actions and inactions are identified, the connection is not made by non-Aboriginal writers between these practices and CDIES. This is perhaps best illustrated in the influential writing of Farley Mowat, whose popular books *People of the Deer*[6] (1968 [1951]) and *The Desperate People* (1975 [1959]) drew international attention to the threat to the Ahiarmiut (a group of Caribou Inuit) from what the government was doing (see Tester and Kulchyski 1994: 56–57).

Like other White "travellers" to the Arctic, Mowat overgeneralized from his highly specific and atypical experiences in terms of Inuit culture and popularized CDIES in emotional, evocative statements such as the following:

The old people stand at the lowest point of the scale. The men whose arms are no longer strong and the women whose wombs are no longer fecund—these live on the thin edge of time, with death always before them. When the choice of living and dying comes upon a camp of the People; when starvation announces the coming of death, then the aged ones must be prepared to go first, to seek death voluntarily so that the rest of the family may cling a little longer to life. The old ones seldom die a natural death and often they die by their own hands. Suicide is not lawful in our eyes but as it comes to the People it is a great, and a very heroic, sacrifice—for it is the old who fear death most and who find it hardest to die. (Mowat 1968: 172)

In 1975, Mowat published a book of stories, *The Snow Walker*, whose title story was based on CDIES. I used to read that story to my anthropology and sociology students at Humber College to teach them about cultural relativism.

The Deep Roots of CDIES

CDIES has deep roots in White literature about the Inuit, roots that may go as far back as 1767, when David Crantz published his *The History of Greenland: Including an Account of the Mission Carried on by the United Brethren in That Country*. Certainly it had become a well-known image in 1824, by which time Captain William Edward Parry and his second-in-command Lyon had published their accounts of experiences with the Inuit in and around Igloolik Island.[7] Both commented on the Inuit practice of abandoning their elders (Rasing 1994: 19–20). Their work had a definite impact. According to Rasing (1994: 3), for example, they were a major reference point for Franz Boas when he came to write his well-read and often reprinted classic work on the Inuit, *The Central Eskimos* (1964, originally 1888). Interestingly, for all the times Boas has been used as evidence for CDIES, he actually only made one short reference to it, almost an afterthought that I suspect was prompted more by his reading of Parry and Lyon than by his experience with the

Inuit. At the end of his section on "Burial Customs," with no mention of anything he had seen or heard among the people (unlike his typical context-loaded field notes), he wrote:

> I may add here that suicide is not of rare occurrence, as according to the religious ideas of the Eskimo the souls who die by violence go to Qudlivan, the happy land. For the same reason it is considered lawful for a man to kill his aged parents. In suicide death is generally brought about by hanging. (Boas 1964: 207)

During the nineteenth and twentieth centuries, the vast majority of White travellers to the Arctic seemed compelled to remark on the practice, even if they hadn't witnessed it themselves and hadn't heard of recent examples from reliable informants (see Jenness 1922: 236).

The neighbouring, newly cleared fields of sociology and social anthropology provided fertile soil for the growth of this simulacrum. In 1894, S.R. Steinmetz published a paper entitled "Suicide Among Primitive Peoples," in the then-as-now most prominent North American anthropological journal, *American Anthropologist*, whose introduction states:

> It is the opinion of many sociologists, who, perhaps have not given especial thought or study to the subject, that the act of self-destruction is infrequent among savage peoples. The purpose of my inquiry is to determine whether this opinion has the support of well-authenticated facts, and, if so, to what degree. (Steinmetz 1964: 53)

He then proceeded to demonstrate that the Inuit practiced CDIES. He did not do his own fieldwork, but relied on earlier works, including Crantz, Fridtjof Nansen (1929 [1893], in translation), and Captain Charles Francis Hall's *Life with the Esquimaux: A Narrative of Arctic Experience in Search of*

Survivors of Sir John Franklin's Expedition (1970 [1864]). This work was based on Hall's experiences of the harsh winters of 1861 and 1862. Hall's book was republished twice more in the next two years, so it can be said to have sold well. In his often melodramatic writing, two deathly ill Inuit elders are "buried alive" in the "living tombs" of igloos (Hall 1970: 161–64 and 444–53). There is little in the way of Aboriginal voice to give an insider's explanation of what this traveller was seeing in terms of traditional Inuit culture or how exceptional the circumstances might have been. One wonders what conclusions Inuit writers might have reached had they gone to the London of that period and witnessed the conditions many of the living and dying poor (old and young) faced in that industrial city during those brutal years. Certainly, they would have seen enough signs of people being abandoned to die that they might have been led to conclude that such was an "English cultural tradition."

ALTRUISTIC SUICIDE: BEING AN ELDERLY TEAM PLAYER

Three years after the publication of Steinmetz's work, Emile Durkheim published his ground-breaking *Le Suicide: Étude de Sociologie*. Near the beginning of one chapter, he wrote the following. Note how the first sentence mirrors (or was mirrored by) Steinmetz's words:

> It has sometimes been said that suicide was unknown among lower societies. Thus expressed, the assertion is inexact. To be sure, egoistic suicide, constituted as has just been shown, seems not to be frequent there. But another form exists among them in an endemic state. (Durkheim 1966: 217)

This form of suicide he termed "altruistic suicide," a form in which "social integration is too strong," when an individual makes the ultimate sacrifice as it is "imposed by society for social ends" (Durkheim 1966: 220). Moreover, "lower societies are the theatre par excellence of altruistic suicide" (Durkheim 1966: 227). His examples do not include the Inuit, but come from ancient Europe (e.g., the Vikings, Goths, Visigoths, and Spanish Celts), the high-caste Hindu practice of suttee or wife's suicidal burning in her husband's funeral pyre, and, not surprisingly, the Japanese ritual suicide of hara-kiri. Nevertheless, he was aware of CDIES: Steinmetz is cited first in his bibliography for this chapter. While Durkheim did not use the explanation of ecology or conservation of food for altruistic suicide, other sociologists who accepted his equation of "folk," "lower," "non-literate," or "primitive" society with altruistic suicide did, as can be seen in the following quotations from the same page of a text-book on the sociology of deviance:

> Among folk societies, suicides tend to be altruistic in that people take their lives with the idea that by doing so they will benefit others....
>
> Suicides occur in certain folk societies where limited food supplies make an old or infirm person a burden to the tribe. Among the Eskimos and the Chukchee, for example, old people who could no longer hunt or work killed themselves so that they would not use food needed by other adults in the community who produce it. (Clinard and Meier 1985: 278)

One can see the impact of linking Durkheim's concept of altruistic suicide with Inuit suicide in what Kirmayer and colleagues rightfully point to as the "first systematic examination of Inuit Suicide" (1998: 189: Alexander H. Leighton and Charles C. Hughes "Notes on Eskimo Patterns of Suicide" (1955)). This article was based on Leighton's fieldwork in the summer of 1940 with the Inuit of St. Lawrence Island, Alaska, and a review of the literature, including the primary sources Birket-Smith (1929), Boas (1888), Moore[8] (1923), Rasmussen

(1927 and 1931), and Thalbitzer (1914), and the secondary source, the often-cited Weyer (1962 [1932]: 138 and 248). It includes some discussion of the Chukchee, a Siberian people related to the Inuit. When a textbook writer includes both the Chukchee and the Inuit together in a discussion of CDIES (see Mann 1968b and Clinard and Meyer 1985), it suggests that the writer has read Leighton and Hughes.

Concerning the Inuit of St. Lawrence Island, the last case of suicide the authors could document occurred in 1902 (Leighton and Hughes 1955: 330). Still, they felt confident in declaring that "the killing of aged or infirm parents by dutiful children was evidently a common occurrence" (1955: 329). Dealing with the abandonment of elders, they made the following statement, disturbing in both the lack of evidence within the authors' experience to support it and the certainty with which it was expressed despite that lack of evidence:

> No clear-cut information on patterns of abandoning the aged (which, if practiced, might have increased the prevalence of suicides, especially among old women) is available, although the practice probably did exist. (Leighton and Hughes 1955: 334)

The authors relied on Durkheim for their CDIES certainty, for they point out (with indirect reference to the cultural relativism to be discussed below):

> It may be recalled that Durkheim [1951] examined several different forms of suicide, and one generalization he reached was that the form which he called "altruistic suicide" occurs when social integration is too strong." It would seem that Eskimo suicide can be placed in this general class, although one can leave off, for scientific purposes, the value assumption implied in the phrase, "too strong." (Leighton and Hughes 1955: 336)

CDIES AND (THE CULTURAL) RELATIVITY (OF DEVIANCE): THE DEVELOPMENT OF A TRADITION

Like the potlatch (to be discussed in Chapter Five), CDIES came into being, at least in part, as a creature of the teaching of cultural relativism. It is an exotic practice that dramatically demonstrates the lengths to which cultural, as opposed to biological, determinism can go, a conceptual weapon for social scientists to use against biologists. It connects well with the key sociological subject matter of deviance, illustrating the important pedagogical point that "deviance is relative," that it is subject to particular cultural determination. The rulebook is different in each culture.

Textbook relativity "one liners" that relate Inuit abandonment to mainstream North American practices that the author appears to oppose are not uncommon in the discussion of the cultural relativity of deviance. It is a well-established tradition in both the disciplines of anthropology and sociology. We can see its strength in anthropology in the following two examples. The first comes from Gary Ferraro's *Cultural Anthropology: An Applied Perspective* (1995), in his section on "Cultural Relativism." Note how he draws upon anthropological discourse on the subject (Friedl and Pfeiffer 1977) to justify his statement:

> Some Eskimo groups practice a custom that would strike the typical Westerner as inhumane at best. When aging parents become too old to contribute their share of the workload, they are left out in the cold to die. If we view such a practice by the standards of our own Western culture (that is, ethnocentrically), we would have to conclude that it is cruel and heartless, hardly a way to treat those who brought you into the world. But the cultural relativist would look at this form of homicide within the context of the total culture of which it is a part. Friedl and Pfeiffer (1977: 331) provide a culturally relativistic explanation of this Eskimo custom:

It is important to know...that this...[custom is not practiced] against the will of the old person. It is also necessary to recognize that this is an accepted practice for which people are adequately prepared throughout their lives, and not some kind of treachery sprung upon an individual as a result of a criminal conspiracy. Finally, it should be considered in light of the ecological situation in which the Eskimos live. Making a living in the Arctic is difficult at best, and the necessity of feeding an extra mouth, especially when there is little hope that the individual will again become productive in the food-procurement process, would mean that the whole group would suffer. It is not a question of Eskimos not liking old people, but rather a question of what is best for the entire group. We would not expect—and indeed we do not find—this practice to exist where there was adequate food to support those who were not able to contribute to the hunting effort." (Friedl and Pfeiffer, cited in Ferraro 1995: 24–25)

The second comes from a recently published Canadian anthropology textbook edited by Miller, Van Esterik, and Van Esterik. After talking about Jane Goodall observing chimps not helping polio-inflicted members of their own troupe, but leaving them behind, the authors state:

Humans also sometimes resort to isolation and abandonment, as seen in the traditional Inuit practice of leaving aged and infirm behind in the cold, the stigmatization of HIV/AIDS victims, and the ignoring of the homeless mentally ill in North American cities. (Miller, Van Esterik, and Van Esterik 2001: 62)

Given this well-established anthropological tradition then, it should not be too surprising to find that when anthropologists enter the field of gerontology, they take their simulacra with them. The following comes from an American gerontology textbook written by two anthropologists. Although most of their discussion about elders among the Inuit is positive concerning the respect that elders received, and despite the fact that they discuss the limited application of CDIES, still, in their textbook, *Other Cultures, Elder Years*, anthropologists Ellen R. Holmes and Lowell D. Holmes, under the heading of "Relativistic Perspective," make the following incautious, unqualified reproduction of the cultural relativism of CDIES:

> Although the common biological heritage of human beings and the inevitability of senescence create elements of common experience, anthropologists are extremely cautious about declaring that the customs in one society are more acceptable or more honorable than those in other societies. Who is to say that locking the elderly up in nursing homes is more humane than allowing them to wander off on the ice floe and freeze to death as Eskimo elders are sometimes permitted to do? Cultural behavior that may imply low status for the aged in one society may mean something entirely different in another. (Holmes and Holmes 1995: 10–11)

As American and Canadian anthropology textbook writers appear to feel free to reproduce CDIES when discussing relativism, so, too, do American and Canadian sociology textbook writers. That this is true can be seen in the following quotation from an American introductory textbook. Note the use of the "mainstream we" in the first case used in opposition to the "exoticized other" of the Inuit "they":

> We view the custom of certain Eskimo tribes of leaving old people behind to die as particularly cruel and inhumane, but they no doubt view our own custom of warfare between nations as incredibly crude and barbarous. (Smith and Preston 1977: 25)

Evidence of its presence in the Canadian literature is evident in the following quotation from sociologist James Teevan, who edited two, long-running, similar series of Canadian introductory sociology textbooks. In a chapter on "Deviance" he wrote:

> Probably most behaviors have been defined as deviant somewhere, at some time, or under certain circumstances, and as not deviant elsewhere, at other times, or under other circumstances. Cavan (1968) noted that in the Inuit culture, for example, the hoarding of food is considered theft and hence a deviant act, because such selfishness threatens the survival of Inuit society. In the rest of Canada, on the other hand, the more that individuals can amass and the greater their wealth, the more successful they are considered to be and the more they are appointed to positions of honor and trust. Similarly, *the Inuit defined infanticide and the killing of old parents as acceptable means to protect a limited food supply.* The rest of Canada does not allow such behavior. The different outlooks can be explained partly by the different amounts of resources in the two societies, but explainable or not, *they illustrate the relative definition of deviance, that what is deviant is specific to time and place and circumstances.* (Teevan 1982b: 63⁹; emphasis mine)

MORES, THE RELATIVITY OF DEVIANCE, AND CDIES: THE DEVELOPMENT OF A SOCIOLOGICAL TRADITION

Teevan was following a long sociological tradition in connecting CDIES and the relativity of deviance, a tradition based on the development of the sociological term "mores." The American sociologist who introduced the word to the sociological literature, Yale professor of politics and social science William Graham Sumner, incorporated CDIES into his work. In chapter seven, "Abortions, Infanticide, Killing the Old," of his highly influential work, *Folkways: A Study of the Sociological*

Importance of Usages, Manners, Customs, Mores and Morals (originally published in 1906), he writes the following under the heading "killing the old in ethnography":

> The Hudson's Bay Eskimo strangle the old who are dependent on others for their food, or leave them to perish when the camp is moved. They move in order to get rid of burdensome old people without executing them [Turner 1894]. The central Eskimo kill the old because all who die by violence go to the happy land; others have no such a happy future [Boas 1888]. Nansen [1893] says that "when people get so old that they cannot take care of themselves, especially women, they are often treated with little consideration" by the Eskimo. (Sumner 1934: 325)

In their textbook entitled *A Handbook of Sociology* (1964; first published in 1947), William Ogburn and Meyer Nimkoff, in chapter eight, "Social Control and Conformity," under the somewhat exaggerated heading "The Mores can make anything seem Right," wrote, "The mores made it right for the Eskimos to kill their old people" (Ogburn and Nimkoff 1964: 148).

This tradition transferred quickly into Canadian sociology. In what appears to have been the first Canadian textbook dedicated to the subject of deviance, *Deviant Behaviour in Canada*, edited by W.E. Mann (1968b), there is a chapter entitled "Suicide in Canada" written by Mann himself. Note that when he is speaking of "strong and unqualified identification with the tribe," he is referring to one of the "textbook" features of altruistic suicide:

> The mores on suicide have, as might be expected, varied considerably between cultures.... In many primitive or peasant societies it seems that a great number of suicides are a consequence of the individual's strong and unqualified identification with the tribe or group and its welfare. Thus, among Eskimoes, and the Chuckchee Tribe,[10] it is expected

that old people, when the supply of food runs very short, will kill themselves. (Mann 1968b: 214–15)

CROSS-CULTURAL COLLECTORS SPREAD THE TRADITION: CAVAN AND HOEBEL

Influential in passing on the idea of connecting CDIES and the cultural relativity of deviance was Ruth Cavan, who, as shown above, was cited by Teevan. She wrote two major works that promoted that connection: *Suicide* (1965; originally 1928)[11] and, 40 years later, *Delinquency and Crime: Cross Cultural Perspectives* (1968). In the latter work, the one cited by Teevan, in the chapter tellingly named "The Eskimos: Delinquency and Crime in a Primitive Society" (Cavan 1968: 13–41), while noting that Inuit groups indulged in CDIES, she perpetuated the cultural relativity of deviance with the following:

> [An] accepted method of reducing tensions was in the approved killing of members of the community who were not self-supporting as judged by the amount of work they could do. These persons were the very old whose days of usefulness, were over.... The killing of the old had no sacred connotations; it was a practiced expedient, practiced in only some of the Eskimo tribes. Where it was customary, the son who took his parent to a remote place and left him (or her) with a small amount of food, soon to die from the cold, was regarded as having performed a meritorious act. (Cavan 1968: 19)

It is important to notice that, in her development of CDIES, Cavan made no mention of the respect for elders that was clearly stated in two of the three primary sources[12] she drew upon to talk about Inuit suicide. For instance, she cited Kaj Birket-Smith's work on the Caribou Inuit:

> An elderly, skilful hunter with great experience always enjoys great esteem as *primus inter pares*. When a number of families are gathered in camp, there is often an elderly *pater familias* who is tacitly looked upon as [ihumataq], i.e., he who thinks, implying: for the others. (Birket-Smith 1929: 258–59)

Another of her primary sources emphasizing respect for elders was Riley D. Moore (1923), who in 1912 visited the Inuit of St. Lawrence Island in the Bering Sea. His discussion of Inuit suicide was limited to describing the methods through which ill "strong men"[13] in particular, and generally "all incurables," killed themselves. Interestingly, like other writers, he refers to the hypothetical suicide not as being practiced at the time he was there, but as a practice that was "formerly quite common" (Moore 1923: 364). When his observation is made in this way, it suggests that this "information" came from what he had read prior to his trip to Inuit country. Within his experience, however, was respect for elders:

> The older members of the family, especially fathers and older uncles, are treated with extreme reverence and respect, accorded them because of their age and the wisdom garnered from years of experience. (Moore 1923: 373)

Another social scientist, involved as Cavan was in developing CDIES and connecting it with cultural relativism (without having done any fieldwork), was the often cited anthropologist E. Adamson Hoebel (including by Cavan 1968; see also Bohannan 1992). His early work on the subject of CDIES (1941) was cited by Leighton and Hughes (1955: 327, fn 2). His *The Law of Primitive Man, A Study in Comparative Legal Dynamics* (1965) included a chapter dedicated to the Inuit: "The Eskimo: Rudimentary Law in a Primitive Anarchy" (1965: 67–99). His project in this book was to make the cultural relativist point that all societies have law—some are written down, while others are not. Putting what he felt were Inuit laws in a form familiar to mainstream North American readers, Hoebel wrote "underlying postulates of jural significance in Eskimo culture" in the following way: "Postulate III. Life is hard and the margin of safety small. Corollary I. Unproductive members of society cannot be supported," (Hoebel 1965: 69) later stating that "Infanticide, invalidicide, senilicide, and suicide are privileged acts: socially approved homicide" (Hoebel 1965: 74). The sources he consulted were Holm (1914), Rasmussen (1929), and Weyer (1962).

ECOLOGICAL CAUSATION: WHEN A SOLO PERFORMANCE BECOMES A TEAM SPORT

Serena Nanda, in the fifth edition of her introductory anthropology textbook, *Cultural Anthropology*, wrote:

> Sometimes, methods of increasing a group's survival seem harsh to us, but they are necessary because of extreme food shortages. In particularly hard years when food was scarce, some Inuit groups, for example, would leave old people on the ice to die. Sometimes it was an old person who suggested this course of action. These suicides of "mercy killings" indicate not a lack of concern for human life but rather a commitment to the survival of the group. (Nanda 1994: 160)

She was reproducing an aspect of CDIES that blames a neutral factor, the harshness of the environment, while rendering blameless the non-Inuit who in a number of significant ways made that environment a more difficult place in which to live. Trading companies early in the twentieth century made the Inuit dependent on Arctic fox, an inedible species whose numbers fluctuated like the price of their furs. Caribou were killed off in record numbers when non-Inuit came north to build the DEW line stations. And government relocation schemes, guided by non-Inuit anthropologists and following the scientifically unsound notion that all Arctic environments (especially their resources) are all alike, moved Inuit into environments in which they were unaccustomed to making a living.

Reproduction of CDIES seems to nullify discussion of the high degree of respect that Inuit had for their elders. It also leaves unexamined the notion of what the "productivity" of an elder might be, more or less confining it to the merely physical.

The development of the ecological argument with its concomitant denial of the intellectually productive role of the elder and the general respect the Inuit have for elders becomes clearer when it is contrasted with the early literature. Ernest Hawkes's *The Labrador Eskimo*, published in 1916 and reprinted in 1970, is one oft-cited primary source (e.g., by Kirmayer et al. 1998: 195, 209) that has had an impact in telling this part of the story. After three years working with the Inuit in Alaska, Hawkes spent the summer and fall of 1914 in Labrador. His reference to CDIES appears as a generalized comment, not based on any events discussed, so we don't know whether he relied on ethnography or the narrative traditions of his predecessors. Like his near contemporary Hutton, and unlike introductory sociology textbooks, he stresses Inuit respect for elders. Notice that, again unlike the introductory sociology textbooks, he brings no ecological argument into his discussion:

> The aged are treated with great respect, and the word of the old men and women is final. The Eskimo say that they have lived a long time and understand things in general better. They also feel that in the aged is embodied the wisdom of their ancestors. This does not prevent them, however, from putting the old folks out of the way, when life has become a burden to them, but the act is usually done in accordance with the wishes of the persons concerned and is thought to be a proof of devotion. (Hawkes 1970: 117)

Hawkes's work is the key primary source used by Edward Weyer in his oft-cited compilation *The Eskimos: Their Environment and Folkways* (originally published in 1932, reprinted in 1962). He is referred to by Balikci in his article in the introductory sociology textbook edited by Blishen et al. (Balikci 1961: 581). Weyer summarized most of the important sources such as Hawkes's books that refer to Inuit suicide and then framed the material in terms of an ecological model. If death is the elder's wish, it is because the elder wishes death as a team player, not for any personal reasons. Weyer discussed CDIES in the chapter tellingly entitled "Reaction to Population Problem," under the heading of "Killing the Aged and the Infirm." It should be noted that the related terms "productive years" and "unproductive" stay undefined, so that readers can impose their own culture's notion on what that might mean.

> Infanticide, we have seen, is customary on occasion in all groups of Eskimos,[14] with the effect of ameliorating the stress which accompanies scarcity of food. At the further end of the life span is the period of old age, when people have passed their productive years. Therefore, we may rightly expect to observe some similarity between the group attitude toward the aged and toward infants. Like the newborn babe, the person who is infirm, either by reason of years or physical disability, is likely to be eliminated under the stress of poverty.
>
> Recourse to abandoning or killing outright such unproductive members of the group is a response to stringent, inexorable life-conditions. Such action, it should be understood, does not indicate a wholly heartless discrimination against the helpless. Devotion among friends and relatives comes into strong conflict with the deliberate elimination of members of a group. The disposing of one who is aged and infirm sometimes seems, indeed, to be more the will of the fated one than of those devoted to him who will live on. (Weyer 1962: 137–38)[15]

Anthropologist Lee Guemple, in his "The Dilemma of the Aging Eskimo," published in Crysdale and Beattie's *Sociology Canada: An Introductory Text* (1974),[16] likewise subtly alters Hawkes's point to suit his resource-based theory. He links the idea of "survival of the fittest"—killing the outsider-defined "unproductive"—to Hawkes's commentary about the wishes of those elders who feel for personal reasons that they are ready to die:

> ... [W]hen the elderly became a drain on the resources of the community, the practical bent of the Eskimo asserted itself. To alleviate the burden of infirmity, the old people were done away with. As Hawkes (1916, 117) points out, this was done when life has become a burden but the act was usually in accordance with the wishes of the persons concerned and thought to be a proof of the devotion of the children. (Guemple 1974: 211)

Thus, Guemple essentializes the Inuit according to a capitalist model, seeing the people as the ultimate pragmatists, coldly calculating the worth of each individual in terms of that person's value as a resource to the community. The elders are not being killed, the community is being "downsized":

> This essay is concerned with the social position of old people in Eskimo society. More specifically, it views old people as a kind of exploitable resource which has value to those who run Eskimo society, the adults. (Guemple 1974: 203)

Although Guemple had engaged in fieldwork with the Qiqiktamiut of the Belcher Islands in southeastern Hudson Bay, and appears in the quotation below to be making an indirect claim on an insider's view ("it is best to consider them as do the Eskimo themselves"), this claim is suspect as no Inuit voice appears in the work. The people aren't doing the explaining here, Guemple is, with his social Darwinist theorizing, plus what appears to be a slightly different version of the "they are good with their hands" trope. While he mentions that Inuit elders have worth, he damns that worth with faint praise by making it that which is calculable using outsider scales. The word "respect" is not written.

> Eskimo are extremely practical. They highly esteem those who make the greatest contribution to the welfare of family and community. This is true for the old and the young as well as the adults. Sentiment is not absent in Eskimo life. Although they are not demonstrative, Eskimo do feel very strongly about family and relatives, and will go to great lengths to be hospitable even to a stranger. But the margin for sentiment in the Arctic is very narrow; the pragmatic business of making a living takes precedence over sentiment. People, then, are judged in terms of their worth as producers. If we are to evaluate the position of the old in Eskimo society, it is best to consider them as do the Eskimo themselves, names, as a special kind of resource. Viewed in this light, the old make two important contributions: (1) a source of extra labour for the camp, and (2) a source of knowledge and wisdom essential for order and continuity in the society. (Guemple 1974: 205)

Social Implications of the Simulacrum CDIES

There are three main implications in Canadian society today of CDIES as a simulacrum in Canadian introductory sociology textbooks. These are:

1) that it contributes to the notion that the Inuit, who have the highest suicide in Canada, are somehow "culturally determined" to commit suicide (i.e., the culturalist notion of suicide);

2) that it contributes to the denial or erasure of the important role of the elder in Inuit, and more generally in contemporary Aboriginal, society; and

3) that it contributes to the carry-over of CDIES into the new and growing field of gerontology.

The Danger of CDIES: The Culturist Notion of Suicide

One of the great dangers of CDIES as a sociological simulacrum is that it has a life beyond the "merely academic" world of the sociology classroom and the academy. It can, and has, been used as an explanatory tool in a "blame the victim" portrayal of one of the most tragic aspects of contemporary Inuit life in Canada: their high rate of suicide. Consider the following figures. In 1992, the suicide rate for the overall Canadian population was 13 per 100,000.[17] A Health Canada study (Isaacs et al. 1998) discovered that the suicide rate for Inuit in the Northwest Territories for the years 1986 to 1996 was 79 per 100,000, or slightly more than six times the Canadian figure. This compares negatively not just to Canadians in general, but to other Aboriginal groups as well. In the study's look at the Dene of the Northwest Territories during the same period, the suicide rate was only 29 per 100,000.

Appealing to "cultural reasons" to explain this phenomenon unrealistically downplays such compelling factors as historic and contemporary colonialism, as well as more general social, political, and economic conditions. Kirmayer, Fletcher, and Boothroyd point this out in their excellent article, "Suicide Among the Inuit of Canada" (1998). While they, unfortunately, seem to accept CDIES in the past,[18] they are astute enough to see that the "culturalist" argument cannot be used to explain away contemporary youth suicide and rightly are critical of studies that do. They note two such studies (Minor 1992 and Boyer et al. 1994) as being flawed in following this logic:

Minor (1992: 83) states: "In the case of the young Inuit, it may be that the victims were making an effort to return to a traditionally accepted and respected death. Or the burden of life may have been so great and the confusion of cultural transition so frustrating that they acted irrationality. One could argue either that suicide expresses traditional attitudes or is a result of their collapse. I am firmly convinced that there is a traditional component in most of the suicides among the youth." (Kirmayer, Fletcher, and Boothroyd 1998: 200)

In a recent epidemiological survey of the Nunavik Inuit of Quebec, in a section on culture and history, Boyer et al. rely on the short entry on the subject in Boas's work of 1888 as justification for writing:

> Suicide could be considered a culturally adapted behaviour because it is associated with an ancient ritual which was performed by the elderly, resourceless people who relieved the community of the burden created by their dependence. Is it not true that current suicides by young people bespeak of Inuit identity and a sense of community belonging? In that sense, could suicide among young Inuit be perceived as the statement of a double paradox, namely the merging with Inuit culture and identity, and the necessity of severing the merging process? In the Inuit cosmogony, violent death enables the soul to reach a better world. (Boyer et al 1994: 140, as cited in Kirmayer, Fletcher and Boothroyd 1998: 200–01)

One further, connected danger lies in the partial sense in which such writers might be expressing a grain of truth in the salt shaker of CDIES. This is not to say that I believe that CDIES is in any way an Inuit cultural tradition; however, it is possible that Minor's "traditional component" comes not from the Inuit themselves but from the traditional approach to Inuit elder suicide used by sociologists and anthropologists who have the power to define the nature of a culture not their own. What if, to a certain extent, the people themselves, listening and reading the "experts," accept the outsider opinion about their own traditional culture? Evidence that at least some educated Inuit have credited the CDIES theory comes from a powerful and revealing article, "Suicide is Price Inuit Paid for Tradition of Competency," recently published by Igloolik Inuit writer Rachel Attituq Qitsualik (2001). In this article, she makes an impassioned plea to her people not to follow the traditional path in committing suicide, something she, herself, once considered. Here, she appears to have accepted as authoritative the writings of outsiders:

> Early explorers and anthropologists were shocked at the high suicide rates among various Inuit groups. *It seemed standard* for the old and infirm, believing themselves to be a burden upon their families, to do away with themselves, sometimes going so far as to recruit their own friends or family members in assisting with the suicide. (Qitsualik 2001; emphasis mine)

CDIES as One Form of Erasure of Aboriginal Elders

As we have seen, the important role of Inuit elders in their traditional society and the respect given to them are erased in Canadian introductory sociology textbooks.

Inuit elders are measured not by the yardstick of their own culture, but by some mainstream North American culturally constructed notion of "usefulness." Not coming from a society in which elders are considered socially useful to a significant degree as repositories of environmental, social, spiritual, or technical knowledge important to succeeding generations, the writers of introductory sociology textbooks are in a poor position to understand, without listening to the words of such elders (or their equivalents in other indigenous or more tradition-minded cultures), how "useful" traditional Inuit elders can be.

Not surprisingly, then, that this erasure is not confined to Inuit elders. The voices of Aboriginal elders are generally missing from Canadian introductory sociology textbooks, their knowledge disqualified. The words of these elders are almost never presented, and in those few instances where they are permitted to speak, they tend to be so marginalized that they are not accepted as serious sources of knowledge. As mentioned in Chapter Three, James J. Teevan's extended quotation from Inuit elder Minnie Aodia Freeman is marginalized by omitting both her name from the index of (non-Aboriginal) experts in the back and her book from the "Suggested Readings" list at the end of the chapter, a site confined to non-Aboriginal knowledge producers.

It should be pointed out that, for writers generating intro-ductory sociology textbooks during the 1990s and the twenty-first century, the exclusion of Aboriginal elders does not come from a lack of awareness of their presence as sources of infor-mation. During the last two decades, university and college campuses across Canada increasingly have been providing access to Aboriginal elders, either through programs of Elders-in-Residence or of Visiting Elders. Some institutions, particularly those with a significant number of Aboriginal students and with a number of Aboriginal programs have both, while others, with a lower percentage of Aboriginal students and fewer (if any) such designated Aboriginal programs opt for the latter. A good example of the former is Lakehead University in northwestern Ontario, deep in the traditional country of the Ojibwa or Anishinabe people. Lakehead has an Elders-in-Residence Program, a Visiting Humanities Fellowship in Native Philosophy, an Annual Elders Conference, and Elder/Healing Circles. On the other hand, the University of Ottawa, which has an estimated 100 Aboriginal students, runs a Visiting Elders program through their Aboriginal Resource Centre. During the 1998–99 academic year, eight elders from various First Nations participated in this program for periods of a few days each. The stated goal of the program is "to provide Aboriginal students with support and also to educate non-Aboriginal peoples in an effort to promote respect and awareness of Aboriginal culture" (Heartfield 1998).

Statistical Erasure of the Existence of Aboriginal Elders

Not only do Canadian introductory sociology textbooks avoid using the words of Aboriginal elders as informed sources, but they typically also suggest that, speaking with statistical authority, few elders even exist. How can elders be seen as playing an important role in contemporary Aboriginal life when, as Henslin and Nelson highlight (as others do in slightly different ways) amidst a flurry of statistics on Aboriginal mortality rates, that "Native people have proportionately fewer elderly than any other racial or ethnic group in Canada" (Henslin and Nelson 1996: 358). Himelfarb and Richardson (1991) exemplify the usual sociological practice:

> Within Canada ... there remain large differences in life expectancy indicative of unequal social and economic conditions. In 1981, one estimate placed life expectancy of Indian men at 62.4 [years] which was the male life expectancy for the general Canadian population in 1941. Similarly, life expectancy at birth for Indian women [was] estimated at 68.9 years in 1981, close to the 1951 figure of 70.8 for Canadian women as a whole.
>
> Life expectancy figures present a similar picture for the Inuit populations of Canada. One estimate for the Northern Quebec Inuit placed expectations of life at birth at 62 years for both sexes combined for the period 1971–1981. Life expectancy for both sexes combined was estimated at 66 years for the Inuit of the Northwest Territories. (Himelfarb and Richardson 1991: 233)

Erasing Aboriginal Elders by Relegating Them to the Past

Another sociological form of denial or erasure of Aboriginal elders is to relegate their role to the past. When the social stature of Aboriginal elders is referred to at all, it is typical to say that elders used to be respected, but, as helpless, agency-less "victims" of harsh, social Darwinist circumstances, they can be respected no more (for a contrasting model, see below, p. 125). It does not take a great deal of imagination to envision the effects on sociology student readers of the following quotation taken from a recent textbook currently being used at my college. I have emphasized the key elements of this quotation:

> Native Canadians are often among the most economically deprived members of our society, and suffer discrimination and prejudice, resulting in high rates of unemployment, inadequate housing, and family instability. As one researcher says, "under these circumstances, identification with traditional cultures suffers, and their central familistic values of kin solidarity, *respect for elders*, and the welfare of children have been *weakened*" (Nett, 1993: 101). Morever, because of their political and economic subordination by Europeans, the family norms of many native people have been threatened.
>
> Throughout the early 1900s, most native people lived on reserves or with extended families in isolated regions. Child care was the responsibility of the extended family and *highly respected elders taught the young their languages and traditions*. Christian missionaries, who had made concerted efforts to assimilate and Christianize native peoples, took children away from the reserves to church-run residential schools to learn another language, religion, and culture, while also learning to despise their own. Traditional family values began to erode: *the elders lost their authority*, and the extended families lost their responsibilities for nurturing and caretaking. (Macionis and Gerber 1999: 443; emphasis mine)

It may be difficult for student readers of this passage to believe that elders can still play an important role in Aboriginal society today.

In Crysdale and Beattie (1977), while some respect for the position of Aboriginal elders relative to the mainstream aged is suggested, the impact of this respect is diminished by locating them in the past and by ending the discussion with Guemple's Western utilitarian construction of "elders as physical resources":

> Among the Mistassini Cree (Edward and Jean Rogers 1960) and the Canadian Inuit (Guemple 1969; [the original publication of the Guemple's piece in Crysdale and Beattie 1974]) the elders are the leaders who decide when and where to hunt or move and are regarded as having more skills and religious lore. Young persons are expected to respect, learn from, and be on close terms with the elders. Yet, despite the esteem for the elderly in these traditional societies, sometimes mistakes and slowness brought on by old age make the person the object of amusement. This leads the person to resist being classified as "old." Lee Guemple (1969) reports that the Inuit practice delaying tactics[19] and renewal activities. Since the focus of attention in Inuit society is on the male hunter, older men will try to mask their failing skills through spurts of activity or by taking a young wife. The woman in Inuit society is expected to play a secondary part as the one who raises children or prepares the game caught by the men, so the elderly women will often adopt a male baby to care for in order to show her continued social worth.[20] Yet, elderly Inuit normally remain part of the community, are given important tasks to perform, and in their own eyes and in the eyes of the community are useful, autonomous persons.[21] (Crysdale and Beattie 1977: 182–83)

Respecting Aboriginal Elders: A Three-Part Presentation

There are three necessary components for a balanced presentation of elders: traditional, colonial, and contemporary. This can be demonstrated by considering two quotations, the first from Rosalind Vanderburgh and the second from Margaret Ward, who relied on Vanderburgh's information for her discussion of aging among the Anishinabe or Ojibwa people:

> Traditionally, the grandparent generation among native people in North America was responsible for socializing the children. They had both practical knowledge and a wealth of cultural information they could pass on. Much of their teaching of core values and survival techniques was transmitted through storytelling. In return, their grandchildren had the honoured responsibility of helping them to remain independent. If they had no grandchildren themselves, they became informal grandparents to other children, who filled the grandchild role. (Vanderburgh, 1987)

> The elder role was eroded through the coming of Christian missions, with their accompanying boarding schools, which removed children from their homes and cultures. In addition, during the 1960s and 1970s, many children were apprehended by child-welfare authorities and placed with white foster and adoptive families. As a result, elders were no longer vital members of society because the socialization of children had passed to other people. Since children were no longer available to provide practical assistance, it also became more difficult for the old to retain their independence. Many ended up in nursing homes, out of touch with their culture....

> In recent years there has been a renewal of interest in traditional native ways. Elders are once again valued as transmitters of culture. They are, however, filling a role that

is somewhat different from the traditional one. They no longer act only within the confines of their family, but also in the context of voluntary groups such as elders' circles. Valuable life experience has been redefined to include how to deal with schools, social-service agencies, health-care facilities and the legal system. Indeed, such knowledge may be just as important for survival as traditional methods of hunting, fishing, or agriculture. In addition, elders are seen as custodians of the traditional culture, from which the younger generations are alienated. (Ward 2002: 198)

Presenting just one or both of the traditional and colonial elements not only misses a discussion of the contemporary, but also directs the reader away from surmising that the contemporary even exists. Talking only about the traditional role makes it merely a creature of the past, a simulacrum that denies a traditionally based but innovative elder role today. Further, while it is necessary to recognize that colonialist oppression has threatened the full functioning of the elders in contemporary Aboriginal culture,[22] this oppression can be stated in such a way as to deny the possibility that there is a culturally valuable role that elders still play.

TEACHING GERONTOLOGY IN CANADA

There is a sociological component in the teaching of gerontology. For instance, the anthropologists Holmes and Holmes mention CDIES in their American gerontology textbook, *Other Cultures, Elder Years* (1995). Does this happen as well in Canadian textbooks written by sociologists?

The two major writers/editors of gerontology textbooks in Canada—Victor Marshall and Mark Novak—are sociologists. Both repeat the CDIES story.[23] In the first edition of his *Aging in Canada: Social Perspectives* (1980, second edition 1987), Victor Marshall includes an essay written for that publication by anthropologist Lee Guemple, to whom reference has been made above. In it, Guemple attempts to reconcile the perceived paradox he sees: how can the Inuit take good care of their elders, while at the same time practicing CDIES. He states the purpose of his essay in the following quotation. Note these two facts: first, he locates CDIES in the "precontact period." This is misleading in several senses. All of his sources, and his own field-work, are decidedly post-contact. More destructive is the fact that by establishing this location, he erases the possibility that the impact of colonialism forced the people into desperate meas-ures in some extreme circumstances. Second, the word "respect" is not used in the quotation or generally in the article. The treat-ment of the elders is presented as if it is an act of generosity (like the keeping of a pet) that cannot be afforded during difficult times. Not entertained is the notion that the elders play an important role even then:

> The treatment the Inuit (Eskimo) traditionally accorded their old people *during the precontact period* has been a source of some consternation to members of the Euro-North American cultural tradition because of a seeming paradox. We know that Inuit lavished[24] care and concern on their old people and invested considerable interest in them. But we also know that they sometimes abandoned them on the trail (Rasmussen 1908: 127). Our own notion of what people are like makes it difficult for us to see how they could be so affectionate in one context and cold-hearted in another, when the chips are down.
>
> The aim of this essay is to try to resolve the paradox; to show how the attitude of love and affection is not incom-patible with the idea of killing one's own parents or helping them to kill themselves. To do so we must make a brief foray into the cognitive universe of the Inuit—into their own notion of how the world (of people and things) works. Only then can we fathom how they manage to mix sentiment

with seeming cruelty without a sense of contradiction.
(Guemple 1980: 95; emphasis mine)

His "brief foray into the cognitive universe of the Inuit" involves stating that "old people do not, in Inuit cosmology, really die" (Guemple 1980: 99), but instead the "name substance" (the spirit of the name they bear) lives on in others who receive that name. This seems to me akin to stating that many North American Christians put their elders into institutions where they are sometimes ignored, not because they are heartless, but because they believe their elders will not die, but will live on in heaven in the next life. It does not stand as a justification. And it too easily lets off the hook the colonialists who imposed their influence on the Inuit world. Fortunately, the 1987 edition does not contain this article, but does include the Vanderburgh piece referred to above.

More consistent in its replication of CDIES, and in its use of Guemple, is Mark Novak's *Aging and Society: A Canadian Perspective* (Novak 1988, 1997, 2001). In a section on the Inuit that is part of a discussion of hunting and gathering societies,[25] the author begins with a more respectful presentation than Guemple of Inuit elders, but follows this with a Guemple-influenced utilitarian spin (which, among other flaws, over-generalizes or essentializes from a few, scattered references), followed by a clear statement of CDIES:

> In Inuit society ... older people keep their status as long as they do some useful work for the group. Their status drops if illness makes them dependent. People make fun of the frail elders, say nasty things to them, or ignore them. The "over-aged" get the worst cuts of meat,[26] have little money, and have to do without trade goods. A stranger may take in an Inuit who outlives his or her spouse, children, and close relatives, but the old person will get no respect and will have to do the worst work (Guemple 1977). (Novak 1988: 29–30)

The Inuit also abandon their aged when the older person becomes a liability to the group. They do this as a last resort, and they encourage the older person to make the decision (Guemple 1980), but sometimes the group will withdraw its support rapidly, thus hastening death (Glascock and Feinman, 1981, 27). (Novak 1988: 31)

Summary

In this chapter we have seen the development of a simulacrum about Inuit, one that I have termed culturally determined Inuit elder suicide (CDIES). It is rooted in a strong sociological tradition, from Durkheim's notion of "altruistic suicide" to Sumner's concept of "mores," the latter linked to the notion of the relativity of deviance. Then it was nurtured through collections of data such as those of Ruth Cavan, Adamson Hoebel, and Edward Weyer, and flowered in both anthropology and sociology introductory textbooks in both Canada and the United States.

Simulacra develop as tools to silence other, contradictory visions of reality. CDIES silenced the many reports that Inuit elders were consistently treated with a respect that differed from the treatment of elderly in the mainstream culture from which the non-Inuit sociologists and anthropologists came.

Further, reflecting Dorothy Smith's theory of relations of ruling and Tuhiwai Smith's ideas about colonialism, at the same time that both the environment and Inuit culture was (and is) being blamed for killing elders, the government of Canada was complicit in their deaths (and that of other Inuit) through its neglect, its ill-conceived relocation programs, and its lack of opposition to colonialist capitalistic practices that were deadly to the Inuit (e.g., the creation of dependence on the Arctic fox trade). Sociologists and anthropologists have been complicit in replicating the simulacrum while failing to mention these factors.

Further, we have seen some contemporary social implications of the replication of CDIES in Canadian introductory sociology textbooks. These include using CDIES as an explanation for the incredibly high suicide rate among Inuit today, an explanation that involves "blaming the victim" and that denies the impact of colonialism (past and present). Also included is the involvement of the reproduction of CDIES in the general erasure or denial of the contemporary role of all Aboriginal elders in Canada, something that is reinforced through statistics and the location of any positive elder role in the past. Finally, we have seen how the reproduction of CDIES has had an impact on textbook production in the growing and related discipline of gerontology, with potentially negative repercussions for the future treatment of Aboriginal elders.

NOTES

1 Unfortunately, Hughes did not use this well-made point to try to deconstruct CDIES. Instead, he was challenging the notion of "the Inuit culture," as opposed to distinct Inuit cultures or ethnicities.

2 The source of this story is not given in the text, nor can I find it in the literature on the Inuit. As far as I know, the authors made this up as an illustrative example.

3 Netsilik is one of the cultural divisions of the Inuit of Canada, a distinction made by anthropologists based on location, language, and other cultural features. These cultural divisions have no collective corporate existence.

4 In a paper, entitled "Research on Arvilik-juarmuit Suicide Patterns," read at the Department of Psychiatry of McGill University in January, 1960, Balikci interpreted the then high rates of suicide and attempted suicide among the Arvilik-juarmiut (a Netsilik group) as "indicating collective inability to control aggressions combined with a low level of social integration" (reported by Boag in Boydell, Grindstaff, and Whitehead 1972: 451).

5 The reference here is to David T. Hanbury's *Sport and Travel in the Northland of Canada* (1904), written about the Copper Inuit. Hanbury was an early popularizer of CDIES and of other outsider-emphasized exoticized traits of Inuit culture (e.g., wife-lending and nose-rubbing). His ethnocentric lack of respect for the people he was visiting is often seen in his work. When the people failed to find caribou, because the animals, for a number of reasons unexamined by the author, did not follow their usual route, Hanbury presents it as an example of the people's lack of knowledge of caribou (Hanbury 1904: 121).

6 An excerpt from this book is found in Crysdale and Beattie. For my first assignment in my first anthropology class (as a student), I wrote a (glowing) review of this book.

7 It is situated between the western side of Baffin Island on the east, and, to the west, the Melville Peninsula.

8 Moore also did his work on St. Lawrence Island.

9 In the most recent version of this presentation of the connection between deviance and CDIES, Teevan articulated the same ideas in a slightly different way, as follows:

Indeed, anthropologists have shown that most behaviors have been designated as deviant somewhere, at some time, or under certain circumstances,
and yet have been accepted elsewhere, at other times, or under other circumstances. For example, in traditional Inuit culture, infanticide and the killing
of old people were seen as acceptable means to protect a limited food
supply.... Most other Canadians would have severely condemned such
behavior. Although the different outlooks are understandable given the
unique conditions facing the Inuit, they illustrate the relative definition of
deviance, that what is deviant is specific to time, place, and circumstances.
(Teevan 1995: 115–16)

10 As is typical for CDIES, the words of two textbooks are very similar. The Clinard and
Meier textbook, quoted above, was first published in 1963, so Mann was either quoting from the same source as the Americans, or was paraphrasing what they had to say.

11 In this work, she drew upon the Inuit-themed writings of Boas, Hall, Nansen, and
Steinmetz.

12 She cited 20 references at the end of her chapter on the Inuit. Only three of them were
primary sources that discussed Inuit suicide.

13 This seems to me to owe more to Durkheim's stories of Vikings and Goths than it
does to Inuit ethnography.

14 Like the assertion of the ubiquity of CDIES, this is a questionable assertion.

15 One can see this type of population dynamics frame in the American sociology textbook *An Introduction to the Study of Society*, by Blaine E. Mercer (1958). In a chapter entitled, "Population Characteristics and Trends," under the headings, first "Some
General Population Policies" and under that "Restrictive Policies," Mercer wrote:

Closely related to infanticide as a restrictive population policy is the practice of killing the aged, the sick, or other persons believed useless or dangerous by the people of a community or society. Among many American Indian
tribes, some Eskimos, and some Africans, the practice was—and to some
extent still is—used. (Mercer 1958: 161)

16 This work is a revised and abridged version of what first appeared in *Sociological
Symposium* 2 (Spring 1969): 59–74.

17 See Health Canada 1995.

18 In interrogating the "culturalist" argument, they still demonstrate acceptance of
CDIES by saying that youth suicides of the present cannot be compared to suicides
of the elderly in the past, as the youth are not the "burden" the elders were (Kirmayer,
Fletcher and Boothroyd 1998: 201).

19 I wonder whether these can only be considered as "delaying tactics" if the mainstream
North American model of old age is set as the standard. Did the people say that was
what they were doing? Is that the way they framed their own activities? Asking the
people how they saw such practices might have been a useful research strategy.
Perhaps these "tactics" are merely performing traditional respected elder roles.

20 Again, how do we know that this is a "show" or demonstration and not merely an elderly
woman doing what she enjoys, or is expected to do, and is fully competent to do?

21 These final comments appear to me to be contradicting the "for show" comments
earlier made by the authors and by Guemple.

22 This would involve a discussion of such institutional attacks as the residential schools,
federally funded, church-run institutions that, during the better part of the twentieth
century, separated Aboriginal children from their homes, parents, elders, culture, and
identity, in an often brutal and brutalizing amalgam of physical, emotional, sexual,
and culture abuse.

23 This seems different from the case with American textbooks. Although, admittedly, I have only looked at a handful of American gerontology textbooks in the Humber library, none of these mentions CDIES.

24 I find interesting Guemple's use of monetary metaphors to describe treatment in a non-monetary culture. Here, as elsewhere, his own culture intrudes too much on his analysis of the Inuit.

25 The Inuit fare somewhat better in this framing than do the Chipewyan, who in his negative (and inaccurate) portrayal he claims "do not value knowledge or tribal lore or craftwork" (Novak 1988: 29).

26 Holmes and Holmes point out that sometimes elders are permitted to eat those foods that the hunters cannot eat because of food taboos (Holmes and Holmes 1995: 153).

CHAPTER FIVE

The Potlatch in Canadian Introductory Sociology Textbooks

Potlatch ... [Chinook Jargon, fr. Nootka *patshatl* giving, gift] ... a ceremonial feast or festival of the Indians of the northwest coast given for the display of wealth to validate or advance individual tribal position or social status and marked by the host's lavish destruction of personal property and an ostentatious distribution of gifts that entails elaborate reciprocity.

— *Webster's Third New International Dictionary*
of the English Language

WHITE PEOPLE CREATE *THE* POTLATCH

During the 1800s, various peoples of the Northwest Coast[1] of British Columbia held a number of ceremonies that included a connection to the spiritual, to the artistic (with song, dance, theatre, and carved wood), and to traditional narratives (personal and familial that extended to the clan and moiety; cultural and shared across cultures). In addition, there was the practice of "giveaway,"[2] a feature shared across cultures throughout Aboriginal Canada, but which was highlighted in the Northwest Coast culture area because the people there were relatively richer in natural resources. Gift-giving demonstrated the core Aboriginal value of generosity common in all First Nations. There was no single name for the giveaway ceremonies cross-culturally, just as there is no single term in English that encompasses Irish wakes, Christmas mass for French-Canadians, Easter celebrations among Ukrainian Canadians, confirmation for Italian-Canadians, and Thanksgiving for the American family.

As agents of Western culture, especially government agents and Christian missionaries, encountered these diverse giveaway ceremonies, they did not know what to make of them. During the 1860s to 1880s, they did have relative consensus on one thing: they almost universally opposed the ceremonies, for a variety of reasons. They were interpreted as "foreign," "savage," and, given the recent history of conflict,[3] somewhat threatening. Missionaries opposed them because they took potential converts away, particularly with regard to practices and spiritual beliefs. All Western agents seemed to agree that the ceremonies impeded the "progress of civilization," particularly with the large amounts of goods being given away.

In order to fight the ceremonies, the Western agents had to give them a unifying name and description. As Christopher Bracken ably demonstrates in *The Potlatch Papers: A Colonial Case History* (1997), this took a number of years and many dispatches and letters to accomplish. The name arrived at was "potlatch," said to be derived from a verb meaning "to give." It cannot now be known conclusively to which ceremonies in what cultures the word traditionally referred. The term came from the Chinook trade language, the native tongue of no one, but a language that was understood cross-culturally among linguistically diverse peoples for communication in the fur trade.[4]

Establishing the term was relatively easy. Defining it entailed more work. Even after ceremonies named as "potlatch" were banned under a change in the federal Indian Act in 1884 (which took effect in 1885),[5] officials and Aboriginal peoples alike were not sure what it was that was being banned. Most influential in this definition process was the early work of Franz Boas, rightly named one of the "founding fathers" of social anthropology. He was involved in a long-term study of the people he referred to as "Kwakiutl," people whose lands were relatively southern in the world of the Kwakwaka?kw, or People Who Speak Kwakwala (one of the Northern Wakashan languages). Like the term "potlatch," the term "Kwakiutl" was extended beyond its traditional use to include a number of related or similar referents.[6]

Very early in his extensive work with the Kwakiutl, Boas produced a very preliminary, and, because of that, flawed study that nevertheless became an anthropological classic. Unfortunately, it has had far greater impact on the writing of anthropology and sociology textbooks than did his much more carefully developed, detailed, and in-depth later works.[7] The study was entitled "The Social Organization and the Secret Societies of the Kwakiutl Indians" (1897), reprinted for the most part in 1966 as *Kwakiutl Ethnography*. His student Irving Goldman noted that in fairness to Boas, the paper was published early in his work with the Kwakiutl, before he became fully engaged in his long term, detailed research with the people. Goldman perceptively remarks that, "It is a tribute to Boas's extraordinary reputation for accuracy that even his first impressions were taken by fellow scholars as flat truths" (Goldman 1975: 163).

Two main features of this work were exaggerated in their importance in characterizing Kwakiutl ceremonies, thus cartooning this spiritual people as solely and intensely materialistic fanatics. One was that notion that "Kwakiutl potlatches" involved ever-increasing loans with fast-escalating interest that built up the wealth and power of certain individuals. Boas begins his discussion of the potlach by describing how a youth borrowing blankets within the "tribe" for a potlatch does so in order to distribute property at an intertribal gathering. In Goldman's terms:

> The purpose of these internal loans, which Boas understood to be some form of debt-hiking, is to allow the youth "to amass a fortune." ([Boas 1897]: 342). (Goldman 1975: 165)

Goldman goes on to note that Boas's early impression of the usurious function of potlatch goods was unsubstantiated. Goldman did not find in the published Kwakiutl texts any record

> to substantiate Boas's account of escalation of loans in the course of which the youth borrows at 100 percent, and lends out at 100 percent until the entire accumulation comes his way. (Goldman 1975: 165)

This flawed notion was reproduced in other writings, including textbooks, but it did not have the same force to mislead, nor the same capacity to showcase the Kwakiutl in a negative light as did the second major error. Specifically, Boas painted "the potlatch" of the Kwakiutl (they had several ceremonies that outsiders such as Boas lumped together under that one "foreign" name) in the bold colours of socially and physically intense and destructive rivalry: "fighting with property."

This notion, which was repeated often in sociological and anthropological treatises and textbooks, to ill effect on "the public's" conception of the Kwakiutl and related peoples, sprang essentially from a speech made in one highly particular circumstance during the Winter Ceremonial of 1895–96, a gathering of Kwakiutl and other Kwakwaka?kw peoples against whom the Kwakiutl occasionally used to fight. Much of what was said had no relevance to ceremonies in which only the Kwakiutl participated, the majority of which were termed "potlatch." Most "potlatches" were for validation of, rather than competition for, names and statuses that were, to use a term usually found in introductory sociology textbooks but never used to refer to the potlatch, more "ascribed"—that is born into, like gender, race, and European royalty—than "achieved." The "person of noble birth" was as much a stock figure in traditional Northwest Coast stories as princes and princesses are in traditional European stories.

Boas recorded the words of a dancer who belonged to the Koskimo, a Kwakwaka?kw people who spoke a different dialect than the Kwakiutl, who were former enemies of the Kwakiutl, and who, in Goldman's apt terms, "were not part of the traditional congregation" of Kwakiutl ceremonies:

> Oh friends! turn your faces this way. Look at me! Treat me and my cedar bark ornaments in the right manner. In former times I and my people have suffered at your hands, Kwakiutl. We used to fight with bows and arrows, with spears and guns. We robbed each other's blood. But now we fight with this here (pointing at the copper which he was holding in his hands), and if we have no coppers, we fight with canoes or blankets. That is all. (Boas 1897: 571)

Qoalxala, a Kwakiutl, replied in kind with the following:

> When I was young, I have seen streams of blood shed in war. But since that time the white man came and stopped up that stream of blood with wealth. Now we are fighting with our wealth. (Goldman 1975: 170)

Elsewhere in the description of that intertribal Winter Ceremonial, a Kwakiutl fool dancer[8] made a statement that became accepted across the decades as an intellectual commodity:

> The time of fighting has passed. The fool dancer represents the warrior, but we do not fight now with weapons; we fight with property. (Boas 1897: 602)

Goldman makes two important points about this phrase "we fight with property." First, it appears nowhere else in the voluminous collection on Kwakiutl ceremonies produced by Boas and his informant and co-collector George Hunt (a part-Tlingit, part-Scottish man adopted by the Kwakiutl).⁹ This is an important point, as, over more than 40 years, the two collected, edited, and published some 4,500 pages of "verbatim text" on the Kwakiutl (Michelson 1982: 1). Second, the words are recorded as spoken by "commoners engaging in 'fight talk'" (Goldman 1975: 171). Those who typically threw potlatches were not "commoners" in this status-ranked society, but what can aptly be called "nobility" or even "aristocracy."¹⁰

Unfortunately, Boas, who rarely made generalizations, generalized these speeches by the Kwakiutl and Koskimo dancers, thus misleading generations of scholars and students since:

> Formerly feats of bravery counted as well as distributions of property, but nowadays, as the Indians say, "rivals fight with property only." The clans are thus traditionally pitted against each other according to their ranks. (Boas 1897: 343)

Helen Codere further enshrined the expression by calling her influential book *Fighting with Property* (Codere 1950). A sense of her exaggeration can be seen here:

> The Kwakiutl potlatch, throughout the historical record, was always a form of rivalry and fighting and it could absorb and command anything in warfare and would add to its impressiveness. It was ridden with the imagery and drama and meaning of Kwakiutl warfare and it was empty of physical violence and destruction except occasionally toward property. (Codere 1950: 129)

P?A'SA: FLATTENING DIFFERENCES

Before we look at the replication of this statement in sociology textbooks, it is useful to note certain specific misleading elements that have contributed to the popularity of Boas's phrase "fighting with property." One is the Kwakiutl word Boas writes as "pʔa'sa" and which he uses as "*the*" term for "*the* potlatch":

> This festival is called p'a'sa, literally, flattening something (for instance, a basket). This means that by the amount of property given the name of the rival is flattened. (Boas 1966: 8)

This sense of the term has been reproduced religiously by those such as Ruth Benedict and Helen Codere who followed Boas and accepted his early interpretation without doing their own fieldwork with the people. Benedict wrote: "The object of his endeavours was to 'flatten' their pretensions by the weight of his own, to 'break' their names" (Benedict 1959: 221).

In Codere's words:

> The usual word for potlatch was "p!Esa," to flatten, and it came to mean to flatten a rival under a pile of blankets or "means of flattening," for the word "potlatch blanket" took its origin from the same root and had this literal meaning. (Codere 1950: 120)

This interpretation was taken up by anthropology textbooks, the following being an illustrative example of how it could be interwoven into the "fighting with property" stereotype:

> In the 1880s, after the Canadian government began to suppress warfare between tribes,[11] potlatching also became a substitute for battle. As a Kwakiutl man once said to the anthropologist Franz Boas, "The time of fighting is past.... We do not fight now with weapons: we fight with property." The usual Kwakiutl word for potlatch was *p!Esa*, meaning to flatten (as when one flattens a rival under a pile of blankets), and the prospect of being given a large gift engendered real fear. Still, the Kwakiutl seemed to prefer

the new "war of wealth" to the old "war of blood."
(Cronk, originally 1989, reprinted in Spradley and
McCurdy 1997: 165)

While this interpretation well served the purpose of emphasizing destructive rivalry, it is mistaken. This can be seen in the
following from Goldman, who was the first to undertake an
extensive study of how the word was used in context, and who
did not set out to reinforce the notion of destructive rivalry. He
noted the difference in Boas's interpretation of the word from
"flattening the name of a rival" (Boas 1897: 343) in his earliest
works to the non-aggressive reference to the gradual flattening
of a soft basket by removing objects from it (Boas 1935b: 40).
In Goldman's thinking, this is consistent with Boas's belief that
the *pasa* distribution was largely restricted to intratribal ceremonies, a context in which one could not "flatten the name of
a rival." he points out that

> [P]*asa* introduces a concept of self-divestment, of empty-
> ing out in behalf of a name, the contrary of "flattening" an
> opponent. (Goldman 1975: 132–133)

Even contemporary Aboriginal writers are not immune to the
authority of Boas's misinterpretation of the potlatch. In her otherwise excellent article "Kwakiutl" in Frederick Hoxie's
Encyclopedia of North American Indians (1996), Namgis[12]
writer and founding director of the U'mista Cultural Centre,
Gloria Cranmer Webster wrote: "Each cultural group has its own
word for the [potlatch] ceremony. In Kwakwala, the word is
pasa, literally meaning "to flatten"—that is, to flatten one's
guests under the weight of the gifts given to them" (Webster
1996: 320). Trusting the validity of this statement as coming
from an Aboriginal author who had significant understanding of
the ceremony and was the curator responsible for sacred potlatch
items, I "learned" error myself, taught it in my sociology and

anthropology classes, and then reproduced it in a book that I co-authored (Steckley and Cummins 2001: 170).

DESTRUCTION OF PROPERTY
The Destruction of Coppers

Coppers were the physical objects that possessed the highest value in traditional Northwest Coast culture. Mined in Alaska, they were shaped somewhat like shields and covered with designs painted with black lead. Consistent with the high respect with which the people held these items, they had names, just as humans do. One copper is particularly famous to anthropologists and to students in anthropology classes, as a part of its story was recorded by Boas in his stay with the Kwakiutl in the winter of 1894–95. Its name was Maxtsolem, meaning "One of whom all (other coppers) are shamed (to look at, i.e., because they are not Maxtsolem's equal)." At a ceremony held that winter, a high-ranking man named Owaxalagilis attempted to buy Maxtsolem. He placed 1,200 blankets in front of the chief who was hosting the potlatch, but was eventually talked into paying about 4,200 blankets (then worth about 50 cents each).

A key element in the Boasian depiction of the Kwakiutl potlatch is the destruction of property, which is carried out in his sketch of this event:

> The rivalry between chiefs, when carried so far that coppers are destroyed and that grease feasts are given in order to destroy the prestige of the rival, often develop into open enmity. (Boas 1897: 355)

> The rivalry between chiefs and clans finds its strongest expression in the destruction of property. A chief will burn blankets, a canoe, or break a copper, thus indicating his disregard of the amount of property destroyed and showing that his mind is stronger, his power greater, than that

of his rival. If the latter is not able to destroy an equal amount of property without much delay, his name is "broken." He is vanquished by his rival and his influence with the tribe is lost, while the name of the other chief gains correspondingly in renown. (Boas 1966: 93)

However, the chief value of coppers existed in their acquisition, not in their possession, nor their destruction. While Boas was correct to note that coppers were sometimes broken in ceremony, that does not necessarily mean destruction of the whole copper, as David Michelson noted:

When destruction did take place only very small pieces were destroyed which did not greatly affect the copper's value. In many cases these pieces were recovered, and new coppers were fashioned from them. (Michelson 1982: 67)

The large-scale destruction of coppers was important to Codere's explanation of potlatches, which also involved her acceptance of the Boas-constructed notion of the spiraling costs of "potlatch loans." If coppers were destroyed in significant numbers, then the spiral stopped, and the people could start from scratch, a process similar to tearing up an IOU. In Codere's words:

It is only in the total destruction of a copper that a profitless act can be found. Then credits were destroyed. Then, the continuous series of cycles where each succeeding peak was twice the height of the one before was finally broken. (Codere 1950: 75–76)

Both Michelson and Goldman, sifting through the evidence of Boas's later collected texts, are careful to note that the breaking of coppers was relatively rare (Michelson 1982: 67; Goldman 1975: 218–19). Goldman points out that one text, the Elgunwe text, assumed to be "typical" by Benedict and Codere, was the only source he had found in reading Boas's Kwakiutl texts that referred to coppers being destroyed and thrown into the sea in an act of putting down a chief (Goldman 1975: 218).

Burning Down the House

One aspect of the focus on the destruction of property that really caught the imagination of later writers was the burning of a house in the potlatch ceremony. This is a misinterpretation of a ceremony known in English by the unfortunate and somewhat degrading (and degraded) name, "grease feast." In a ceremony high in symbolism and theatre, the host used various devices to pour large quantities of oil made from the eulachon or candlefish (so named because of all the oil in its body), a traditionally rich resource for Northwest Coast peoples, into a fire to demonstrate his wealth and to make other important metaphorical statements. Guests then presented gifts as metaphoric attempts to "put out the fire." Because it fit with her psychological profile of the Kwakiutl as "Dionysian" megalomaniacs, Ruth Benedict, one of Boas's students, put in the anthropological spotlight the single recorded instance in which the fire got so out of hand that a house burned down:

> *On one occasion* within the lifetime of men now living, the chief tried to "put out" the fire of his rival with seven canoes and four hundred blankets, while his host poured oil upon the fire in opposition. The roof of the house caught fire and the whole house was nearly destroyed, while those who were concerned kept their places with assumed indifference and sent for more possessions to heap upon the fire. (Benedict 1959: 199–200, emphasis mine)

Benedict's spotlight ignited the imagination of a good number of uninformed but influential writers and teachers[13] to spread the fire from text to text. The following two examples illustrate how this single example is falsely generalized. The first comes from literary critic and postmodernist Jacques Derrida (writing too far from his area of expertise), the second from the author of an American introductory sociology textbook who mistakenly believed that burning down the house in that instance (and other fictional ones) was a deliberate act:

> Whole boxes of olachen (candle-fish) oil or whale oil are burned *as are houses* and thousands of blankets. (Derrida 1992, in Bracken 1997: 160; emphasis mine)
>
> The most successful potlatches were those in which a chief would give away all his property and, to demonstrate his true greatness, *pour oil on his house and burn it to the ground*. (Sanderson 1988: 87; emphasis mine)

RUTH BENEDICT

Ruth Benedict (1887–1948) was one of Boas's most famous and influential graduate students. As a mature student of anthropology at Columbia University shortly after the end of World War I, she was raised academically on "Papa Franz's" Kwakiutl and potlatch material and began her teaching career there by giving a class on the Northwest Coast. She used Boas's study of the Kwakiutl in an important intellectual battle of the time: the battle between biology and culture in explaining the nature of human beings, particular classifications of human beings (e.g., races, ethnic groups, classes). Biological explanation ("nature" in the nature/nurture debate), strong in the 1920s and 1930s when Benedict produced her works, gave academic credibility to biological definitions of race,[14] racism, eugenics, and social Darwinism. Benedict, however, was on the side of cultural relativity. Her main weapon was her best-selling book *Patterns of Culture*; published in 1934; by 1974, it had sold an estimated 1.6 million copies and had been translated into at least 12 languages.

Following sociological tradition since Durkheim's *Rules of the Sociological Method* (1938, originally 1895), Benedict worked with the notion that "normal" and "abnormal" are culturally defined, extending that to mean that different cultures frame as ideals different personality types. In order to illustrate clearly the truth of this concept, and to demonstrate that culture was as powerful as she believed it was, she pushed cultural relativism to the limit by engaging in a discussion of three cultures she considered to be "extremes." One of those was the Dobu, a Pacific Island people (studied by a friend, Reo Fortune) that Benedict labelled (seemingly with no intention of being judgmental) as "Paranoid." She contrasted them with two Aboriginal groups— the Zuñi (with whom she had done her own fieldwork) and the Kwakiutl (from Boas's fieldnotes, publications, and her talks with him)—using terms relating to Greek tragedies and that had been used earlier by Friedrich Nietzsche. She labelled the Zuñi "Apollonian," with the sense of balance and emotional calm of the Greek god Apollo. The Kwakiutl were labelled "Dionysian," megalomaniacs who indulged in wild demonstrations of emotional extremes in pursuit and display of wealth. Thus, Benedict considered the potlatch to be their primary theatre. Unfortunately, she caricatured both the Kwakiutl and their ceremonies, often taking as literal their rich metaphors and symbolism. Concerning this caricature, Goldman commented that, "Boas once remarked to me, 'The words are those of the Kwakiutl, but they have nothing to do with the Indians that I knew'" (Goldman 1975: 146).

The narrative of the destructive mania or madness of the potlatch was a theme picked up by Marcel Mauss, the nephew of French sociologist Emile Durkheim and an influential sociologist in his own right, in his most famous work, *Essai sur le don* (1950), translated as *The Gift: the Form and Reason for Exchange in Archaic Societies* (1990). In his useful look at this narrative, Bracken shows how Mauss's idea of the "madness" of the competition was adopted by Jacques Derrida. In the latter's extravagantly exaggerated interpretation of Mauss's narrative is this unthinking (and "undeconstructed") reproduction of the Western narrative of "the Kwakiutl potlatch" as madly destructive competitive rivalry:

It is a competition to see who is the richest and also the *most madly extravagant* [le plus follement *dépensier*]. Everything is based upon the principles of antagonism and of rivalry. The political status of individuals in the brotherhoods and clans, and ranks of all kinds are gained in a "war of property," just as they are in real war, or through chance, inheritance, alliance, and marriage. Yet everything is conceived of as if it were a "struggle" for "wealth." Marriages for one's children and places in the brotherhoods are only won during the potlatch exchanged and returned. They are lost at the potlatch as they are lost in war, by gambling or in running and wrestling. In a certain number of cases, *it is not even a question of giving, and returning, but of destroying, so as not to want even to appear to desire repayment....* The most valuable copper objects are broken and thrown into the water, in order to crush and to "flatten" one's rival. In this way one not only promotes oneself, but also one's family, up the social scale. (Derrida 1992, as presented in Bracken 1997: 159–60; emphasis added by Bracken)

Bracken's comment sums up well the cumulative effect of Benedict, Mauss, Derrida, and others: "It seems the more Western European observers describe the potlatch, the more extravagant their narratives become" (Bracken 1997: 160).

The Kwakiutl: A People of the Past

In his discussion of the nature of simulacra, Baudrillard (1983) talked about the effectiveness of silencing contemporary indigenous people by ethnographic descriptions focussed on the past as the only time when the culture of the people was *real*. I discussed in Chapter One how Aboriginal writers and the Native Studies approach in general opposes this tendency. Ruth Benedict articulated the view that the Kwakiutl she describes existed as a complete culture and flourished ceremonially only in the past. This reflected the then-prevalent belief that Native Americans were the "Vanishing Americans."

> The culture of the Northwest Coast fell into ruin during the latter part of the last century. Our first-hand knowledge of it therefore as a functioning civilization is limited to those tribes that were described a generation ago, and it is only the Kwakiutl of Vancouver Island whose culture we know in great detail. For the most part, therefore, the description of this culture will be that of the Kwakiutl, supplemented by the contrasting details that are known from other tribes and by the memories of old men who once took part in what is now a vanishing civilization. (Benedict 1959: 175)

Every Canadian introductory sociology textbook that mentions the potlatch keeps it as a practice confined to the past.

THE POTLATCH IN CANADIAN INTRODUCTORY SOCIOLOGY TEXTBOOKS

Not surprisingly, considering the close connection between sociology and social anthropology in Canada and the United States, the potlatch has long been featured in introductory sociology textbooks in North America. The most comprehensive look at the potlatch in such a text appears in an early work by Carl A. Dawson, then professor and chair of the department of sociology and anthropology at McGill University (Dawson and Getty 1948). In the third edition of this work, almost an entire chapter, "Cultural Integration in Specific Societies," is dedicated to looking at the Kwakiutl (1948: 42–60). Dawson and Getty steer clear of the extreme interpretation of loan payments and destructive rivalry, being more inclined to present a broader context. However, they still speak of the potlatch as if it only existed in the past and do not identify its banning as ethnocentrism.

In textbooks with potential impact on college and university students, the portrayal of the potlatch is neither so central nor as balanced as in Dawson's early work. Paul B. Horton's *Sociology and the Health Sciences* (1965), used to teach Sociology for Nursing at Humber College in 1974, replicates Benedict's extreme contrast between the Kwakiutl and the Zuñi (Horton 1965: 255) and makes the following comments concerning the potlatch. Note the stress placed on competition and the destruction of property and the inaccuracy of the Western capitalist analogy of bankruptcy and "American dream" social mobility:

> The Kwakiutl work very hard to accumulate wealth which is used primarily to establish status rather than for material comfort. The competition for status reaches its height at the famous potlatch in which the chiefs and leading families vie with each other to see how much they can give away or destroy.... A family may spend a lifetime accumulating wealth, then bankrupt themselves in a single potlatch, thereby establishing the social status of their children. A family that persisted in keeping their wealth would be criticized for their unwillingness to "do anything" for their children. (Horton 1965: 255)

While the present tense is used, the story told is of the "ethnographic present" of an earlier period and does not accurately reflect the potlatch as it existed at the time of the book's publication.

The first exclusively Canadian introductory sociology textbook to mention the potlatch is Crysdale and Beattie's *Sociology Canada: An Introductory Text* (1977). The authors speak of the potlatch exclusively in the past tense, and the destructive rivalry is stressed. The potlatch is framed in terms of Thorstein Veblen's theory of "conspicuous consumption," usually applied to North American society, with the Kwakiutl past being presented as more restrictive than the mainstream North American present, a very debatable point:

Both the conspicuous destruction of goods by the Kwakiutl and the conspicuous consumption of goods by modern North Americans are patterns that impose constraints on members of society. But the modern North American has more options open to him that [sic] were available in Kwakiutl culture or in his own culture several generations ago. (Crysdale and Beattie 1977: 61)

Kenneth Westhues (1982) presents his discussion of the potlatch in Mauss's terms. Of the sociologist authors considered here who discuss the potlatch, he alone makes reference to the banning of the ceremonies. However, instead of speaking of this as the ethnocentric act it was, he considers the legislation in the social Darwinist sense of the inevitability of the extinction of the ceremony. And, of course, he writes about the potlatch in the past tense, for it cannot exist in his frame of the present:

In his *Essay on the Gift*, he [Mauss] wrote that in archaic societies, objects "are never completely separated from the men who exchange them; the communion and alliance they establish are well-nigh indissoluble." The most celebrated example was the potlatch of the Kwakiutl Indians in nineteenth-century British Columbia. This was a joyous ceremonial festival where the host reduced himself to virtual poverty by giving away his possessions to his guests. But he had not at all made himself poor in the context of Kwakiutl culture, for his friends and kin had accepted the host's very self into their lives along with his gifts. The norm of reciprocity in gift-giving would ensure, moreover, that others would soon invite him to partake of their own possessions.

When the Canadian government outlawed the potlatch in 1883,[15] it furnished thereby a poignant symbol of the fate of gift giving in more economically advanced societies. (Westhues 1982: 223)

Rosenberg, Shaffir, Turowetz, and Weinfeld (1983) so convincingly describe the potlatch as existing solely in the past that student readers might easily come to believe that the Kwakiutl are no more. While destructive competition is not stressed to the same extent as in other works and status is recognized as primarily ascribed, the potlatch is still made to fit into a narrow frame that sees only the materialist, economic part of a ceremony (the word "material" appears four times in the following quotation):

> Even an emphasis on *material* possessions need not take the exact form it does today in Canada. The native Indians of Canada's west coast, prior to Westernization, *were* concerned with *material* goods, but with giving them away rather than with acquiring them. In large ceremonies we know of as the *potlatch*, a host and his kindred *would* give gifts—in latter years, most often blankets made by the Hudson's Bay Company—to guests and in so doing *would* earn social honour. The system of the Kwakiutl, *who lived* in the area north of Comox between Vancouver Island and the mainland, has been well described. (See Codere, 1950) People's names in this society *were* like the aristocratic titles of England, carrying status in a completely explicit way so that it *was* possible to talk of such and such a name as being the sixth highest in the whole society. The status of these names *was* maintained by the giving of gifts. Status *could* be improved by excelling in gift giving, so the system included provision for social mobility.
>
> The stratification system of the Kwakiutl *was* in some ways the opposite of our current system, since it *emphasized* giving away *material* goods rather than consuming them. But in other ways it *was* curiously similar since it *was* based on *material* goods and since acquisition *had* to precede distribution of them. (Rosenberg, Shaffir, Turowetz, and Weinfeld 1983: 350; emphasis mine)

Finally, Murray Knuttila (1993) follows Benedict's work, which he discusses at length, by picking up the narrative of the destructive competition and in presenting the potlatch in the past tense: "it was essentially an opportunity for individual men to demonstrate their superiority either by giving more wealth to a rival than the rival would be able to return, or by publicly destroying their own wealth" (Knuttila 1993: 40).

Anthropology Textbooks

Although they are not strictly part of the corpus of texts analysed here, it is important to emphasize that introductory anthropology textbooks suffer from the same faults as introductory sociology textbooks when it comes to the presentation of the potlatch. The following are illustrative examples, one, unfortunately, relatively recent:

> An example in which warfare may have been successfully replaced by another activity was the case of the North American Pacific Coast Kwakiutl Indians. As the Kwakiutl themselves put it, "wars of property"—*potlatches*—replaced "wars of blood," and fighting was done with wealth instead of weapons. (Miller and Weitz 1979: 542)

> To an individual raised in a culture where economic individualism and the market mechanism of exchange are taken for granted, it may be intriguing to find in the anthropological literature so many accounts of transfer transactions that do not conform to this norm. Some of the transactions seem to be irrational. One example is the *kula* exchange of the Trobriand and neighboring islanders of the southwestern Pacific.... Equally baffling were the potlatches of the Indians of the northwest coast of America in which huge quantities of goods that had been acquired were given away and even destroyed. Whatever was involved in these

transactions, it was not like the buying and selling of auto-mobiles in modern America. (Nash 1999: 129)

POTLATCH: ALTERNATIVE VIEWS
Looking at the Potlatch in Holistic Rather Than Partial Terms

The simulacrum of the destructively competitive potlatch blinds the reader to other views that are generated from a more complete knowledge of the ceremony and the people, a knowledge that reflects more accurately the people's views of it. Texts by anthropologists such as Drucker and Heiser (1967), Goldman himself (1975), and Michelson (1982) provide a critical alternative view of the potlatch, an alternative available during the period in which all the analysed introductory sociology textbooks were written

Goldman introduced his epic study of the potlatch with the following powerful commentary on how writings about the Kwakiutl and their ceremonies were only partial, selective,[16] and especially negligent in failing to include the important context of the spiritual or religious so abundantly supplied by Boas and Hunt:

> *Only a backward sociological tradition dares postulate general theory from only a partial examination of available data....*
>
> The proverbial committee of blind men could not conjure up the shape of a real elephant. Thus scholars who have examined only portions of the Kwakiutl cultural anatomy have inevitably produced a bizarre image. They have projected Kwakiutl character as pathological. They have seen in distribution and exchange archaic forms of welfare and old age insurance, or primitive banking complete with investments earning very high rates of interest. They have seen distressing forms of materialism together with distasteful manifestations of aggressive invidiousness and status climbing. Some have had to defend the

Kwakiutl by pointing out examples of an "amiable side."[17]
By and large, however, the Kwakiutl "image" has been
harshly drawn by writers who have viewed the parts rather
than the whole. (Goldman 1975: ix–x; emphasis mine)

In addition, knowledge of great significance is generated by the
people themselves, in three readily accessible but ignored autobiographical works composed by Kwakiutl, in which the hand of the
outsider researcher appears to be only lightly felt, and the Kwakiutl
are more than mere "informants." These works are Charles James
Nowell's *Smoke from Their Fires: The Life of a Kwakiutl Chief*
(1941 and 1968); James Sewid's *Guests Never Leave Hungry: The
Autobiography of James Sewid, a Kwakiutl Indian* (Spradley 1969);
George Clutesi's *Potlatch* (1969); and, more recently, Harry Assu's
Assu of Cape Mudge: Recollections of a Coastal Indian Chief
(1989; see also the excerpt published in 1996).

James Sewid's Autobiography: Aboriginal-Produced Knowledge About the Potlatch

Anthropologist James Spradley collected two years of interviews
with James Sewid to produce *Guests Never Leave Hungry*. Most
of the book (1969: 16–267) is written in the first person. It is
clear that it was a project to which Sewid was deeply committed:

> I have always tried hard to live up to all the things that I have
> done and I think that others can learn from hearing about my
> experiences. I thought that if I could put my life story in a
> written book, then even people that I know in distant places
> could read about it and it might help them. That was why I
> thought it necessary to make this book. (Spradley 1969: 5)

In this book, readers learn important lessons about the
potlatch, lessons that are missing from introductory sociology
textbooks. For instance, in Sewid's story about the potlatch that

celebrated his birth in 1913, we learn about the significance of
its connection to naming (Spradley 1969: 16). This connection
is repeated in at least one other anthropological autobiography:
Harry Assu refers to a 1977 potlatch in which a significant
number of children received names:

> When you continue the names of the people in the family
> who have gone before, you feel part of something bigger
> that goes way back in time. Some of our people believed in
> reincarnation. I know I still do. Maybe that is part of why
> this custom is so important to us. But mainly it is impor-
> tant because it keeps the family together, the way we want
> it to be. We want them to be strong in the Indian culture.
> (Assu 1996: 357)

In another instance, Sewid successfully resisted efforts to crim-
inalize the potlatch that inducted him as a 16-year-old into the
important Hamatsa or Cannibal Society. The potlatch had been
reported in advance to the police, and an RCMP officer had
been sent from Ottawa to investigate. He asked the people to
show him what the performance entailed. According to Sewid:

> He demanded to see it that night, so we put on a good show
> for him. The dances we did were all mixed together and not
> in the right way we had been doing them. I was dancing with
> a fool's mask on along with a group of [people wearing]
> masks. The mounted police was standing on one side of the
> house while the big dance was going on and one of our
> people was interpreting to him what it was all about.... [At
> the conclusion of the ceremony, the RCMP officer declared:]
> I'd like to see the young man that went through this thing.
> I'd like to see him dance for me tonight because I was sent
> here to investigate this young man. I want him to dance with
> everything he had on, all his masks and everything. I want
> him to do it just like the way he did it last week.

The village leaders told Sewid that he would have to dance for the officer. He did so, and the officer said, "It was a wonderful dance. I really enjoyed it. I can't see anything wrong with it." And then he returned to Ottawa. (Spradley 1969: 92–93)

Sewid tried to revive the ceremony in 1951, when the ban was lifted (Spradley 1969: 158–62). This report of the people's work to make the potlatch strong again is also in Assu's book.

Opportunities Lost

The simulacrum of the potlatch is not only to be criticized for valorizing a partial view of what it was and is. It also illustrates well the critical insights of both Dorothy Smith and Linda Tuhiwai Smith concerning the politics of the production of knowledge. In terms of the theorizing of the former, the simulacrum efficiently serves the relations of ruling, denying the readers of the textbooks an awareness of the fairly blatant ways in which the state (through federal agents and missionaries) abusively exercised power over the Aboriginal peoples of the Northwest Coast. Key missing features are the government's banning of the potlatch, the continued persecution of the peoples because of their religion, and the use of the ban to "legally" steal the most sacred items of the people. In terms of Tuhiwai Smith's analysis of colonialism, the simulacrum misses an opportunity to serve the indigenous research project of "remembering," of creating "dangerous memories" concerning Canadian history that, I will argue, has lasted up until recent times.

In the four Canadian introductory sociology textbooks that mention the potlatch, not one mentions the ban. It is not included in the sociological "story of the potlatch." The only reference I found in any sociology (or anthropology)[18] textbook was a rather offhand remark presented in Dawson and Getty's early textbook, part of their comprehensive look at the potlatch. They quote the eminent British social anthropologist, A.R. Radcliffe-Brown, an African specialist:

> For the politicians of Canada the potlatch of the Indians of
> the northwest of America was simply wasteful foolishness,
> and it was therefore forbidden. For the anthropologist, it
> was the machinery for maintaining a social structure of
> lineages, clans and moieties, with which was combined an
> arrangement of rank defined by privileges. (Dawson and
> Getty 1948: 45)

This seems more an exercise in demonstrating how social
scientists are able to see more than do mere politicians than it is
a means of taking politicians, federal agents, and missionaries to
task for colonial practices. Of course, Radcliffe-Brown, a British
anthropologist studying cultures in Africa then under the sway
of British imperialism, would be unlikely to make such a point.

Completing the Story of the Banning

There is more to the critical telling of the story of colonialist
oppression of the potlatch than just mere mention of the
banning of religious practices. There is the more general anti-
colonialist point that this was not an isolated act, but one wholly
consistent with other practices. Examples that spring to my mind
(there are many more) include the banning of the Sundance of
the Prairies (see Appendix C), the institution of the legally questionable pass system (also practiced in the Prairies; see Appendix
D), the residential schools, and the way in which a succession of
British Columbia provincial governments (unlike their counterparts in most of the other provinces) have refused to make
treaties with the Aboriginal peoples in that province.

More specific to the telling of the potlatch story is "remembering" the people's resistance to the banning. When Franz Boas
came to study the Kwakiutl in 1886, he was told that if he was
there to oppose the potlatch, he should leave. Here is the
Kwakiutl's statement to him:

We will dance when our laws command us to dance, we will feast when our hearts desire to feast. Do we ask the white man, "Do as the Indian does?" No, we do not. Why then do you ask us, "Do as the white man does?"

It is a strict law that bids us dance. It is a strict law that bids us distribute our property among our friends and neighbors. It is a good law. Let the white man observe his law, we shall observe ours. (Nabokov 1991: 227)

Along the same vein, in 1896, three Nisga'a elders sent the following petition, which was published in the *Victoria Daily Colonist*:

If we wish to perform an act moral in its nature, with no injury or damage, and pay for it, no law in equity can divest us of such a right.... We are puzzled to know whether in the estimation of civilization we are human or fish in the tributaries of the Na'as River, that the felicities of our ancestors should be denied us. (Dickason 1997: 261)

Likewise specific to an anti-colonialist telling of the potlatch story is discussion of the practices surrounding the enforcing of the potlatch ban, including reference to the repercussions of the largest "potlatch bust" ever made. This report of the incident from a Kwakiutl perspective comes from an Aboriginal-based website:

[F]ollowing a large potlatch held at Village Island in December 1921, forty-five people were charged under Section 149 of the Indian Act. Of those convicted of offenses including making speeches, dancing, arranging articles to be given away and carrying gifts to recipients, twenty-two people were given suspended sentences. The sentencing was based on the illegal agreement that, if entire tribes gave up their potlatch paraphernalia, individual members of those tribes who had been found guilty would have their sentences suspended. Three people were remanded for appeal and twenty men and women were sent to Oakalla Prison to serve sentences for two months for first offenders and three months for second offenders. (www.schoolnet.ca/aboriginal/umista2/potlatch-e.html; see Webster 1996: 321 for a slightly different wording, and Steckley and Cummins 2001: 173 for a similar discussion)

The taking of the sacred potlatch items is an important dangerous memory to tell, as it represents a colonial practice whose impact remained (and still remains) long after the potlatch ban was ended in 1951. In the potlatch bust of 1921, the local Indian Agent gathered together the ceremonial potlatch gear, including coppers, masks, headdresses, curved boxes, belts, rattles, and whistles—altogether around 600 pieces (Assu 1996: 354)—and sent these sacred items to Ottawa and to American collector George Heye in New York (who eventually left them to the National Museum of the American Indian). The Ottawa collection was divided between what is now the National Museum of Civilization, the Royal Ontario Museum, and the personal collections of Duncan Campbell Scott, the Superintendent General of Indians, the much-hated official responsible for the institution of the residential schools and a number of similar colonialist practices.

The Kwakiutl fought hard to get the items back. The curator of the U'mista Cultural Centre tells the story not told by sociologists or anthropologists:

> Convinced that the surrender of our treasures had been illegal, we began in 1969 to negotiate with the National Museum of Man for the repatriation of its portion of these objects. By 1975, the museum had agreed to return our treasures on the condition that two museums be built to house them. The Kwakiutl Museum at Cape Mudge opened in 1979; the opening of the U'mista Cultural Centre at Alert

Bay followed, in 1980. The Royal Ontario Museum returned its part of the collection in 1988, and in 1993 the National Museum of the American Indian repatriated some of our treasures. (Webster 1996: 322; see also Assu 1996: 353–6)

Not all the sacred items were taken by governmental officials. Missionaries, too, were able to take potlatch ceremonial gear from the people. They did so by applying religious/colonialist pressure. The following, excerpted from Steckley and Cummins (2001), discusses how certain potlatch items were taken from the Tsimshian people in this way and looks at how, as capitalist commodities, the treasures of the Tsimshian people were made inaccessible to them:

In the 1860s, Rev. Robert Dundas, a young Anglican missionary from Britain, received some goods. The person believed to have given him those goods was Tsimshian Chief Paul Legaic of Fort Simpson, the richest and most powerful of the Tsimshian leaders.... Giving away the objects was a condition of becoming a Christian.... Legaic wanted to maintain his strong position in the trade. To do so, he sacrificed his people's traditions. It would not be fair to judge him harshly. We don't know how much freedom of choice he really had.

Dundas took these items to Britain, sold some, gave away some to museums, but kept the better part of his collection.... When his daughter died in 1948, they were saved from being discarded by Dundas' great-grandson Simon Carey. He kept them at his place, and his children played with them.

Carey... has been trying to sell the collection in one piece. He has entertained Canadian offers from the Museum of Civilization, the Royal Ontario Museum and Canada Heritage, but they could not pay the price he was asking.

He has put the collection, now worth an estimated

$5,000,000, in the hands of the prestigious auction house of Sotheby's, who will publish a catalogue and will mount an exhibit that will ... give Native scholars and anthropologists an opportunity to study the pieces ... [but] only [in] London, Paris and New York. They fear that the Canadian government will seize the collection. The director of Sotheby's American Indian art department says "We wouldn't want to put the collection at risk." (Steckley and Cummins 2001: 173–4)

Summary

In this chapter I have shown how the potlatch became a sociological simulacrum. The process began when diverse ceremonies in the culture area of the Northwest Coast were lumped together as "*the* potlatch" by agents of the state opposed to the religious practices of the local Aboriginal peoples. Lumping them together in this way facilitated the move to making the religious practices illegal, a move that succeeded in 1884.

The next step in the process, one linked with the first (although not the intent of the social scientists involved) was the canonizing of an early, flawed attempt by Franz Boas to interpret the potlatch of the Kwakiutl. That ceremony became the archetype, as did Boas's capitalist framing of the ceremony as primarily a vehicle for a complex usurious system of loans through which individuals became rich, or as a way in which former enemies were "fighting with property," even involving the destruction of property.

The popularization of this simulacrum was achieved primarily through the work of Ruth Benedict, who, in her psychological/anthropological best seller, *The Patterns of Culture*, cast the Kwakiutl in the potlatch as megalomaniacal competitors and positioned the potlatch only in the past. The writers and editors of Canadian introductory sociology textbooks uncritically reproduced this simulacrum. In doing so, they have framed the potlatch as destructively competitive, thus erasing the more holistic picture contained not only in Boas's later work, but, more importantly, in what the people themselves say about the potlatch in their lives.

The portrayal of the potlatch is also partial in that it does not put the state (as reflected in the government, federal agents, and missionaries) into the frame. In so doing, these textbooks follow a pattern predictable from the insights of Dorothy Smith, in serving the relations of ruling, and of Linda Tuhiwai Smith, in serving colonialist purposes rather than those of the indigenous research project of "remembering."

NOTES

1 Anthropologists have traditionally grouped Canadian First Nations into seven "culture areas," areas in which Aboriginal cultures bear a significant number of similarities: Northwest Coast, Plateau, Western Subarctic, Plains, Eastern Subarctic, Woodlands, and Arctic.

2 In my experience with Aboriginal peoples, the term "giveaway" is often used to talk about gift-giving in the context of ceremony.

3 In 1864, the so-called Chilcotin War (see Appendix B) was much exaggerated in the press and induced great fear among White colonists.

4 There are a great variety of languages along the west coast of North America. In British Columbia alone, there are the language isolates of Kutenai, Tlingit, Haida, and Tsimshian, along with the language families of Athabaskan, Salishan, and Wakashan, seven of the 11 Aboriginal language varieties in Canada. The other four are the language families of Eskimo-Aleut (that includes the various dialects of Inuktitut spoken in Canada), Siouan (that includes Dakota and Nakota or Assiniboine in the Prairie Provinces), Iroquoian (that includes Mohawk, Oneida, Onondaga, Cayuga, Seneca, Tuscarora, and the extinct language of Huron), and Algonquian, the largest language family.

5 Also included in the banning were Salish ceremonies lumped under the terms "Tamanawas" or "Spirit Dance."

6 It is not unusual to find the term for one First Nation overgeneralized to refer to related peoples. The Mississauga, for example, were one of several Anishinabe or Ojibwa groups that moved into Southern Ontario from their traditional home by the northern shores of Lake Huron during the late seventeenth century. Non-Aboriginal officials and writers dubbed all such groups as "Mississauga."

7 This was to a certain extent due to Boas's adherence to a school of thought known as "historical particularism," which emphasized description over generalizing analysis. Michelson captures a good part of the nature of this situation: "The texts have been literally fair game for the numerous interpreters of the various aspects of Kwakiutl life. The reason for this situation is the lack of definitive statement by Boas" (Michelson 1982: 47).

8   A fool dancer is a figure in ceremonial story-telling/dancing who dances in a way that appears foolish. In this context, the individual mentioned may have belonged to the Fool Society, a prestigious organization among these people.

9   Boas 1909, 1921, 1925, 1930, 1935, 1943, and 1966.

10 It is a little misleading to use this Eurocentric terminology, in that Kwakiutl "nobility" did not monopolize access to basic resources as European aristocracy often did. They would not let their people starve or do without, as often happened in feudal Europe.

11 It is debatable whether the Canadian government had such a policy. Certainly, the statement appears as a kind of justification (without solid evidence) of government policies among the Kwakiutl and their neighbours.

12 This is one of the Kwakwaka?kw or Kwakwaka'wakw peoples inaccurately labelled as Kwakiutl.

13 I remember being enthralled when I was told the story in my first anthropology course (York University, 1970–71), and I likewise spread the story in my first years of teaching anthropology at Humber College.

14 Ruth Benedict dedicated a book to attacking the purely biologically defined notion of race: *Race: Science or Politics?* (1940).

15 He is mistaken in the date assigned. As I have pointed out above, the potlatch was banned in Canada in 1884, a change to the Indian Act that came into effect in 1885.

16 See Michelson 1982: 47–48 for a continuation of this theme.

17 What is being referred to here is Helen Codere's "The Amiable Side of Kwakiutl Life: The Potlatch and the Play-Potlatch" (1956).

18 Anthropology textbooks that discuss the potlatch, but fail to mention the ban include Barnouw 1987, Ember and Ember 1999, Howard 1986, and Park 2000.

Oka:
Background

CHAPTER SIX

WHAT HAPPENED AT OKA

In the spring of 1990, the city council of Oka, a non-Aboriginal town adjoining Kahnesatake, a Mohawk community in south-western Quebec, moved to expand their municipal golf course on to land claimed by the Mohawk as a sacred burial ground. On March 11 and 12, women of the Kanehsatake Longhouse built a barricade across a dirt road leading to the golf course. Negotiations dragged on, and the barricade was reinforced by armed members of the Akwesasne Warrior Society. On July 11, 100 fully armed SQ officers confronted the protesters; shots were fired, and an SQ officer was killed; it is still uncertain whether the bullet was fired by the SQ or the Warriors. The SQ fell back, and the Mohawk used captured police vehicles to block a nearby highway and then seized the Mercier Bridge, a major transportation link for the city of Montreal. Angry non-Aboriginal residents and commuters staged noisy and often violent protests against the bridge barricade, protests that were met in force by the SQ. On August 28, while the bridge was still occupied, a convoy of women, children, and elders was attacked by non-Aboriginal youth as they fled the prospect of increasing violence in Kahnawake; six people were hurt, but no one was arrested. The next day, the bridge barricades came down.

The SQ was eventually joined by a large force of RCMP and then by Canadian army troops who basically laid siege to Kahnesatake. The confrontation continued until September 26 when the Mohawk surrendered after burning their weapons.[1]

THE ROOTS OF THE CONFLICT

There are four key components to understanding the issues surrounding the conflict in Oka in 1990. Not one of these elements is part of the discussion in the eight Canadian introductory sociology textbooks that touch on the subject, as I will argue in the next chapter.

The first element is the *Gayanerengo:wa* ("It is a Great Good") or Great Law of Peace (hereafter referred to as the Great Law[2]), a centuries-long tradition that is the oral and written foundational document of traditional Mohawk and Iroquois government and politics. In Foucauldian terms, excluding mention of the Great Law is a fundamental disqualification of Aboriginal-produced knowledge. Had Mohawk or Iroquois writers been given a chance to contribute to the sociological discussion of the Oka conflict, reference to the Great Law most probably would have been made. Discussing Mohawk politics without making reference to the Great Law of Peace is like discussing the relationship between the federal and provincial governments without grounding it in the British North America Act.

Another key is to understand that the conflict goes back in time. It is not merely, or arguably mainly, the product of the late twentieth century, as writers and editors of Canadian introductory sociology textbooks have stressed. To use the metaphor of a fire, the Oka conflict was first lit in the early 1700s. It blazed up and subsided numerous times over the centuries and never was without hot coals. It merely required the type of fuel fed to it in the

1980s to catch fire again. As will be demonstrated in the next chapter, the coals are still there in the early twenty-first century.

The third key comes from the relationship between policing agencies and Mohawk communities and how that relationship differs from that between police services and mainstream Canadian communities. Generally, it can be said that outsider police forces involved with the Mohawk (as with other Canadian First Nations) have long lacked the functionalist legitimacy of "serving and protecting the people" that such forces have had elsewhere in Canada.[3] This lack springs mainly from the fact that these police forces have been used as tools of colonialist oppression in Mohawk communities by federal and provincial governments, as will be clearly demonstrated in the relevant histories of four Mohawk communities. This is, of course, not a situation unique to the Mohawk, but is part of the institutional racism of the Canadian justice system with respect to Aboriginal peoples that has been noted several times in a non-Mohawk setting over the last 20 years (e.g., the Manitoba Aboriginal Justice Inquiry of 1988–89 and the Hickman Commission that investigated the Donald Marshall case at about the same time).

An important aspect of this third component is that, since outsider policing agencies lack legitimacy, the Mohawk have developed their own agencies, with a great deal of opposition from the federal government and the provincial governments of Ontario and Quebec and their respective policing agencies. The Mohawk forces have experienced a range of (dis)respect by outside governments and policing agencies from labelling the Mohawk Warrior societies as criminal to the suspicion shown toward Mohawk services that have pursued more readily recognized policing channels and forms in their establishment.

The fourth component is the factionalism in Mohawk communities, itself to a significant degree the product of colonial oppression. Their centuries-old government forms, based on the Great Law of Peace, were made deviant by the federal government and had to go "underground," helping to create a division in the communities between supporters of traditions and supporters of the "White man's government." This, of course, is not unique to the Mohawk situation; similar factionalism is likely to occur wherever colonialism oppresses a people. As a result of this factionalism, there was no uniform support for what the Mohawk Warriors did in Oka or in Kahnawake. Nonetheless, as will be shown in Chapter Seven, Canadian introductory sociology textbooks have essentialized the Mohawk and, in fact, all Aboriginal peoples by speaking of the Mohawk Warrior actions as if all Aboriginal peoples supported that stance.

I argue that, had the introductory sociology textbooks incorporated Aboriginal voice in their discussion of the Oka conflict, these four key points probably would have been mentioned, and a far greater understanding of this conflict would have been made possible for students.

In order to write this chapter, I have made extensive use of Aboriginal voice through Mohawk writers Gerald Alfred (1995), Darren Bonaparte (2002a, b, and c), Ronald Cross and Hélène Sévigny (1994), Dan David (1992), Andrew Delisle (1984), Doug George (2000), Brian Maracle (1996), Mike Mitchell (1989 and 2000), and Patricia Monture-Angus (1995); and through Tlingit writer Jennie Jack (1991); Métis writer Olive Dickason (2002); and Ojibwa writers Gail Guthrie Valaskakis (2000) and Richard Wagamese (1996). More indirectly, my account has been influenced by the writing of non-Aboriginal journalists Rick Horning (1991), Geoffrey York, and Loreen Pindera (1991), and academic Edna Garte (1981) who quote Mohawks who played a significant role in the Oka situation.

THE GREAT LAW
Introduction

The Great Law is centuries old,[4] predating Aboriginal peoples' contact with Europeans. It is both a story and a collection of teachings concerning the establishment of what is termed in English the

League or Confederacy of the Iroquois. The people did not refer to themselves as Iroquois; [5] their own name, *Haudenosaunee* (Monture-Angus 1995: 249), usually pronounced something like "hoh-deh-no-show-neh," means "they are of the extended house" or "they build a house," signifying that all the initial five (later six)[6] peoples are together under one roof. References to this form of government, or the teachings of the Great Law, often use the word "Longhouse" (e.g., Longhouse government or Longhouse religion), partially because of the peoples' name for themselves and partially because the traditional houses of the Iroquois were long and narrow.

The story[7] begins with a woman and her adult daughter, worried about the warfare that surrounded them, who go to live on their own.[8] The daughter gave birth to a boy known as the Peacemaker. As a child, he experienced a vision in which he saw a way for the combatting peoples to achieve peace. When he became an adult, he decided to share this vision of peace with the warring five Iroquoian nations (from east to west, the Mohawk, Oneida, Onondaga, Cayuga, and Seneca) living in what is now the state of New York.

The Peacemaker went first to a Mohawk community, where his words were accepted by a peace chief,[9] Hiawatha ("He makes wampum"). Hiawatha spoke for him and helped to bring about acceptance of the Peacemaker's vision. Next, the two men successfully convinced the neighbouring Oneida to follow suit. As their greatest obstacle was a powerful Onondaga sorcerer, Thadodaho, the Peacemaker arranged that the middle of the five nations would be the last visited by the peace delegation. With the four other nations on side, it would be more difficult for Thadodaho to oppose the proposed confederacy. The Cayuga became convinced by the Peacemaker's words. After them came the Seneca, although their war leaders were initially uncertain.

When the five nations eventually met together in peace, they developed the Peacemaker's vision in a form through which they could be brought together in one confederacy. They were divided into two moieties or halves. One, referred to as the "fathers" (sometimes the "older brothers"), was made up of the Mohawk, Onondaga, and Seneca. The other, referred to as the "sons" (less often as the "younger brothers"), was made up of the Oneida and the Cayuga. The sachems[10] would sit in council with the "fathers" on one side of the meeting (long)house and the "sons" on the other side.

The council was made up of 50 sachems: 14 Onondaga, 10 Cayuga, nine each from the Mohawk and Oneida, and eight Seneca. With decision by consensus rather than by majority rule, this is more an honouring distribution of sachems than one that gave power to the nations with the greatest numbers. The Onondaga were further honoured by being named the Firekeepers, or hosts of the meetings of the council. The Seneca war chiefs, who were finally convinced to accept the Peacemaker's vision, were honoured by being named the Doorkeepers, controlling access to the council meetings.

It is important to understand how the sachems were chosen and how they could be removed. Each of the sachem positions belonged to a matrilineal clan (i.e., determined along the mother's side). For the Mohawk, there were three sachems from each of their three clans (Wolf, Turtle, and Bear). One was considered the "head chief," and the other two were "sub-chiefs." The sachem position did not automatically fall to one person, such as the eldest son of a particular mother. The clan leaders responsible for the position could exercise choice. Neither was the position of sachem always a position for life. Each clan also had three clan mothers, who spoke for the women if a sachem was thought to be self-seeking or otherwise corrupt or incompetent. They could impeach him, a process known as "de-horning."

Two Strands of Interpretation of the Great Law

To understand what took place at Oka and at Kahnawake in 1990, one needs to be aware that there are two basic traditions or strands of interpretation of the Great Law. They can somewhat simplistically be labelled a peace tradition and a warrior tradition. Journalists York and Pindera, in *People of the Pines*, a good book on the conflict at Oka, unfortunately not consulted by writers of introductory sociology textbooks, liken the division to that between the pacifist Martin Luther King and the "warrior" Malcolm X in the fight for civil rights for African Americans in the 1960s (York and Pindera 1991: 268). As those two leaders fought for justice for their people using different strategies, so do those adhering to the war and peace traditions of the Great Law.

Near the end of the story of the Great Law it is told that a great white pine tree of peace was planted, with weapons thrown under its roots, symbolizing that the five nations would no longer fight each other. Those who interpret the Great Law along the warrior tradition point out that this "pacifism" only applies within the longhouse, while those of the peace tradition interpret it as applying more generally. In the words of Jake Swamp, a Longhouse chief at Akwesasne for more than 20 years, his adoption of the latter strand came with the realization that:

> If anyone picks up a weapon, he's breaking the Great Law, because all the weapons were buried. If people truly believe in peace, they will never pick up weapons. (York and Pindera 1991: 265)

When the Mohawk felt the need to police themselves, the policing agencies they developed were formed along the two lines of war and peace. In terms of major conflicts like the "Battle for Akwesasne" and the standoff at Oka, both taking place in 1990, the two traditions were evident in the positions people took concerning the Mohawk Warriors.

The Peace Strand of the Great Law

The peace strand is rooted, in part, in the teachings of Handsome Lake (1735–1815), a Seneca sachem. In 1799, he had a series of three visions. During the last, he received instructions from the Creator to maintain traditional ceremonies and positive family values, to oppose alcohol and witchcraft, and to counsel peace with non-Aboriginal peoples. During the remaining years of his life, Handsome Lake preached those instructions. After he died, his words were recounted and formed an oral tradition that came to be known in English as the Code of Handsome Lake (hereafter referred to as the Code).

This strand of the Great Law was first written down in 1912, when John A. Gibson, who bore the sachem name Handsome Lake, dictated some 500 pages of oral text to the anthropologist Alexander A. Goldenweiser. It was not published until 1992 (Woodbury, Henry, and Webster 1992). However, versions of this strand have been taught over the years by influential cultural and spiritual leaders such as Cayuga sachem Jacob Thomas,[11] who maintain the oral tradition of the Great Law. Some of them have felt that something important but indefinable would be lost if the Great Law were to be reduced to writing.

The Warrior Strand of the Great Law

As is the case with the peace strand, the warrior strand also has a written tradition. It was first published in 1916 by Arthur C. Parker (1881–1955), a Seneca anthropologist. Although his family was closely connected with followers of Handsome Lake, and he published a version of the Code, his version of the Great Law has become a text used in the warrior tradition, probably because its 117 wampums[12] or articles, literally translated, feature instructions to warriors on how to act to defend the Confederacy (see Appendix E: "Wampum 81 of the Great Law"), especially wampums 36–41 ("Names, Duties and Rights of War Chiefs") and 79–91 ("Rights and Powers of War") (www.constitution.org/cons/iroquois/txt, 2003).

A more recently published document in the written tradition of the warrior strand is the *Warriors Handbook*, a collection of sometimes tongue-in-cheek humourous, sometimes serious, and often outrageous statements by Kahnawake Mohawk Longhouse chief, artist (he created the Mohawk Warrior flag), and writer Louis Hall.

The warrior strand of interpretation of the Great Law is more commonly adhered to among traditionalist Mohawk than among traditionalists among other member nations of the Confederacy. In part, this is because neither Handsome Lake nor his early followers made substantial contact with the Mohawk. His influence, therefore, has been least felt among these people of all the Six Nations. The nature of the conflicts that the Mohawk communities have had to face is another factor in this.

THE COLONIALIST TRAIL: A TALE OF FOUR COMMUNITIES

The stories of four communities are directly relevant to understanding the background of the conflict at Oka: three Mohawk communities[13], Kahnawake, Kanesatake (Oka),[14] and Akwesasne; and Six Nations, an Iroquois community with a strong Mohawk component. I begin with Six Nations because, although it did not play as significant a part in the Oka conflict as the others did, its history mirrors the colonialist experience of the others and it was the first community to form a group called "Mohawk Warriors."

Six Nations

In 1923, Six Nations still used the traditional government system, despite federal government opposition. They wanted their system and their sovereignty to be officially recognized, and so they sent representatives that year to the League of Nations to apply for sovereign nation status. They received the support of Estonia, Ireland, Panama, and Persia (all nations who understood colonial oppression), but Britain intervened, and the proposal to have their status recognized was dropped.

That same year, Colonel C.E. Morgan, a former South African colonial administrator, was appointed as the Indian Superintendent at Brantford. In the fall of 1924, Morgan arrived in the community in force with 20 RCMP officers. They interrupted a meeting of the sachems and declared the Six Nations government abolished. Then, they broke open a safe and seized the legal records of that government, including wampum belts, the sacred symbols of Iroquois treaty-making and governance. The police even went so far as to go into homes to remove loose shell beads that might be used to make new belts. In 1920, the population of Six Nations was recorded as 4,615, but in the federal government-imposed election staged on October 21, 1924, only 52 people voted. The community has been divided on that issue ever since. Some community members do not recognize the authority of the elected band council, while others look upon supporters of the traditional system as unrealistic dreamers or troublemakers. This division, as we will see, exists in various forms at Kahnawake, Kanesatake, and Akwesasne as well.

The RCMP never quite won the trust of the Six Nations people. On March 5, 1959, about 1,300 community members marched to the council house, led by a group calling itself the Mohawk Warriors. The elected council fled out the back door as the Warriors removed the locked front door from its hinges. A community meeting was held, attended by roughly 5,000 people. They drafted a proclamation in which the elected council was abolished and the Longhouse council was restored. They also appointed a 133-member police force to replace the unwelcome outsider force.

The federal government moved quickly. A week after the takeover:

[A]t three o'clock in the morning, sixty RCMP officers attacked the council house, where about 130 people had gathered to resist the expected raid. A riot quickly developed, led by the Iroquois women, who tried to push the police out. As television cameras recorded the scene, the police clubbed the Iroquois and dragged them out.... (York and Pindera 1991: 165)

Kahnawake: Two Solitudes in Quebec

There are few positive connections between the Kahnawake Mohawk, whose territory is near Montreal, and the French-speaking majority in Quebec. The long history of conflict between Mohawk and French began in 1609 when the "Father of New France," Samuel de Champlain, decided to strengthen his alliance with the Montagnais, Algonquin, and Huron by joining a raid on the Mohawk. In the battle that ensued, 50 Mohawk warriors were killed, and about a dozen were taken prisoner. History textbooks in Quebec valorized the French fight against the Mohawk during the seventeenth century. Students were fed racist descriptions, such as those of historian François Garneau,[15] who wrote that the Mohawk (and other Iroquois) were "des loups alteres du sang [bloodthirsty wolves]" (Smith 1974: 28). Unfortunately, about the same time as French-Canadian historians began to rethink and rewrite this aspect of their history, a new conflict concerning competing notions of sovereignty arose between the two people. Most Mohawk did not (and still do not) speak French, so many Québécois considered them to be Anglos, or at least allied to the English-speaking Quebec minority in opposition to French sovereignty. At the same time, Mohawk sovereignty was (and is) shown little respect in Quebec. Therefore, few firm institutional links joined the two peoples. In the words of Mohawk educator and writer Gerald (Taiaiake) Alfred:

Quebec poses a clear and present threat to the Mohawks' efforts to develop autonomous institutions in such areas as policing and education. Kahnawake Mohawks have rejected the legitimacy of Quebec institutions within their community and responded to the perceived danger of an imposed Quebec sovereignty in their community by developing "alterNative" institutions. (Alfred 1995: 17)

The Beginnings of Conflict

You could rightfully say that Kahnawake was a community born of violence. In 1666, Alexandre de Prouville de Tracy led an invasion force of more than 1,000 into the heart of Mohawk country. Luckily, when the French army approached, the 300 to 400 Mohawk warriors, along with the more numerous women and children, easily eluded their less woods-wise antagonists. Unfortunately, however, the French torched the Mohawk villages, fields, and much of their crucial winter supplies of food, primarily corn.

In 1667, Jesuit Father Pierre Raffeix, feeling that de Tracy had "pacified" the Mohawk, believed that an Iroquois mission could be established in the Montreal area, on the edge of Mohawk country. He encouraged half-a-dozen visiting Oneida to winter on the south shore of the St. Lawrence River. The mission, named St. François-Xavier, became a success, at the cost of a significant depopulation of the Mohawk communities in what is now New York State. Ten years later, the mission village moved upriver to the Lachine Rapids and was renamed Kahnawake ("At the Rapids"), both after the location and after the Mohawk community in more traditional territory from which it drew most of its population and which was eventually abandoned.

There has been a long history of conflict between the Mohawk of Kahnawake and outsider police agencies. For the most part, this is owing to three factors: expropriation of land, cigarette sales, and different notions of how the village should be governed. In the following historical presentation, these three factors will be interwoven chronologically.

Concerning expropriation, section 35 of the Indian Act allows for the federal government to expropriate any reserve land it chooses. Band consultation or permission are not legally required. The reserve, being close to Montreal, has long been a particular target of expropriation, as the original 17,800 hectare reserve has been shrunk to less than one-third that size, or 5,260 hectares. Railways, highways, bridges, and the St. Lawrence Seaway have all been established on land taken from the Kahnawake Mohawk. The result has often been Mohawk resistance, and the reaction has not always been peaceful. In 1922, two Kahnawake chiefs were shot by RCMP officers during protests against a federal construction project restricting Kahnawake access to the St. Lawrence.

The Diabo Case and the Jay Treaty

The most persistent customs issue concerning the Mohawk and the police forces of Canada and the United States is the cigarette trade. First Nations people can purchase for personal use an unlimited amount of tax-free cigarettes in the US. There are high taxes on cigarettes in Canada, but cigarette manufacturers in Canada make the same profit per package regardless of taxes paid by the consumer. These manufacturers ship a great number of cigarettes to the United States, not unaware that many of those cigarettes will make their way back to Canada by boat or, when the St. Lawrence is frozen, by truck or snowmobile. Although this is primarily the case in Akwesasne, the illegal cigarette trade has caused problems in Kahnawake as well.

In 1926, a watershed event occurred. Paul Diabo, a Kahnawake Mohawk, was arrested in Philadelphia as an illegal alien. His defense was based on the Jay Treaty of Amity and Commerce, enacted in 1794 to deal with several border issues between the United States and Britain. Both governments were concerned that trading posts on the border between British land (now Canada) and the United States would lose business if Aboriginal peoples were not allowed to move freely to bring furs for trade. The Jay Treaty allowed them to cross the border with their personal "goods and effects" without having to pay customs duties. Lieutenant-Governor John Graves Simcoe, speaking to the Six Nations representatives at Fort Erie on August 28, 1795, worded the people's rights in the following way:

[Y]ou have a right to go to the British Settlements, or to those of the U. States, as shall suit your convenience, nor shall your passing or repassing with your own proper goods and effects of whatever nature, pay for the same any impost whatever. (Mitchell 1989: 113)

The American federal judge handling the Diabo case upheld the Jay Treaty (Canada has yet to do so officially).[16] Since then, there have been unofficial understandings that have allowed the border-dwelling Mohawk of Kahnawake and Akwesasne the right to cross without a customs check. Passports issued by the Mohawk or Six Nations have been recognized. However, there has been conflict over this, mainly over bringing cigarettes into Canada.

Another important consequence came from this case. The Mohawk of Kahnawake had been politically separated from the other Iroquois for some 250 years. The Grand Councils at Onondaga, New York, and Six Nations, in Ontario, rallied to support the Kahnawake people in the Diabo case. The Longhouse had returned.

The St. Lawrence Seaway: The Community Divides

In the 1940s and 1950s, a sharp division cut the community in two. On the one hand, a group that referred to itself as the "Intelligent Party," who were educated, devoutly Catholic, and spent a great deal of time off-reserve, wanted greater integration into Canadian society. The other side was a somewhat loose alliance of the growing number of traditional Longhouse people and the elected council. It is rather unusual to see the latter group as part of this alliance, as in other Mohawk communities, members of the band council were more likely to oppose the Longhouse. These allies wanted a more traditional style of government and wished for greater political independence for the *Kahnawakeronon* ("people who live by the rapids"). They grew in power during the 1950s with the development of the Seaway, along with Mohawk resistance to that development.

The development of the Seaway meant that land had to be expropriated along the St. Lawrence River. In part because the Kahnawake reserve was considered to be "federal land," and thus easier to obtain than privately owned land, portions of it were expropriated. The loss of 526 hectares hit the Kahnawake people hard. It also cost them symbolically as the loss of this land separated them from the river that had been part of their lives for hundreds of years before European contact.

The band council fought the expropriation every peaceful way it could, including petitioning Great Britain and the United Nations. Some people found resistance more difficult than others and succumbed to the carrot of cash settlement and the stick of government pressure. Resentment against those families continues to this day.

The experience radicalized the community along traditional lines. In the words of Gerald Alfred:

> If the Seaway is viewed as the catalyst for the community's rejection of the Canadian government's legitimacy, then ... the Seaway is responsible for activating the traditionalist movement in Kahnawake. The legacy of the Seaway betrayal in Kahnawake thus contributes to the high intensity of the Mohawk assertion of independence. (Alfred 1995: 162)

The Need to Create a Mohawk Police Force

The RCMP enforcement of the expropriation contributed to their pariah status as tools of government oppression. This negative reputation had been building since the 1940s. During World War II, although many Kahnawake Mohawk volunteered to enlist, others resisted conscription (ironically something they shared with their French neighbours), feeling that it violated their sovereignty. Fights ensued between Mohawk and RCMP officers, and Longhouse meetings were raided by the RCMP. Alcohol was a contentious issue also. In the 1940s, the Mohawk could not legally drink anywhere, so the RCMP often raided Mohawk restaurants and weddings where alcohol was suspected. In one storied incident in 1948, a group of Mohawk men beat up an RCMP officer as he was trying to make arrests for drinking in a restaurant.

For a short while, three Mohawk Special Constables (Big Six Jocks, Tom Lahache, and Frank Lahache) were sworn in under the RCMP Act, but their positive effect was limited by the inferiority of their position relative to "real" constables.

As much as the RCMP were outside oppressors, the Sûreté du Québec (SQ), the provincial police, were even more so. In 1969, the federal government tried to offload some of its Aboriginal responsibilities to the provinces. That included policing. The Kahnawake Mohawk quickly responded by creating their own police force, the Kahnawake Peacekeepers, the first Aboriginal-controlled police force in Canada. The federal and provincial governments, and their respective police forces, initially resisted this development. An elected councillor and chief of the Kahnawake Mohawk, interviewed in the 1990s, described this resistance and how it was overcome. The Mohawk leaders were asked to go to the local RCMP headquarters. They entered a room where the RCMP stood on one side, the SQ on the other: it was like running a gauntlet. They were told that their police force was illegal, merely a group of "vigilantes":

> But we had done our homework by contacting several judges on the Superior Court and got them on our side. They were looking for a solution to the problems here too, and we told the police brass that we would stop it on the condition that we work toward establishing an Indian Police Force in Kahnawake. And they said, "all right." So we called a big meeting with all the people, the police brass and the judges. We had the Attorney General on our side too. And then the government had to agree to establish the Indian Police here. (Alfred 1995: 112)

A Divided Longhouse

The first real test of the Kahnawake Peacekeepers revealed a major division in the community and within the Longhouse. More than one tradition of interpreting the Great Law of Peace emerged as the Longhouse garnered support during the 1950s over the Seaway dispute. Mohawk writer Gerald Alfred writes about the situation in Kahnawake:

> There has been no unified movement toward or interpretation of Iroquois tradition in Kahnawake. Beyond the consensus that the Indian Act and Western political values are inappropriate, there has been no singularly acceptable framework established within which a standard interpretation of the Kanienerekowa's principles could be achieved. This lack of consensus has manifested itself in mainly negative ways and has led to serious confrontations within the community. (Alfred 1995: 83)

The Longhouse in Kahnawake divided into three (see Alfred 1995: 66, 82–87). One division was the Warrior Longhouse, from which the Mohawk Warrior Society developed during the early 1970s. The person most often connected with this Longhouse and with the Mohawk Warrior Society is Longhouse chief Louis Hall, although I believe that his influence has been overestimated by outsider journalists. Second is the Mohawk Trail Longhouse, which is strongly influenced by the Code of Handsome Lake and by its connections with the Longhouses of the Iroquois Confederacy outside the Mohawk nation. Its message is primarily one of peace. Third is the Five Nations Longhouse, which in a sense can be called the "fundamentalist" branch, following as closely as possible to the letter of the Great Law. According to Alfred, it focusses on injustices perpetrated by non-Aboriginal society and is against any form of cooperation with non-Aboriginal authorities and institutions.

The Development of the Kahnawake Mohawk Warriors: A Second Kahnawake Police Force

In August and September 1973, a showdown between factions over evicting band members from the territory involved a conflict between Mohawk police forces. The people to be evicted were non-Aboriginal peoples who had married into the community. According to Alfred, the confrontation was not over whether or not the people should be evicted,[17] but that they consisted of "non-desirable elements." The real issue was over who had the authority to kick them out.

The newly formed Mohawk Warrior Society made the first move. The band council opposed this taking of authority, and the opposition became violent. The Mohawk Warrior Society attacked the band council building, and the tension escalated. Legionnaires armed themselves to protect the local legion hall. The 10 members of the Mohawk Peacekeepers, lacking support from the RCMP or the SQ, resigned. The desperate chief and council sent a formal request that the SQ enter Mohawk territory. This did not resolve the issue, but created deeper trenches of separation between the Kahnawake factions. The chief later resigned, tainted by the act of bringing the SQ into Kahnawake.

The Confrontation of 1979

In 1978, the Quebec government established the Amerindian Police Service (APS) as a way for Aboriginal communities, with provincial governmental and SQ supervision, to police themselves. Kahnawake joined the APS in its inaugural year, but this did not last. According to the Kahnawake Mohawk Peacekeepers' website:

> [O]ur force was accountable to the Quebec government. This was unacceptable and in 1979 the Mohawk contingent withdrew from the Amerindian Police and formed an independent law enforcement body. (www.kahnawake.com/ peacekeepers/past.htm, 2003)

In 1979, a tragic event distanced the Kahnawake Mohawk even further from the SQ. An SQ officer, Constable Robert Lessard, caught a vehicle speeding. The driver did not stop, but drove away. A chase ensued, leading into Mohawk territory. The driver ran into his house, leaving his passenger in the car. The officer arrested the passenger, Matthew Cross, and put him in the back seat of the police vehicle. The driver, David Cross, Matthew's brother, came out of the house carrying a pool cue to try to rescue his brother.[18] In the course of that attempt, he smashed the windshield of the police car; Lessard shot him two or three times in the upper chest, killing him.

An inquest was held. The coroner ruled that Constable Lessard was criminally responsible for the death of David Cross, that the shooting was an "abusive use of force," and that his handling of his weapon was "negligent, unskillful and acting without think-ing." He was charged with manslaughter in 1980, but was acquit-ted by the Quebec Superior Court. The Kahnawake community was furious, none more so than David Cross's cousin Ron, later to become known at Oka as the Mohawk Warrior, "Lasagna."

The Kahnawake Mohawk Warriors Gain Power

One effect of the shooting was a certain amount of bridge build-ing between factions at Kahnawake, although the unofficial two-police force situation, overt and covert, did not change, but became a fixture. Although people still disagreed about some issues, a summer meeting of people from all factions resolved— and this resolution was made official by the elected council—that they should move toward a more traditional form of government.

In 1981, a clash between the SQ and another Aboriginal group, the Mi'kmaq of Restigouche (on the Quebec/New Brunswick border) furthered Kahnawake concern about how potentially oppressive and dangerous to their community the provincial police could be. Heavily armed SQ officers twice raided Restigouche to enforce provincial fishing regulations on salmon. Helicopters, bulldozers, tear gas, and clubs were used to confiscate fish and nets and to quell Aboriginal protests against the raids. A number of Mi'kmaq men, women, and children were hurt in the police raid.

The shooting of David Cross and the SQ invasion of Restigouche caused some of the people to begin to seriously think of arming themselves against the outsider police. The elected band council and the Warrior Longhouse (often referred to by writers and community members as the Longhouse) spent approximately $10,000 to purchase about a dozen rifles and semi-automatic weapons to be put in the hands of trusted community members, some of them Mohawk Warriors, in the event of an SQ raid on Mohawk territory. When the cigarette trade came to Kahnawake in 1985, with cigarettes supplied largely through Akwesasne, key figures in the trade financially supported the development of the Mohawk Warriors as a policing agency to protect the community from the provincial and federal governments.

It is important to note that the advent of the cigarette trade and, eventually, gambling (Super Bingo) did not divide Kahnawake as it did Akwesasne. The recent histories of the two communities have taken different paths in that way. The people of Kahnawake did not have to contend with the jurisdictions and laws of two countries, and their gambling was limited to Super Bingo and not the more volatile casinos and slot machines. Thus, the Kahnawake Warriors Society more readily developed into an institution that presented itself as having the support of the majority of the community; it did not merely represent a faction, which was the case with their fellow Mohawk Warriors of Akwesasne.

By 1987, the Kahnawake Mohawk Warriors had developed a formal code that forbade the consumption of alcohol and drugs and that strictly controlled the use of firearms. Their discipline and organization was tested the next year. On June 1, 1988, around 200 RCMP officers, complete with helicopters, semi-automatic weapons, and bulletproof vests, staged a massive raid on six cigarette stores in Kahnawake. They arrested 17 people and confiscated some $450,000 worth of cigarettes. Within an hour of that attack, the Warriors seized the Mercier Bridge, which has its southern point in Kahnawake and crosses the St. Lawrence and is one of the main bridges for traffic entering and leaving the city of Montreal. The Warriors were well armed and successfully kept the bridge closed for about 29 hours. They lifted their blockade only when the province and the federal government promised to negotiate on the cigarette issue.

This earned the Warriors more support than they had ever had before, even from those who had opposed the "buttleg" cigarette industry. As they had acted decisively, and as the Mohawk Peacekeepers had looked ineffective in resisting the police raid, the Warriors looked to many to be the Aboriginal police force most worthy of respect in Kahnawake.

The cigarette industry continued to grow and with it the influence of the Mohawk Warriors. Cigarettes financed a force of 30 Warriors (twice that of the Mohawk Peacekeepers), who were paid $335 per week for four shifts of 12 hours. They patrolled the territory in 10 vehicles, establishing checkpoints and looking out for more outsider police raids. Also, the masks they wore to preserve their anonymity (a practice that was continued in Oka in 1990) intimidated people suspected of being drug pushers or other forms of social predators.

Relationships with the Mohawk Peacekeepers

The relationship between the Mohawk Peacekeepers and the Mohawk Warriors in Kahnawake was essentially that of an uneasy truce. For instance, they communicated with each other about people they both regarded as criminal. Following orders from the elected band council, the Peacekeepers did not act upon the arrest warrants for Kahnawake people involved with the cigarette trade or with the barricades on the Mercier Bridge.

Mohawk Peacekeepers and outsider police agencies during the 1980s leading up to 1990 shared a mutual respect of territory, but had no solid working connection. Ronald Cross (a.k.a. "Lasagna") described that relationship as follows:

For a lot of years up till '90 the Peacekeepers were pretty
well respected by the RCMP and the SQ. They kind of
worked together hand in hand. I mean, they weren't
allowed to come here, the SQ and the RCMP, so if a car
was chased onto the Territory they would be in touch with
the Peacekeepers here in Kahnawake and the Peacekeepers
would take over from there because they knew if they did
try to come into Kahnawake there would be people who
would have stopped them and who knows what would
have happened. So they would go up to the borderlines of
Kahnawake, and there the Kahnawake Peacekeepers would
take over. (Cross and Sévigny 1994: 48)

During the Oka Crisis, however, the outsider police agencies
treated the Peacekeepers more as "Mohawk, therefore suspect"
than as fellow police officers. In Cross's words:

In 1990, during the crisis, the SQ pulled over the
Peacekeepers and had them kneeling on the ground and
took their guns and arrested them and charged them with
weapons charges. These guys were Peacekeepers here in
Kahnawake, and this is what the SQ did. It was on the
front pages of the papers. But they recognized them from
the time the SQ left here in the late '70s until the crisis in
1990. They were even recognized in their courts when they
took our people out of their courts and brought them over
here. They were recognized. And all of a sudden now the
governments don't recognize them—because of all the stuff
that went on in '90. (Cross and Sévigny 1994: 49)

Kanesatake (Oka)

During the early 1700s, there were Mohawk living in the
Montreal area who did not live in Kahnawake. Along with some
Algonquin and Nipissing, they were forced to leave the island

of Montreal, which was then being developed as a French trade centre, and live in one community a short distance to the north-west: Lac des Deux Montagnes (Lake of Two Mountains). The mission there was developed by the Sulpicians, a Catholic reli-gious order with powerful connections in France, who had been granted a seigneury in 1717 by Louis XV. By 1721, nearly 900 Aboriginal peoples had moved into the mission; by 1735, a second grant of land had been added.

If it can be said that Kahnawake was born of violence, it can equally be stated that Kanesatake was born of a broken prom-ise. The Sulpicians enticed the Mohawk, Algonquin, and Nipissing with verbal promises of collective land ownership. In the words of an eighteenth-century Mohawk chief, Aughneeta, speaking to a government official in an effort to get the Kanesatake people's rights recognized:

> [O]ur priests ... told us ... that if we should consent to go and settle at the Lake of Two Mountains we should have a large tract of land for which we should have a Deed from the King of France as our property to be vested in us and our heirs forever, and that we should not be molested again in our habitations. (York and Pindera 1991: 86)

Unfortunately for the Kanesatake people, these promises were spoken, but not written. This severely hampered their claims to the land for more than 250 years. The Sulpicians, although they allowed Aboriginal families to settle on the land and build homes, kept control over the resources. They used the lack of written deeds in the Aboriginal peoples' names along with their power-ful connections with governments in France, Britain, and Canada to force the Aboriginal peoples to ask permission to use land, sell crops, and—a major source of conflict between the priests and the Aboriginal peoples on a number of occasions—to cut wood.

Over the years, the people of Kanesatake saw other Mohawk mission communities gain reserve status, while they remained with no land rights and under the tight control of the Sulpicians. Time after time they petitioned for recognition of their rights, only to be turned down. In 1868, the people felt that they had a good chance for some recognition, as the new Superintendent General of Indian Affairs sounded sympathetic to their cause. But the Sulpicians used their connections in high places to have that year's bid fail. That brought about a major turning-point in the community. The next year, tired of the constant confrontation, the Algonquin left to form a community elsewhere in Quebec: Maniwaki (now known as Kitigan Zibi). The Sulpicians sold the land the Algonquin had occupied to White settlers, who later founded the town known as Oka.

The Mohawk reacted differently. First, in February 1869, Chief Joseph Onasakenrat ("White Feathers"), accompanied by 40 armed Mohawk, warned the Sulpicians that they had eight days to leave the community. The police arrived before the deadline was up, in the early hours of the morning, and arrested four of the Mohawk. They were released, but told that their cause could only be served through legal channels and by obeying the Sulpicians.

The Mohawk's next move was both religious and political. As the Mohawk were Catholic, the Sulpicians had made effective political use of excommunication as a tool to keep them in line. To counteract this power, most of the community converted to Methodism. The new Protestant majority was thus divided from the minority who remained Catholic and who wanted to maintain a good relationship with their spiritual mentors, the Sulpicians. In 1872, the Mohawk began to build a church, but were arrested for cutting the wood necessary to build it. They had not asked permission, not that they would have received it had they asked. Previously, the Sulpicians had been able to "legally" have Mohawk homes torn down if the builders had not asked permission to cut the wood. So, it is not surprising that in December 1875, the Sulpicians successfully obtained a court order to have the Methodist church torn down.

In 1877, the conflict between the Mohawk and Sulpicians

escalated. The Mohawk had fenced in a pasture on common lands they had been using for over a century and chopped down some trees to obtain building materials for the fence. The Sulpicians reacted by relying on force. In the evocative words of York and Pindera:

> It was three o'clock in the morning when the Quebec provincial police arrived in Oka, armed with warrants for the arrest of forty-eight Indians. They burst into homes and dragged the sleeping men from their beds, firing off pistols in their ears. Eight suspects were rounded up altogether and hauled off to jail. (York and Pindera 1991: 82)

The Mohawk gathered together and armed themselves. Chief Joseph Onasakenrat counselled resistance, "If the police come to take you without warrant, fire at them" (York and Pindera 1991: 83). The next morning the Catholic church was burned down. Fifteen Mohawk were arrested for arson. After five unsuccessful trials, with hung juries (divided basically along French/English linguistic lines), an English jury acquitted them.

The federal government wanted so much to defuse the problem that they arranged for land in the Muskoka area of Ontario to be acquired for the Kanesatake Mohawk. In 1882, about one-third of the people left for the community now known as Wahta. Not all of them stayed when they discovered that the land was not what it had been described as being. The Kanesatake problem was not resolved.

In 1912, a Mohawk land claim went all the way to the Privy Council in Britain, only to fail yet again. In 1936, the Sulpicians sold the rest of their land to a wealthy Belgian baron. In 1945, the federal government bought 32 separate lots of land scattered throughout the area, comprising about 1 percent of the original seigneury. They did not consult with the Mohawk about this land transfer, nor did they create a reserve from the land: it remained as Crown land with individual Mohawk families being issued "certificates of possession." In 1947, the government of Quebec authorized an expropriation of some of the baron's land, which included the area known as "The Pines." In 1961, after the town of Oka began clearing trees to make room for a nine-hole golf course, a joint Senate-Commons Committee on Indians Affairs met and recommended that the Kanesatake land issue be settled quickly. That recommendation was ignored. In 1975 and 1986, two land claim cases were launched by the Kanesatake Mohawk. Both were rejected by the federal government.

As with the other Mohawk communities discussed here, division is part of the story of Kanesatake. The Catholic minority differed from the Protestant majority not only on religious grounds but linguistic ones, in being more likely to be French-speaking than English-speaking. The Longhouse existed in this community as well. Early on, it was a small group, misunderstood and even ostracized by the Christians in the community. Both, however, lobbied for more traditional government during the late 1960s. In the fall of 1969, a meeting of fewer than 100 people approved the adoption of a hereditary system complete with clan mothers and a council of nine chiefs (three chiefs from each of the clans), with a Head Chief coming from the Turtle clan. The people were divided in their acceptance of this new system. Longhouse people did not approve of official connection with the Indian Act and Indian Affairs. Opposition came as well from those who favoured an elected band council. They formed the Kanesatakeron ("people of Kanesatake") League for Democracy. By 1977, further complications were added. The clan mothers deposed a set of traditional chiefs, but the chiefs refused to step down, creating two sets of chiefs and clan mothers for a while. During the last years of the 1980s, chiefs were appointed and deposed several times.

Helping contribute to the tense atmosphere developing in Kanehsatake, in September 1989, the SQ raided a newly opened bingo hall, coupling the raid with a search of Mohawk homes in the community. This meant that, by 1990, all three Mohawk

communities had had recent experience with the SQ as an invad-
ing force.

Akwesasne

Akwesasne ("Where the Partridge Drums") is also a community
divided. To begin with, it exists in two countries and two provinces:
its territory, which straddles the St. Lawrence River, extends into
Ontario, Quebec, and New York State. In addition, there are the
critical faultlines—Christian/Longhouse, warrior/peace tradition
Longhouse, elected council/traditional government, cigarette
trade/anti-cigarette trade, and gambling/anti-gambling—that
provide ripe conditions for the growth of factions.

Fierce factionalism, such as that which developed at
Akwesasne, has its own dirty logic. Originally fair and reasonable
ideals such as unity, sovereignty, and peace become tainted. Noble
causes become temporarily forgotten in the amnesia of personal
and family vendettas. Power and wealth, originally pursued to
further worthy causes, can become more purely selfish goals.

Sources of information about Akwesasne, therefore, also take
sides, particularly when dealing with the events leading up to
and including the "Battle of Akwesasne." Three of my major
sources clearly represent the views of one faction—New York
journalist Rick Hornung, in his sensationalistic but nonetheless
useful work, *One Nation under the Gun: Inside the Mohawk
Civil War* (1991) shows definite preference for the pro-
gambling/Mohawk Warrior side of the clashes during the late
1980s to 1990, portraying the casino owners as more innocent
entrepreneurs than they were and failing to draw adequate attention to their criminal connections and dealings in hard drugs and
guns. Likewise, he seems to have been seduced by the rhetoric
of the Mohawk Warriors (he spent most of his research time
interviewing the Warriors), while ignoring their bullying.
Similarly, two of the insiders on whom I have relied heavily,
Doug (Kanentiio) George and Mike Mitchell, were highly active

players in the faction game, as we will see in the discussion below. I have had to work to create a "balanced picture" in what follows since I, myself, support the anti-gambling/peace strand faction with whom I have had the closest contact.

The First Division: The Imposition of Elected Democracy through Colonialist Means

Although Bonaparte (2002a) speaks of some slight conflict during the 1800s because the people were divided between the two countries, I argue that the first major division among the Akwesasne Mohawk began with the colonialist imposition of a supposed "elected democracy" upon the people. I say "supposed" because the democracy was illusory. All real power belonged to the federal government. At the time of the imposition, and for slightly more than 60 years afterwards (status Indians got the federal vote in 1960), the Mohawk could not vote federally.

The people of Akwesasne had followed a traditional-based system of Mohawk practices from the time the community was established during the mid 1700s. With the Indian Act of 1876 and the Indian Advancement Act of 1884, the federal government of Canada officially gave itself the power to impose its version of democracy upon the Mohawk of Akwesasne in their community government. Further, the Indian Agent was given the power to disallow the election of any person, should he feel the person was unsuitable.

In 1891, in the first election at Akwesasne, the five chiefs who won were all found guilty of following the non-Aboriginal practice (illegal but not uncommon) of dispensing alcohol to obtain votes. Problems also occurred with the chiefs elected the following year. Many of the people wanted to return to less disruptive traditional practices. A petition signed by more than 1,000 Akwesasne, Kanesatake, and Kahnawake Mohawk stated that:

> The Indian Act breeds only sorrow, contention, hatred, disrespect of family ties, spite against one another, and absence of

unity among us Indians. It also creates two distinct parties at the elections.... There is only one way to recover brotherly feelings, that of substituting the seven lords appointed by each of the seven totems[19] according to the ancient customs which we know gave us peace, prosperity, friendship and brotherly feelings in every cause, either for personal good, or to the benefit of the whole community. (Mitchell 1989: 116–17)

In 1898, the Indian Agent, with police backup, failed to enforce the European-style election process at Akwesasne. Nine months later, Indian Agent George Long brought two police officers with him to the local schoolhouse where an election imposed by the federal government was supposed to occur. In the words of the *Montreal Star*:

They found [the schoolhouse] surrounded by about 200 aborigines ... they were refused admittance and a general riot took place. The police were badly assaulted and Indian Agent Long was seized and locked up in the school house ... the Dominion Police [i.e., RCMP] were driven away. At six o'clock at night, Mr. Long was still caged up. (York and Pindera 1991: 160)

A few weeks later, on May 1, the federal government tried a different tactic. A contingent of Dominion Police officers, headed by Lieutenant-Colonel Percy Sherwood, pretended to represent a construction company and sent a message to the leaders or chiefs of Akwesasne, claiming that they (the officers) might want to purchase some stone from the community for the repair of the bridge that crossed the St. Lawrence (and Akwesasne). When the chiefs entered the Indian Agent's office, they were seized and handcuffed. One was Chief Ohnehtotako ("Pine Tar"), known in English as Jake Fire. He was the brother of Saiowesakeron ("The Ice Is Floating"), known in English as Jake Ice or John Fire. According to Akwesasne Mohawk Darren

Bonaparte, in his recently written history of the community (2002b), when Ohnehtotako walked into the building and saw two other chiefs in custody, he backed out, giving a warning cry, only to be tackled and brought back in. Women who heard the warning ran to Saiowisakeron's house.

> Saiowisakeron immediately bolted out of his house and, letting out a mighty shout of his own, ran to the Indian agent's office and pushed his way through the door.... Sherwood's testimony of what took place inside the office has Saiowisakeron coming at him and sneering "Shoot! Shoot!" when told not to come any further. He grabbed Sherwood and pushed him back against a stove. Sherwood then fired his gun, wounding Saiowisakeron in the arm. Saiowisakeron then pushed Sherwood on top of the stove while other Mohawks grappled with the other officers. While the other officers used their guns as billy clubs on the heads of their Mohawk opponents, Sherwood fired his second shot into Saiowisakeron's chest. Saiowisakeron finally let go of his grip on Sherwood and collapsed to the floor, dead. (Bonaparte 2002b)

Over the following few weeks, 15 Mohawk were arrested and jailed. Five of the chiefs were imprisoned for almost a year. After a trial in the spring of 1900, they were released and issued a strong warning concerning resisting "democracy."

Shortly after the arrests, the police took 15 Mohawk to nearby Cornwall to hold an election of councillors. There have been allegations that the police supplied these people with alcohol. In later years, the elected representatives of a community of thousands have been put into office by as few as 20 voters.

The killing of Saiowisakeron is still remembered. In 1986, May 1 was declared a national holiday in Akwesasne. In 1999, there was a parade in his honour, sponsored ironically by the elected council, a system he strongly opposed.

On the American side of Akwesasne, police were also used to impose an elected council on the people. In 1948, the people of that part of the community voted to abolish the elected system and return to traditional governance. The next year, a police guard was used to re-establish the imposed system. The development of a Mohawk Warrior Society in Akwesasne has its roots in a confrontation between this elected council and its supporters and the Longhouse and its supporters. In the spring of 1979, Loran Thompson, a Longhouse sub-chief in his 30s, saw some workers cutting down trees near his home on Raquette Point, on the American side of Akwesasne. They were following orders of the New York elected council, which wanted to build a fence around the reserve. The Longhouse opposed the building of that fence as having the potential to reduce the Mohawk's chances of regaining more of their traditional territory. Thompson confronted the workers and confiscated chainsaws. He was arrested by Akwesasne police officers working with New York State troopers. The Akwesasne Police Force was created by, and answered to, the elected council. Their relationship to the community at the time was not the best, as there were reported beatings of community members (Garte 1981, citing Longhouse chief Jake Swamp). Longhouse followers staged a protest, disarmed the Akwesasne Police, and briefly took over the building that housed the police station and the elected council's headquarters.

Over the months that followed, Thompson's home became the refuge for those Longhouse supporters who feared arrest for their part in the protest. At one point, state troopers arrived with a SWAT team and blockaded the roads leading to Raquette Point. The Mohawk at Thompson's place built bunkers. Tension remained high for some time. When the troopers left, Christian Mohawk vigilantes who supported the elected council built their own barricades and threatened to storm the Thompson house and take the wanted men into custody. The troopers returned, but despite the great potential for violence, nothing serious happened.

In 1980 and 1981, two of the three band council members

were defeated in elections and were replaced by people more willing to cooperate with the Longhouse. They disbanded the Akwesasne Police Force. In 1981, the indictments against Thompson were dismissed.

The Second Division: Customs and Cigarettes

We have spoken before about the Jay Treaty, accepted officially in the United States and unofficially in Canada, that allows Aboriginal peoples to cross the border without paying customs. This has special significance to the people of Akwesasne. The international border is on Kawehnoke ("island in water") or Cornwall Island, which is physically carved up by an 8- to 10-foot chain link fence topped with razor wire. Not surprisingly, customs has long been an issue in this Mohawk community. In 1968, the Canadian federal government decided to levy customs on Mohawk crossing the border; as a result, the people seized the Seaway International Bridge. Forty-nine protesters were arrested by the OPP and RCMP.

The stereotype of Akwesasne is that all its Mohawk people smuggle cigarettes (not to mention drugs, alcohol, and guns) in order to avoid the Canadian tax. However, there is no unified attitude in the community toward the cigarette trade. Some feel it is a matter of rights; some have been forced to turn to the trade when times are hard and cigarette taxes (and therefore profit margins) are especially high; and some are completely opposed to the trade. Very few want the notoriety that the trade has brought to the community, nor the connections that have been formed with organized crime and the smuggling of drugs and weapons.

Attempting to Maintain a Unified Police Force

During the latter half of the 1980s, an attempt was made to develop a council and a peacekeeping force to unify the American and Canadian sections of the community. Those pushing for the unification became, or were already, something of a faction in the community. In a community as sharply divided as

Akwesasne, even unification wore colours. The unified council (known as the Tri-Council) existed from 1986 to 1988, but was voted out when opposition was successfully mounted by those involved with gambling in New York (among other practices).

In 1986, the Tri-Council tried to create a policing agency by appointing conservation officers as constables to enforce the community's conservation by-laws. The by-law establishing these officers was disallowed by the Department of Indian Affairs, which has the power of disallowance. The Tri-Council tried to have their conservation officers trained by the Ontario Ministry of Natural Resources (OMNR), but the OMNR refused. The Council then went to New York authorities to have officers trained by the New York State Police and the US Conservation Authority. The OPP charged one of the conservation officers with unauthorized possession of a restricted weapon when they encountered him with his service revolver. The Tri-Council had tried to register the weapon, but the RCMP had refused to do so because it did not consider the Akwesasne Police Force a law-enforcement agency, even though the officers had been given a measure of policing authority by both the Ontario and Quebec provincial governments. The charge was initially dismissed, appealed, and then dismissed again.

In 1989, Grand Chief Mike Mitchell (holding that position in the Canadian, not the American council) described with great frustration the federal government opposition to the council's attempt to create a strong, local police force:

> Our by-law creating and empowering our police force in 1986 was disallowed because it was felt it was outside the authority of a band council. But what else would the Indian Act mean when it authorizes by-laws for "law and order"? And why have similar by-laws in other communities been enacted without being disallowed? ... [W]e have had eleven by-laws disallowed, having to do with nuisance, trespass, residency, explosives, weapons, and so on. We are

convinced that, if these by-laws had been in force, we would not have experienced the problems we have had recently in connection with the smuggling of cigarettes, guns, liquor, and drugs. (Mitchell 1989: 128)

On October 13, 1988, 250 officers from the RCMP, the OPP, the Cornwall City Police, and the New York State Police and Border Patrol conducted a raid on Akwesasne, sealing off Cornwall Island for four hours. They were looking for cigarettes, illegal drugs, and weapons. They had not consulted the Akwesasne council or their partially recognized police force before this raid. Was it because both organizations were Mohawk and therefore automatically suspect?

That is certainly the impression Chief Mitchell received (Mitchell 1989: 132).

The legitimacy in Akwesasne of outsider police forces was severely compromised by this raid. In Mitchell's words, "we cannot see ourselves trusting these outside agencies again. They have alienated the people of Akwesasne" (Mitchell 1989:131). With the insider police force lacking outsider respect, and the outsider police forces lacking local legitimacy, the climate was ripe for the growth of the Mohawk Warrior Society at Akwesasne.

The Third Division: Gambling
Beginning in the early 1970s, gambling came to the New York side of Akwesasne. As with their involvement in the illegal cigarette trade, the Mohawk Warrior Society felt that they were defending the sovereignty of the people by establishing an independent economy for them through these activities. Bingos and casinos were allowed in New York. Slot machines were not, but they arrived in American Akwesasne anyway. Gambling became an issue over which the Longhouse supporters divided. In 1986, Longhouse sub-chief Loran Thompson proposed a contract to be financed by a private investor to operate a bingo. The Longhouse would receive 51 percent of the profits, and Thompson

would get 19 percent from the private investor's profits. He claimed to have obtained the signatures of three clan mothers in support of this venture. Longhouse chiefs Tom Porter and Jake Swamp and many others in the Longhouse opposed the idea of connecting sacred traditions with gambling. Thompson was removed as sub-chief, and the deal fell through.

In 1987, the Tri-Council held a referendum on gambling, and the majority voted against it. This was ignored. Neither the band council nor its police force had enough local support to enforce the decision.

As mentioned above, slot machines were illegal in New York State. Encouraged and supported by a band council that opposed gambling, the New York State Police made several slot machine raids.

In 1988, the office of the successful Aboriginal journal *Akwesasne Notes* was destroyed by arson. It was the first in an escalating series of blows, both verbal and physical, that were struck by the two major factions that had developed at Akwesasne. The editor, Longhouse supporter Doug George, had been writing editorials opposing gambling, as well as the drug and gun smuggling ring and the organized crime connections that he saw as being established in the community by the Mohawk Warrior Society. In speeches and articles, he questioned the legitimacy of the Mohawk Warrior Society in terms of the Great Law:

> As far as every legitimate Iroquois government is concerned, there can be no such thing as the Warrior Society.... This organization operates outside Iroquois law, without the sanction of Iroquois government. It is, by its essence, illicit. (York and Pindera 1991: 264)

For its part, the Mohawk Warrior Society deeply resented that the anti-gambling faction, which included Doug George, Mike Mitchell, and the band council, would resort to bringing in outsider police to fight gambling. In the words of Mohawk

Warrior Art Montour or Kakwirakeron ("Many Branches Lying About on the Ground"):

> When one group of Mohawks began to express a desire for sovereignty and nationhood by establishing an economy, another group of Mohawks asked the police to come in.... The police are not the source of the problem. It is how we work among ourselves. (Hornung 1991: 16)

On July 20, 1989, more than 400 FBI agents and New York State Police officers stormed the community and arrested 11 people on gambling charges. This was followed by 11 days of police blockades. That summer, about 100 members of the Mohawk Warrior Society met to determine how to prevent such a police raid from happening again; they formed the Mohawk Sovereign Security Force (MSSF). Eight patrol vehicles were painted white and bore the insignia of the MSSF. The officers' pay ($300 a week) was supplied by regular donations from the owners of the casinos and from cigarette retailers. Seen from one view, it was a private police force. That was the way it sometimes acted, as little more than security guards and bouncers for casinos. Sometimes, however, some of their number acted like bullies and criminals, but that is not how they, and their numerous supporters, thought of themselves. Consider these statements from John Boots and Art Montour, two of their number:

> We are peacekeepers, whose only purpose is to protect ourselves from outsiders and traitors. We have no intent to provoke violence, nor do we want to hurt any one of our brothers and sisters in the Mohawk Nation.... (Hornung 1991: 28–29)

The St. Regis Akwesasne Mohawk Police (SRAMP), the police force then recognized by the band council, also had its factional side. On the night of August 26–27, 1989, anti-gambling protesters marched on the Mohawk Warrior Society headquarters and set a newly built casino, the Lucky Knight, on fire. Among those alleged to have been at the scene were Grand Chief Mike Mitchell, as well as several off-duty members of the SRAMP. On a number of occasions, the MSSF claimed that the SRAMP had attempted to provoke them, so that, by retaliating, the MSSF would look bad.

The two forces competed for legitimacy as *the* official policing agency at Akwesasne. In December, Major Leu, the New York State Police Commander of the unit assigned to Akwesasne, met with the band council to discuss making the MSSF the official policing authority on the American side of Akwesasne. The council refused this and asked to have Leu removed from his position.

The Battle for Akwesasne

Violence escalated. On January 20, 1990, SRAMP Police Chief Ernie King said, "We are beyond saying that someone is going to get hurt. We now know someone is going to get killed"(*Toronto Star*). From March 23 to May 1, 1990, there ensued what has been referred to as the "Battle for Akwesasne." It had an impact not only on that community, but helped set the stage for the conflict at Oka. Some of the Mohawk Warriors from Akwesasne—Loran and Larry ("Wizard") Thompson, Francis Boots, and Gordon "Noriega" Lazore, in particular—became leading figures in that conflict. Yet, this Akwesasne connection has not been cited by the writers of introductory sociology textbooks.

The combatants took different positions on several issues, primarily that of gambling. On March 23, the anti-gambling faction, a loose alliance of peace-strand Longhouse members, Christians, and supporters of the band council, took the dramatic step of setting up barricades to block access to a strip of eight casinos on the American side of Akwesasne. They were led by Doug George, who stated that they set up the barricades as they were "determined to hold out until the three councils could assure the people there would be an overall disarmament and ongoing negotiations to resolve the anarchy which was consuming Akwesasne" (George [Kanentiio] 2000). In the telling words of the same writer, "In the end, the absence of a peacekeeping force to keep the sides apart meant a final clash was inevitable."

With the erection of the barricades, battle lines were formally and physically drawn. Sporadic battle ensued, with verbal abuse, fistfights, physical assault, and the firing of guns. Schools were closed, and an estimated 2,000 people temporarily left the community in fear of their lives. The Travelling College (well-known for its work in teaching Aboriginal culture and history across Canada) on Cornwall Island became a refugee camp and communications centre. On April 23 and 24, the MSSF and their supporters attacked the roadblocks. Twenty-four cars were destroyed by fire and bulldozer. The barricades were torn down by April 25. There was a bombing at the tribal police station, and a George family house was turned into a defensive fortress for the anti-gambling faction.

Two Mohawk were killed in gunfights. George was charged with murder, but was freed after a six-day preliminary hearing. The fighting ended on May 1, 1990, when provincial and state police sealed off the community. New York State declared the American part of the community under martial law.

Summary

In this chapter, we have discussed what I strongly feel are the necessary background elements to understanding the Oka confrontation. One of these is the Great Law, which is both the foundational document of traditional Mohawk (and general Iroquois) governance and an important site of contention among contemporary Mohawk. For both those reasons, it ought to be presented in any sociology textbook that discusses Oka. Also indispensable in any textbook description of the Oka situation is an account of the historic roots of the conflict, particularly the colonialist relationship between outsider policing agencies and

Mohawk communities and the attempts of these communities to build self-policing alternatives that are tied to the conflicts concerning interpretations of the Great Law.

In the next chapter, we will see that these necessary elements are absent from Canadian introductory sociology textbooks. Thus, any sociological discussion of the Oka situation can be no more than superficial and as complicit as colonial practices and interpretations.

Notes

1. For a fuller description of the events at Oka, see Chapter Seven.
2. I will be noting later in this chapter that there are two strands of interpretation concerning the Great Law: a warrior strand and a peace strand. Even calling this foundational document "The Great Law of Peace" has been contested as being prejudiced toward one strand. Therefore, in future references, I will be referring to it simply as the Great Law.
3. This is not to say that Aboriginal communities are unique in this regard. Police services have had a similarly problematic relationship with Black communities in urban Canada. I have long found that many Black students have generally had an easier time understanding the Oka situation than most White students.
4. While it is hard to put a precise date on the formation of the Great Law of Peace, most writers estimate the origin as 1451 or 1536, two years in which there was an eclipse of the sun, as is mentioned in the story.
5. This name came from Europeans. It is generally thought to be derived from a Basque word meaning "to kill."
6. They became six nations when the Tuscarora, a linguistically and culturally related people, were driven off their land by White settlers and were invited by the Oneida to share their land.
7. The main written source from which I derived this shortened telling of the Great Law is Woodbury, Henry, and Webster 1992.
8. They are usually said to have been living somewhere around the Bay of Quinte, by the eastern end of Lake Ontario. Along with this interpretation is the belief that they were Wendat (Huron), who then lived in the area.
9. A peace chief (in opposition to a war chief) is a leader who deals with matters of internal government and external diplomacy.
10. This English word used to refer to the 50 leaders of the Iroquois is developed from the Algonquian word "saqmaw" (Mi'kmaq version) meaning "chief" or "leader."
11. Most of my own exposure to the Great Law has been through this tradition, primarily through those who have been taught by Jacob Thomas.
12. Wampum or shell-bead belts have long been used as documents of treaties and other important statements, read through symbols. There are several such belts of significance to the Mohawk (e.g., the Akwesasne Wolf Belt).
13. There are two other Canadian Mohawk communities not mentioned because they did not play a significant role in the Oka conflict: Tyendinaga and Wahta.
14. Kanesatake ("there is plenty of sand") is the Mohawk word for the community, while

Oka ("walleye or pickerel") is the Algonquin name, which is used primarily for the non-Aboriginal community.

[15] His works were first published in 1845, but were republished as recently as 1969–71.

[16] A Canadian federal court in 1997 ruled that the Mohawks did have the right to cross unimpeded, but that ruling was challenged by the federal government, and the decision was overturned by the Canadian Supreme Court.

[17] I suggest that what can be said for sure is that the primary issue was not so much the eviction as it was a struggle for local legitimacy of authority.

[18] Some of my sociology students, being given an early copy of this story, have asked why David Cross thought he would need to "rescue" his brother from the police if, as the passenger, he was "innocent." It is difficult for these students to realize that if the police are "outsider enemies," anyone held by them is captured by the enemy (and therefore needs rescuing).

[19] The clan history of the Mohawk is not a straightforward one. The traditional system consisted of three clans and nine sachems (three to a clan). However, this was altered in different communities. In the early 1800s, the Onondaga of Sawekatsi (sometimes spelled Oswegatchie) joined the Akwesasne Mohawk, adding more clans to the original three. Throughout much of the nineteenth century, the Akwesasne Mohawk had 12 chiefs, with the additional three being added by the Snipe clan. The federal census of 1890 had the Akwesasne Mohawk with nine sachems (www.wampumchronicles.com/hiddenhistory.htm, 2003). Gerald Reid, writing for the Kahnawake publication *The Eastern Door*, instructs us that from 1840 to 1889, the Kahnawake Mohawk had seven chiefs representing seven clans: Turtle, Wolf, Bear, Old Bear, Rock, Deer, and Snipe (Reid 1999).

CHAPTER SEVEN

Oka:
The Warrior Frame

In his critical questioning of the extent to which Canadian sociology has served the unique sociological needs of Canada, John Hofley asked the following:

> [H]ere in 1991, amidst the constitutional debate, the failure of Meech Lake, and the events of Oka in the summer of 1990, can sociologists point to a corpus of research that would enlighten these debates? (Hofley 1992: 113)

Judging from the evidence provided by the way that the Oka confrontation is treated in Canadian introductory sociology textbooks, the answer to Hofley's question is a resounding "no."

INTRODUCTION

The Oka confrontation of 1990 is a popular topic in Canadian introductory sociology textbooks. Of the 25 textbooks printed from 1991 to 2002, 14 mention it. These include Henslin and Nelson 1996; Henslin et al. 2001; Johnstone and Bauer 1998; Kendall, Linden, and Murray 1998 and 2000; Macionis and

Gerber 1999 and 2002; Spencer 1996; Teevan 1995; Tepperman and Rosenberg, 1991, 1995, and 1998; Warme, Malus, and Lundy 1994; and Zeitlin and Brym 1991.

These 14 books resort to what I call the "warrior frame" in their presentation of the Oka situation. This frame, like the treatment of CDIES and the potlatch, is a sociological simulacrum, produced as if there were no meaningful Aboriginal role in knowledge production and erasing the possibility that there may be a different framing to be developed from such knowledge production.

In more specific terms, the simulacrum of the warrior frame posits a narrow view of the Mohawk Warrior at the centre of the Oka situation. It makes any sociological explanation partial, vague, disconnected from any "big picture" explanation of why and how Oka took place, and disconnected from any historical specificities of causation. It is a frame that illustrates well Dorothy Smith's "relations of ruling." Specifically, it serves the federal government's public relations campaign to vilify the Mohawk; helps to defend its inaction on the Kanesatake land question; and obscures its failure to live up to its (admittedly paternalistic) responsibility to stand up for Aboriginal peoples in conflicts with the province by not questioning the highly questionable actions of the Quebec government, especially its police force.

The warrior frame is not unique to the writers and editors of Canadian introductory sociology textbooks; it was produced by the media at the time of the Oka confrontation. In a critique that could just as well be applied to introductory sociology textbooks, Ojibwa educator and writer Gail Guthrie Valaskakis, in her insightful work, "Telling Our Own Stories: The Role, Development, and Future of Aboriginal Communications," criticized the mainstream media's coverage of the Oka situation:

> [I]n all television, radio and newspaper coverage, one image
> emerged as salient in the Mohawk crisis: the image of the

"warrior"—bandanna-masked, khaki-clad, gun-toting Indians who dominated the media.... With few exceptions, media's warriors were exaggerated, monolithic representations of Aboriginal activists: the military masculine, criminalized through association with terrorism and epitomized in the ultimate warrior, code-named "Lasagna" who became both the darling of the media and a willing subject. (Valaskakis 2000: 79)

I agree with Valaskakis and argue that, in a less dramatic but equally consistent fashion, the authors of introductory sociology textbooks walk the same path in portraying the Oka situation in a warrior frame. It is difficult to determine to what extent, in so doing, they are following the media's lead, or, alternatively, whether they are merely reflecting the same non-Aboriginal biases. Certainly, given the fact that the writers do not cite any Aboriginal sources, or even any other books or articles dedicated to discussing the subject, it appears that they have taken the media images and text at face value, adding to it a sociological interpretation, one that does not appear to challenge or question the media's framing of the situation.

Sourcing the Warrior Frame

Not one of the 14 textbooks makes any use of Aboriginal voice to shed critical light on the Oka situation. Henslin and Nelson (1996) refer to Abenaki film-maker Alanis Obomsawin's excellent National Film Board video, "Kanehsatake: 270 Years of Resistance" (1993) in a sideline entry outside the text:

> *Kanehsatake* is an NFB film that chronicles the Mohawks' resurgent attempts to assert their land claims and their right to self-determination and directs focus on the "Oka Crisis." (Henslin and Nelson 1996: 623)

While it is good that Henslin and Nelson mention this video, they fail to identify it as the work of an Aboriginal film-maker and present no material informed by the insights it offers.

Obomsawin's film is an important work[1] that lends an insightful Aboriginal perspective to the Oka situation. In the summer of 1993, when I was teaching in the Native Education Counsellor Program at Cambrian College in Sudbury, my Ojibwa, Cree, Mohawk, and Oneida students were anxiously awaiting the release of this video, so that they could see what "really happened" at Oka, as opposed to the views that came from the mainstream media. Obomsawin being Aboriginal, and having a good track record from earlier works, primarily through her coverage of the SQ raid at Restigouche (see below concerning this raid), was trusted by the students and by me.

Many Aboriginal peoples saw this video as proof of what really happened at Oka as opposed to the view that came from the mainstream media. Obomsawin's earlier films, especially her coverage of the SQ raid at Restigouche, has given her video validity in the eyes of her viewers.

One textbook—Kendall et al. 2000—makes use of Aboriginal voice to talk about cigarette smuggling, a subject that, as we have seen, directly relates to the nature of the Oka confrontation. Unfortunately, rather than contributing to a different framing of the Oka situation, it reinforces the negative stereotype of the Akwesasne Mohawk as cigarette smuggler. They quote sociologist Margaret Beare (1996), who quotes a CBC interview with Mike Mitchell to interpret the smuggling as functionalist strain theory:

> The money—it's unbelievable the money you can make and it's so easy.... You can buy a pack of cigarettes on the American side of the reservation for $1.58 and you go across here in Cornwall and you have to buy it for close to $7.00 a pack, same pack, within a short distance of each other, so no one is surprised that all this is happening. (Kendall et al. 2000: 203)

As explained by Kendall et al., "According to strain theory, people feel strain when they are exposed to cultural goals that they are unable to obtain because they do not have access to culturally approved means of achieving those goals (1999: 203).

This, of course, is not the only Mohawk face that can be put on Akwesasne's relationship to cigarette smuggling. Those Akwesasne Mohawks who oppose the trade in their community could have been quoted, but they appear to be mute sociologically; the writers of introductory sociology textbooks do not let them speak. Mike Mitchell, for example, has spoken out against the trade on a number of occasions. His framing of the situation centres the government lack of support for Akwesasne anti-smuggling initiatives, the pressure from non-Aboriginal criminal elements, and the media stereotyping of the Mohawk. The following, part of an open letter to Prime Minister Jean Chrétien, appeared the same year as the Kendall et al. textbook that includes the previous quote:

> I am writing this letter to you on behalf of the Mohawks of Akwesasne as a means to express our collective concern on the proposed plan to substantially increase the amount of taxes on cigarettes and other tobacco products in Canada. To be blunt, Akwesasne steadfastly opposes the increase in tobacco taxes and words that follow will tell you why.
>
> When the news of the tax increase broke in the national media, one of the first reactions by the newspaper columnists was to the effect that smuggling business would once again be booming in Akwesasne....
>
> Akwesasne is a Mohawk community of hardworking peaceful people. We admit that there is an element of people who were enticed into this activity, but it is clear that the lack of jobs or opportunities played a factor in convincing people to accept the role of low level mules for big money people from the outside. With that being said we must point out that there is no disputing the fact that

the overwhelming majority of Akwesasronon are honest people working for a better life. Instead of reporting this, the media instead chose to sensationalize Akwesasne as a criminal haven without law and order....

My community has had to defend itself too many times from attacks within Parliament itself, as well as the media editorializing Akwesasne as a criminal community and misleading the Canadian public in the process. Your government wants to raise the price of cigarettes. Stop and think what this could do to our community without preventative measures to assist our community in protecting itself. (Mitchell 2000)

It is especially misleading for an introductory sociology textbook published in 2000 to make the Akwesasne Mohawk "the face" of cigarette smuggling, since the legal focus has shifted recently to the cigarette companies themselves for their role in the enterprise. Arrests in 1998 by American law enforcement agencies of a cigarette smuggling ring included an executive from a major American cigarette producer. In December 1999, the Canadian government filed a suit in the US Federal Court against several cigarette manufacturers and the Canadian Tobacco Manufacturers Council for their role in cigarette smuggling.

Further, the connection that Kendall et al. make between cigarette smuggling and Oka is vague and tangential. In talking about the factors that facilitated the smuggling trade, they make reference to "the jurisdictional disputes over law enforcement, which were so apparent during the 1990 Oka crisis in Quebec, [that] reduced the ability of the police to work effectively" (Kendall et al. 2000: 203). They do not state which jurisdictions are disputing: United States/Canada, Quebec/Ontario, Quebec/Canada, Mohawk Warriors/Mohawk Peacekeepers, etc. The only source other than Mitchell found in introductory sociology textbooks to discuss the Oka situation is Lorimer and McNulty's *Mass Communication in Canada* (1991) in Warme,

Malus, and Lundy (1994). Interestingly, while this book also reproduces "the picture," it discusses Oka more thoroughly than any of the introductory sociology textbooks do and at least attempts to perform such necessary but absent sociological functions as contextualizing the picture and making reference to the historically negative relationship between the SQ and the Mohawk.

Given that Frideres is the number one source concerning Aboriginal peoples cited in introductory sociology textbooks, conspicuous by its almost complete absence is reference to his chapter on Oka that appears in the last three editions of his otherwise often cited *Aboriginal Peoples in Canada* ("Conflict in Society," 1993: 365–406; 1998: 326–57; and "Aboriginal Resistance: The Summer of 1990 in Perspective," 2001: 324–50; see also Chapter Three). Perhaps this absence reflects the fact that Frideres moves the focus a few degrees away from the warrior frame, giving, for example, the historical background for the Mohawk's claim to Oka and recognizing the importance of the Longhouse. It should be noted, however, that to a large extent, as he does not draw upon Aboriginal voice and knowledge production,[2] his frame ultimately does not present a view that is radically different from that of the other introductory sociology textbooks. There are, for example, no remembrances of colonial oppression and no presentation of the history of conflict with the outsider police.

COMPONENTS OF THE WARRIOR FRAME

There are seven components of the warrior frame as it is reproduced in the introductory sociology textbooks:

1) reproduction in the media of the famous picture of the "Mohawk Warrior" confronting a soldier without contextualizing it;
2) portrayal of the Mohawk Warriors as criminal outsiders;

3) depiction of the Mohawk Warriors as uniformly "war-like" militants;

4) exclusion of the important role of women from the frame;

5) depiction of a false picture of unity;

6) casting of the Sûreté du Québec as a functionalist, "neutral" organization; and

7) downplaying acts of non-Aboriginal violence.

1. The Picture: Context Free

The warrior frame begins with *the* picture. It appeared first on television and was often repeated in the print media (e.g., the *Maclean's* cover story, "The Fury of Oka"; and Burke et al. 1990: 17). The authors of three textbooks (Henslin et al. 2001: 442; Kendall et al. 1998: 647; and Gerber 1999: 559) include it. In this picture, we see a tough-looking masked Mohawk Warrior, assumed to be the media darling "Lasagna"—it was actually an Ojibwa university student who became involved in the confrontation. The "Mohawk Warrior" is glaring at a young, innocent-seeming, and baby-faced but still resolute-looking soldier. A fourth textbook (Warme, Malus, and Lundy 1994: 206) prints a similar picture, only this time it is of the back of a Mohawk Warrior (who looks like and could very well be Lasagna) holding the Mohawk Warrior flag in his hand.

It is important to note that, consistent with the general use of pictures of Aboriginal peoples in sociology textbooks (see Chapter One), none of the four books tries to contextualize the picture. None discusses the sociological message their pictures convey. They are presented as if they constitute part of a neutral or objective scientific depiction of the series of events that took place, rather than being part of the story of how the non-Aboriginal media (including introductory sociology textbooks) came to establish the discourse of the Oka situation. This is not surprising given Dorothy Smith's critique of mainstream sociologists (1990), as discussed in Chapter Two. They do not see themselves as having a standpoint, as contributing to a subjectively based discourse. Reproducing this picture without discussion involves replicating a non-Aboriginal standpoint that serious restricts the readers' view of the Mohawk involved with the Oka confrontation.

2. The Criminal Outsiders

Another key part of the warrior frame is the portrayal of the Aboriginal participants at Oka as being criminal outsiders. In this way, the introductory sociology textbooks, as predicted by Smith, reflect the relations of ruling; in this case, they are in the service of federal government propaganda. The federal government's expensive public relations campaign[3] presented Oka in an anti-Mohawk light by casting the Mohawk Warriors as criminal outsiders. They were referred to as Americans, as Vietnam War veterans, and as criminals. Calling some of the Mohawk involved American ignores the primacy of Mohawk citizenship for the people involved in the confrontation, the divided nature of Akwesasne, and the finer points of the Jay Treaty (discussed in Chapter Six). Lasagna, the "poster boy" favoured by the media, epitomized this outsider nature with his Brooklyn accent—but it belied his family's deep roots in, and his lifelong close connection to, Kahnawake. As will be mentioned below, there were a number of Vietnam War veterans in the small group that initially blockaded the Mercier Bridge, but their number was not as large as government propaganda (and much of the French press) led people to believe.

None of the introductory sociology textbooks attempted to counteract the image of the criminal outsider, and two of them reproduced the image in some way. Johnstone and Bauer, whose presentation of Oka generally is the least sympathetic to the Mohawk, refer to the almost exclusively Mohawk support for Kanehsatake as coming from "Other First Nation warriors" and reproduce the image of "American criminals," just as the government desired:

Other First Nation warriors, many of whom were US citizens armed with guns that they were not allowed by law to possess and carry in Canada came to support the Mohawks. (Johnstone and Bauer 1998: 52)

Spencer, whose description of the Oka confrontation generally valorizes the Canadian army's role and vilifies the Mohawk Warriors, also introduces the criminal outsider element:

A new surge of support for Native causes was felt in English Canada, where journalists downplayed criminal behavior on the part of the Mohawk Warriors Society. (Spencer 1996: 378)

3. The "War-Like" Militant

The Mohawk Warrior as portrayed in the warrior frame is a subset of the general image of Aboriginal maleness: the warrior. This is the familiar Hollywood figure of a man whose essential nature and upbringing is "war-like," a tough guy who is constantly fighting battles, who does not acknowledge pain or gentler feelings, and who is a warrior for life. The actor who played the nasty Pawnee in "Dances with Wolves" (Wes Studi) and the nasty Huron in "The Last of the Mohicans" epitomizes that figure. In Canada, it has been replicated in the image of the Mohawk warrior in the 1991 movie "Black Robe" and in telling the story of seventeenth-century New France in the recent CBC production "Canada: A People's History."

The warrior is part of an essentializing binary distinction of nasty savage/noble savage. For Aboriginal women, that binary pits the "indian princess" against the "squaw" (see Steckley 1999: 2–5). For Aboriginal men, the distinction is between "warrior" and "noble savage." The latter dedicates his life to peace, art, and ecological responsibility. His representation can be seen in the same movies that replicate the warrior: the Dakota in "Dances with Wolves" and the Mohicans in "Last of the Mohicans."

In essentializing, of course, one part of the image is inscribed at the cost of erasing something else. The binary does not allow for someone to partake of both warrior and noble savage. Therefore, Mohawk Warriors must be warriors and only warriors.

Missing from the introductory sociology textbooks are portrayals, which depart from the essentializing package contained within these books. Kanehsatake Mohawk Dan David wrote in "Razorwire Dreams" about his brother Joe. Joe was an artist—hence, his Warrior pseudonym "Stonecarver"—who became a Mohawk Warrior because of what he saw happening during the course of the summer of 1990. Here is a type of Mohawk Warrior invisible to most mainstream media and to readers of all the introductory sociology textbooks that mention Oka:

> He was the last person I would have predicted to become a "Warrior." He hated guns and violence. Still, he went into the Pines and he refused to leave. He knew the army was coming and what that might mean. He'd made up his mind that some things are worth dying for. (David 1992: 30)

A similar picture of the "warrior convert" Stonecarver comes from the writing of journalists York and Pindera, in their book *People of the Pines: The Warriors and the Legacy of Oka*. It is an insightful book that allows a significant amount of Aboriginal voice to emerge. York had covered Aboriginal issues for some time before Oka and had benefited from the experience. Despite the ready availability of this book, not one of the introductory sociology textbooks mentions it. York and Pindera write about the David brothers:

> Joe had never carried a gun in the long months leading up to the police raid and he had argued against the decision to allow arms into the camp. Now he had a black scarf pulled over his face and an AK-47 in his hand. The two brothers looked at each other in silence. Finally Joe David said to

[Dan], "I know. I don't believe it either." Like so many others who had been opposed or indifferent to the Mohawk warrior movement in the past, Joe David had suddenly become a warrior. (York and Pindera 1991: 194)

4. Excluding the Women

Any discussion of Iroquois politics is incomplete without acknowledgment of the significant role that women play (see Spittal 1990). Clan membership is determined matrilineally, and, as we have seen, clan mothers have a significant role in the choosing and deposing of sachems.

Part of the warrior frame, and integral to essentializing the Mohawk Warriors, is the total exclusion of mention of the women involved at Oka in 1990. They were a significant part of the protest from beginning to end. Women led the way on March 10 and 11, when a number of people, primarily those of the Kanehsatake Longhouse, protested the proposed expansion of a municipal golf course into a Mohawk cemetery by mounting a barricade on a dirt path or side road that connected Route 344 with a cemetery and a lacrosse/baseball field. Their protest was low key. Traditional ceremonies were performed, and there were no weapons.

Aboriginal writers, and Aboriginal peoples involved at Oka who are quoted by journalists, have repeatedly pointed out the significant presence of women in all aspects of the Oka confrontation. Richard Wagamese wrote, in "Indian Wars— Government Never Learns," an article critical of Robert Bourassa, then the premier of Quebec:

Fourthly, and perhaps most importantly, he's had to hide the fact that when the initial storming of the barricades occurred it was only women and children present at the frontlines. The warriors were well behind them and only appeared once the Quebec police made the initial aggressive motions. They returned fire to protect their women and children. (Wagamese 1996: 68)

The introductory sociology textbooks do not tell this part of the story. It would seem that, because there was no armed Mohawk Warrior presence in the early days and because no violence was involved, the domination of women in the early period of the protest is simply not reported in the introductory sociology textbooks. It is out of the frame.

The following example is typical. The author shows the police in conflict only with the Warriors. The women who led the initial protest are nowhere in sight:

[The confrontation] began when a barricade was erected by Indians to save a sacred burial ground from destruction for a golf course. The provincial police clashed with an armed Warriors' Society, resulting in the death of a police officer. (Spencer 1996: 378)

Tepperman and Rosenberg overstate the Mohawk Warriors' early role by referring to the "blockades Mohawk Warriors built at Oka, Quebec" (Tepperman and Rosenberg 1998: 197).

Likewise missing is the long and hard negotiating process that began in the fall of 1989 and stepped up in importance once the violence began. Kanehsatake Longhouse member Ellen Gabriel played a major role in those negotiations (as can readily be seen in the Obomsawin video), but her name is not mentioned.

When some 63 people left the treatment centre at the end of the confrontation, 16 of them were women.

5. A False Picture of Unity

An important essentializing aspect of the warrior frame is the idea that all Mohawk, even all Aboriginal peoples, supported the warrior stance in the Oka situation. We have seen in the previous

chapter that such was not true during the long series of events leading up to the confrontation, and it is equally untrue of the events
during the summer of 1990 at Kahnawake and at Kanehsatake.
Aboriginal sources and those informed by Aboriginal sources are
free in admitting that.

Many Aboriginal writers, while acknowledging the disunity
among their people, also feel the need to resolve these differences. One of the most passionate and articulate arguments for
this stance has been made by Patricia Monture-Angus, a law
professor whose home community is at Six Nations:

> I look at Mohawk territory and I look at young men pick-
> ing up weapons, picking up drugs, arguing that gambling
> and cigarette smuggling is economic development....
> Mohawks have what is called the Great Law of Peace. It is
> not called just the Great Law. It is called the Great Law of
> Peace. The button I am wearing says, "The bravest
> warriors are those who stand for peace." I do not want my
> son ever to have to make the decision about whether he is
> going to pick up some automatic weapons and stand on a
> bridge or at a roadblock. I do not want his mind and heart
> to be forced to think only of violence and resistance. That
> is not a good way for a spirit to be forced to live. As I
> understand it, picking up a weapon is a fundamental viola-
> tion of that Great Law of Peace... I understand about our
> young men who have grown up being lost, and someone
> puts out their hand to them and in their hand is this beau-
> tiful golden warrior image—an image that says a warrior
> is someone who protects the land, protects the people, so
> the young men hungrily pick it up.... the beauty of our men
> and the true meaning of warrior becomes "Rambo-ized."
> I understand that and I pray for those young men that they
> might understand what they are doing. (Monture-Angus
> 1995: 84–5)

Confrontation at Oka

As the negotiations concerning the extension of the golf course at Oka dragged on; as an injunction against the protest was applied, removed, and then applied again; and as the SQ presence lurking not so quietly in the background was increased, the protesters began to worry that their cause would be lost. In May, they contacted the Akwesasne Warrior Society, who had been in communication with them before. This contact was not well received by Grand Chief George Martin and members of the band council, who saw this as bringing in outside agitators. In the words of deposed (but still influential) former Grand Chief Clarence Simon:

> [W]e had some people who practiced our traditional religion who wanted to protest by putting up a little barricade on a dirt path. And it stayed that way until the town got the injunction. Then the Warriors came and ... they brought guns. (Hornung 1991: 226)

On July 11, the situation exploded. One hundred SQ officers, armed with tear gas, concussion grenades, and SWAT gear, approached the barricade early that morning. As they were asking Kanehsatake Longhouse members Ellen Gabriel and Denise Tolley who the leaders of the protest were, tear gas and grenades were set off. The confrontation had begun.

In an exchange of gunfire, an SQ officer, Corporal Marcel LeMay, was shot and killed. It has never been proven whether the gun that killed him was fired by a Mohawk or by an SQ officer. The SQ beat a sloppy retreat, and the Mohawk captured police vehicles and moved the blockade to Route 344, a highway.

The intensity of the situation escalated. More than 1,500 SQ and 500 RCMP officers became involved, eventually to be replaced by some 4,400 troops of the Canadian army, both at Kanehsatake and in the conflict at Kahnawake (see below).

The negotiations for a peaceful settlement were troubled by division. Grand Chief George Martin publicly protested against the fact that band council members were not on the Mohawk negotiating committee,[4] which included representatives from his community, Kahnawake, and Akwesasne. After he issued a statement referring to the committee members from Akwesasne and Kahnawake with the words, "This is not their territory, not their reserve ... [and] they should get the hell out" (Hornung 1991: 230), six Warriors beat him up and fired guns at his house. Ronald Cross (Lasagna), in a book written a few years after the confrontation, stated that:

> A lot of us got fed up with the people from Kanehsatake because they weren't there to help us. They had asked us to help them, and as soon as the shit hit the fan they hid or they ran away. (Cross and Sévigny 1994: 94)

While the confrontation was going on, on September 1, Cross and another Warrior slipped away briefly and beat up Kanehsatake band councillor Francis Jacobs and his son, who had threatened to tell the SQ the names of several masked Mohawks who had burgled a nearby home.

The confrontation ended on September 26, when, after dumping and burning their weapons, the Mohawk Warriors, and the women and children who were with them, left the treatment centre that had become their base, and faced the angry soldiers and SQ officers who took them prisoner.

The Taking of the Mercier Bridge

> Shortly after the SQ raid on the barricades on July 11, about a dozen Mohawk from Kahnawake, some of whom had fought with the U.S. army in the Vietnam War, seized the Mercier Bridge. It was an impulsive act that took the Mohawk community by surprise. The militants had not informed either the band council or the Kahnawake Warriors Society of what they were going to do, but the latter felt they had to support them. (Hornung 1991: 205)

Members of the Kahnawake Mohawk Warriors Society rushed to the bridge to establish a show of solidarity and to try to set up some form of alliance with the people who had taken the bridge. However, not all the community supported the bridge takeover. Joe Norton, chief of the elected band council, initially was opposed to the move, but gradually he changed his mind, perhaps in the interests of demonstrating community unity in the face of outsider opposition.

In the introductory sociology textbooks, the takeover is presented as if it were a unified act of the Mohawk of Kahnawake:

> Increasing their defiance, the Mohawks barricaded one end of a major bridge to the island of Montreal, cutting off a suburb and causing immense daily traffic pileups. (Warme, Malus, and Lundy 1994: 205)

In contrast, the difficulties of managing the differing, even opposing interests in Kahnawake and Kanehsatake, is well expressed by Akwesasne Mohawk Warrior Francis Boots, a prominent figure at Oka during the confrontation, who talks about the different factions with their different concerns:

> The people of Kanesatake were worried that outsiders were taking over the community. George Martin was worried that the people from Kahnawake and Akwesasne would make the battle much bigger than it had to be....
>
> But the men on the bridge had to get amnesty.... [People in Kahnawake] wanted to know, did the standoff affect what started in 1988 when they took the bridge to protest the raid of cigarette dealers? They felt they had to protect these gains. And from Akwesasne, we had our own agenda.... We wanted the Canadian government to formally recognize us as a nation, to deal with us as a country, not a band or tribe. (Hornung 1991: 217)

Not a word of this discord is to be found in any introductory sociology textbook. This illustrates a point made by Dorothy Smith. She speaks of sociology as drawing what she refers to as "mystical connections" that are not only not informed by insider standpoint, but, significantly, preclude information so generated. In her words:

> This ideological practice—the drawing of mystical connections—precludes the development of a body of knowledge resulting from the explication and theorizing of the actual relations coordinating the particular sites of people's lives. (Smith 1990: 50)

The writers of Canadian introductory sociology textbooks have tied the Mohawk together with mystical connections of unity that appear to preclude the notion that any divisions could exist, divisions that would have been made readily apparent by sources informed by Aboriginal voice.

There is a similar situation with the division of Aboriginal opinion outside the three Mohawk communities. Aboriginal writers have expressed concern that any opinions articulated within Aboriginal Canada that were not supportive of the warrior stance would not be tolerated by the Aboriginal community generally. Six Nations Mohawk Patricia Monture-Angus stated that she felt that, "My view of the activities in some of the Mohawk territories [is] not going to make me very popular with some people. I can accept that as long as what I have said is respected as my own view of the situation" (Monture-Angus 1995: 85). Richard Wagamese discussed this need for tolerance of conflicting views concerning the Warriors in Aboriginal Canada:

> Throughout the Oka crisis of last summer it was disturbing to hear native people who disagreed with the armed tactics of the Warriors being slandered by their own people. Charges of being *un-Indian* were flung around as casually as mainstream

opinion. Perhaps some reflection on the grounds for this disapproval might have resulted in a quicker and more beneficial end to the conflict. (Wagamese 1996: 96)

Again, not a word of this division is mentioned in any introductory sociology textbook.

6. Casting the SQ as a Structural-Functional Neutral Institution

You can't have Aboriginal warriors without the cavalry riding to the rescue. It is useful here to recall Sylvia Hale's critique of introductory sociology textbooks. She questioned whether in such textbooks all three of the canonized paradigms of sociology—structural functionalism, conflict, and symbolic interactionism—were in reality collapsed into the former. I contend that all writers of introductory sociology textbooks, no matter what their personal favourite sociological paradigm might be (and I suspect that most of the writers are more inclined in their research and teaching to a conflict rather than a functionalist view), resort to applying a functionalist paradigm in their presentation of the SQ's role at Oka. Thus, this constitutes another aspect of the warrior frame.

The following description by Robert Hagedorn stresses clearly the central tenets of this paradigm or approach to sociological data:

1. that a society cannot survive unless its members share at least some common perceptions, attitudes and values
2. that each part of the society makes a contribution to the whole
3. that the various parts of society are integrated with each other, each part supporting the other parts as well as the whole
4. that these forces keep societies relatively stable (Hagedorn 1983: 12)

Using such an approach, the structure or institution labelled "police force" is considered to be a neutral body that serves the population by performing the function of protecting its members from crime and criminals.

However, as we have seen in the previous chapter, the SQ are not neutral. We must locate it socially when it comes to its dealings with Aboriginal peoples. Members of the SQ are French and so have been raised in a culture that views the Mohawk as the "great enemy" of the classical period of New France (the seventeenth century).[5] The SQ itself has a specific colonialist history in relation to Aboriginal peoples. As I have pointed out, in 1981, 400 heavily armed SQ officers literally laid siege to the Mi'kmaq community of Restigouche in order to enforce fishing regulations (see Dickason 2002: 332). And, as we have seen in Chapter Six, they have a specific history of harsh confrontation at Kahnawake. They are generally considered to be an outsider force by members of Mohawk communities of all factions.

The SQ relationship with Aboriginal police forces can be described as colonial, arguably the worst such relationship between a provincial police agency and Aboriginal police forces in Canada (see Cummins and Steckley, 2002). The Amerindian Police Services (APS), founded in 1978, put the Aboriginal police forces newly developed in 23 First Nations communities in Quebec under the control of the SQ and the provincial government. An early review of the APS stated that the SQ was "autocratic, centralizing, and rejecting almost any consultation or discussion" (Woods and Gordon, cited in Stenning 1996: 154). Little wonder that 10 of the original 23 First Nations communities with APS policing opted out of the organization.

Despite the oppressive colonialist history between the SQ and Mohawk communities, the SQ remain almost anonymous in the introductory sociology textbooks. They are mentioned by name only once (Warme, Malus, and Lundy 1994: 205), otherwise being referred to merely as the "Quebec police" (Macionis and

Gerber 1999: 559 and 2002: 585), the "provincial police" (Spencer 1996: 378, and Teevan 1995: 371) and "the police" (Johnstone and Bauer 1998: 205).[6]

There is no mention of the historically bad relationship, documented in the previous chapter, that existed between the SQ and all three Mohawk communities, or that all three Mohawk communities had been raided by the SQ in recent times. There is no mention of the special implication of the SQ being French in terms of the long history of aggression between French and Mohawk. And there is no discussion of the notion that the SQ (and other outsider police forces) have been often used to implement the political (as opposed to strictly justice) objectives of municipal, provincial, and federal governments, all of whom had a stake in the standoff at Oka.

This lack of critique of the SQ should not be surprising. Police forces as social institutions are only lightly touched upon in introductory sociology textbooks and are rarely mentioned in the index of these books. Not surprisingly, then, there is no serious interrogation of the colonial role they play in Canadian society, both generally and specifically in policing Aboriginal peoples. One major reason for this is the way that the sociological approach or paradigm that would allow for such interrogation—the social conflict (or just conflict) approach—is applied in introductory sociology textbooks.

While there is a great deal of variation in what may be called a conflict approach, a variation that does include Marxism and anti-colonialism, recall that Hale stated:

> Textbook Marxism loses all its critical political edge to become a safe, respectable variant of functionalist conflict theory. In this "Boy Scout Marxism" conflict is an unavoidable fact of social and economic life that must be dealt with piecemeal by the capitalist welfare state. (Hale 1992: 143)

A definition that aptly reflects how the conflict paradigm is represented in introductory sociology textbooks comes from Macionis and Gerber, who write that it is:

> ... *a framework for building theory that envisions society as an arena of inequality generating conflict and change.* This approach contrasts with that of the structural-functional paradigm by highlighting not solidarity, but division based on inequality. Guided by this paradigm, sociologists investigate how factors such as social class, race, ethnicity, sex, and age are linked to unequal distribution of money, power, education, and social prestige. Conflict analysis points out that, rather than promoting the operation of society as a whole, social structure typically benefits some people while depriving others. (Macionis and Gerber 2002: 18; emphasis in original)

While a sociologist using this approach should be able to question the role of the police in their interaction with Aboriginal peoples, the writers of introductory sociology textbooks do not include such questioning. In matters of policing and justice, they are much more likely to focus primarily on class than they are to focus on the dynamics of race and ethnicity. The following is typical in that regard. Note how it identifies only wealth and power as involved in a conflict paradigm of justice:

> Conflict theorists look at power and social inequality as the primary characteristics of every society. They stress that the state's machinery of social control, which includes the *criminal justice system*—the police, courts, and prisons that deal with people who are accused of having committed crimes–represents the interests of the wealthy and powerful. (Henslin et al. 2001: 395)

When writers of introductory sociology textbooks mention race or ethnicity in the context of justice it is usually to talk only about differences in arrest rates, using a proliferation of statistics with no serious and specific critique (e.g., anti-racist or anti-colonialist). Without such specificity to demonstrate the workings of racism or colonialism, suggestions as to how things might be changed or improved are not and cannot be made.[7] In this quotation, an oppressive situation is buried in numbers without providing tools for digging up reasons:

> The conflict perspective reminds us that while the basic purpose of law may be to maintain stability and order, this can actually mean perpetuating inequality. Natives are the most overrepresented group in Canadian jails. According to a report from the Canadian Centre for Justice Statistics, from 1985 to 1990 almost 18 percent of the provincial and 8 percent of the federal prison population has been Native, although the total Native population is only 5 percent (Frideres, 1993: 214). In Ontario, Natives' rate of offending is 4.5 times greater than the rate of all ethnic groups; for liquor violations the rate is 16 times higher. Reasons given to explain the figures include culture conflict, economic inequality, and discrimination (Gomme, 1993: 186–190). Boyd (1988) notes that Natives make up 18 percent of murder victims and 28 percent of murder suspects. In addition, Hartnagel (1992) points out that Natives account for 19 percent of all sentenced admissions to provincial correctional institutions, and Kershaw and Lasovich (1991: 227) note that in a 1988 report of the Canadian Human Rights Commission, Aboriginal women are more likely to go to prison than to university.
>
> On the whole, conflict theories contend that the criminal justice system of North America treats suspects differently, on the basis of racial, ethnic, and social class backgrounds. (Schaefer et al. 1996: 117–18)

As the introductory sociology textbooks are without Aboriginal voice, and do not apply an historically based anti-colonial or anti-racist perspective, or, indeed, do not make any serious attempt to apply a conflict perspective concerning outsider policing of Aboriginal peoples, it is predictable that the oppressive and sometimes racist actions of the SQ in the Oka situation are not called into question in any of them. The actions of the SQ ought to be questioned in particular with respect to two aspects of the Oka confrontation. The first concerns both the initiation of violence by the SQ and how that violence was initiated, neither of which is adequately treated by the introductory sociology textbooks. The precipitating incident was the attack on July 11 by some 100 heavily armed SQ officers on the four-month-old peaceful blockade of a dirt road. As Frideres notes, the road in question was "an unimportant side road. When it was blocked, it inconvenienced no one except the Mohawks" (Frideres 1993: 403). Negotiations were still going on between the SQ and the women guarding the barricade when concussion grenades were detonated and gunfire was exchanged. Officially, there has been no recognition of who gave the order for the SQ to attack. No one in the upper echelon of the SQ formally authorized the assault or submitted any tactical plan for the move (as would normally be done). The head of the union of the SQ officers said that the union did not know who gave the order. In the words of an aide to Quebec Premier Robert Bourassa:

> ... what a mess! More than a hundred policemen were told to attack, and no one knew who gave the order, when they gave the order, and what the attack plan was. (Hornung 1991: 206)

The second aspect also not questioned by any of the textbook writers is the intense psychological and physical violence perpetrated by the SQ during the confrontation. This is well-documented in the non-sociological literature, by both Aboriginal and non-Aboriginal journalists (David 1992: 28–29; Cross and Sévigny 1994; Obomsawin 1993; Wagamese 1996; and York and Pindera 1991: 336). Equally necessary to discuss and equally well-documented is the brutal beating of certain targetted figures among the Mohawk Warriors on September 26, once the men, women, and children at the treatment centre had destroyed their weapons and had walked out, unarmed, to take whatever was coming to them. One of the women was stabbed with a bayonet while protecting a child (Obomsawin 1993).

On October 19, 1999, in response to an official complaint lodged by Ronald Cross, three SQ officers were suspended without pay—two for 30 days, the third for 60 days—for manhandling Cross when he was handcuffed. However, in the words of the Turtle Island Native Network[8] Web-posting on the next day, "The officers are no longer with the provincial force so the ruling carries no monetary penalty but it does go into their service record."

Four textbooks mentioned that an officer (Corporal LeMay) was killed early in the confrontation. They do so as follows:

> The most serious conflict between the Native people and the Quebecois was the "Oka crisis" of 1990. The momentum toward Quebec independence was jarred by this crisis, which began when a barricade was erected by Indians to save a sacred burial ground from destruction for a golf course. The provincial police clashed with an armed Warriors' Society, resulting in the death of a police officer. (Spencer 1996: 378)

> [A]t the Oka standoff in Quebec in the summer of 1990, social conditions such as the tension between the police and Mohawk warriors precipitated the occurrence of a hostile outburst. The expansion of a golf course from 9 to 18 holes would have encroached on sacred native land. After a police officer was killed, more than 1000 police officers converged on Oka (population 1800). (Johnstone and Bauer 1998: 52)

In July, the Sûreté du Quebec (the provincial police), called
in by the Oka mayor, attacked; in the resulting standoff one
officer was killed. (Warme, Malus, and Lundy 1994: 205)

Sometimes acts of civil disobedience become violent even
though it is not the intent of the parties involved. During
what is referred to as the Oka crisis, a police officer was
shot and killed and several people on both sides of the
blockade were injured. (Kendall et al. 2000: 647)

As can readily be seen, none of these references point out that it
was never determined whether the officer was killed by the
Mohawk Warriors or by "friendly fire." Likewise, none even
suggest that if the SQ had not attacked as they did, the officer
would not have died.

7. Downplaying Acts of Non-Aboriginal Violence

When the Mohawk blocked the Mercier Bridge, opposition grew
quickly as commuters living on the South Shore of the St.
Lawrence faced a three-hour commute in order to bypass the
barricade. The nature of the angry response reflected its multiple cause: commuter frustration, mob dynamics, and racism, but
the latter is not mentioned in the introductory sociology textbooks where the extent of the violence is also downplayed.

Crowds of as many as 4,000 people demonstrated their
anger, some yelling obscene and racist remarks. As the summer
moved into August, the non-Aboriginal protesters grew more
violent, attacking and injuring SQ officers. At nightly demonstrations, effigies of Mohawk were burned. United Nations
observers were blocked from going to Kahnawake, and journalists were threatened with violence. One night, 200 demon-
strators, protesting the arrest of one of their leaders, went to
the police station where he was held, broke windows, and
destroyed two squad cars. On August 13, more than 400 pelted

the police with rocks and metal objects and had tear gas canisters lobbed at them.

On August 28, a convoy of 75 vehicles evacuating Mohawk children, women, and elders who feared racial violence left Kahnawake. A local French radio station alerted local residents to this fact, so about 500 came out in force to impede the progress of the convoy. A group of some 20 young men threw rocks at the cars, injuring at least six Mohawk. No one was charged. Ojibwa journalist Richard Wagamese articulated the view of many Aboriginal peoples when he wrote that "the biggest criminals walked away" (Wagamese 1996: 76). That night, the people of Kahnawake voted 80 percent in favour of abandoning the bridge barricade. The next day it came down.

How was this series of events represented by introductory sociology textbooks? Five make mention of it. Not one mentioned that the bridge was on Mohawk land. Not one referred to anyone being hurt. Not one used the words "racism" or "racist" or "criminals" in the description. In the fourth and fifth examples presented below, the actions of the non-Aboriginal peoples are dismissed merely as examples of crowd or mob behaviour. The fifth example denies that any violence took place.

> Increasing their defiance, the Mohawks barricaded one end of a major bridge to the island of Montreal, cutting off a suburb and causing immense daily traffic pileups. Over the summer, the hostility of the suburb's residents increased and Mohawk vehicles were stoned crossing the bridge into the city. (Warme, Malus, and Lundy 1994: 205)

> And support came not only from other Mohawks, such as those who established another barricade on the Mercier Bridge near Montreal, but also from other Indian nations, such as the Hurons, who had fought bitterly with the Mohawks in centuries past. (Teevan 1995: 371)

> Sympathy blockades were set up by other Indians elsewhere, and angry Francophones retaliated by stoning the cars evacuating Indian children and elders. (Spencer 1996: 378)

> In July 1990, during the Oka crisis, an unexpectedly violent clash occurred between the police and 4000 residents of Quebec's South Shore when the latter came out to protest the Mohawk takeover of the Mercier Bridge into Montreal. (Macionis and Gerber 1999: 561 and 2002: 588)

> Mob behaviour in this country has included fire bombings, effigy hangings, and hate crimes. Mob violence tends to dissipate relatively quickly once a target has been injured, killed, or destroyed. Sometimes, actions such as effigy hanging are used symbolically, by groups that otherwise are not violent; for example, during the 1990 Oka crisis on the Kanehsatake reserve in Quebec local non-Aboriginal residents burned an effigy of a Mohawk to emphasize their displeasure with the blockade of the Mercier Bridge to Montreal. (Kendall et al. 2000: 643)

A few small points concerning these references should be considered here. One is the significance of Teevan's mention of the old conflict between the Huron and the Iroquois in the second example, the only reference to violence made in the quotation. It should be pointed out that that conflict ended almost 300 years before Oka (i.e., with the peace of 1701). It had all the relevance (or irrelevance) of commenting on the fact that people in the Highlands of Scotland and in the north of England both voted for the Labour party in the last British election, even though both had fought on opposing sides at Culloden during the mid 1700s (more recently than the peace of 1701).

Secondly, I question Macionis and Gerber's use of the word "unexpectedly" in describing the violence of the non-Aboriginal peoples. Only an analysis devoid of any idea of racism would present the violence as unexpected. It was certainly not unexpected by the Mohawk. Were the authors intimating that the violence was unexpected because the antagonists were non-Aboriginal peoples and not Mohawk? They did not use the word "unexpected" when referring to the actions of the Mohawk Warriors.

SOCIOLOGISTS EXPLAIN THE CONFRONTATION AT OKA
Specific Explanations

In the introduction to this chapter, the way warrior frame is used by Canadian introductory sociology textbooks to explain the Oka situation distorts and muddies the historical causes and actual events. It generally facilitates the avoidance of any analysis based on conflict theory. How is this demonstrated?

Three of the textbooks—Spencer (1996), Teevan (1995), and Warme, Malus, and Lundy (1994)—dig no deeper than to identify the immediate cause: the extension of the golf course onto the sacred burial site.

Four other sets of writers attempt to add some broader sociological explanation, but still do so in disconnected ways. Macionis and Gerber disconnect Oka from its independent historical and current existence by considering it as merely a momentarily foregrounded aspect of the more significant political context of French separatism and the Meech Lake Accord, a "social movement" of the time (Macionis and Gerber 1999: 559), seemingly without deeper cause. Tepperman and Rosenberg limit their discussion to speaking in terms of a concept—self-government—that has little explanatory value as it is not spelled out in terms of specifics of oppression and resistance:

> Many natives feel that Canadian governments have little commitment to solving their problems, and little idea of how to go about doing so. This is one of the reasons that many native people seek self-government. The blockades

Mohawk Warriors built at Oka, Quebec, in the summer of 1990, dramatized this effort. (Tepperman and Rosenberg 1998: 197; see also 1991: 172 and 1995: 163)

In their short attempt to explain Oka, Johnstone and Bauer refer to "structural conduciveness":

> Structural conduciveness refers to the basic conditions that make collective behavior possible. The right circumstances, such as structural differences in society, must be present. For example, at the Oka standoff in Quebec in the summer of 1990, social conditions such as the tension between the police and Mohawk warriors precipitated the occurrence of a hostile outburst. The expansion of a golf course from 9 to 18 holes would have encroached on sacred native land. (Johnstone and Bauer 1998: 52)

The concept of "structural conduciveness" was developed by structural functional sociologist Neil J. Smelser in his book *Theory of Collective Behavior* (1962) to explain the actions both of Americans during times of money market financial strain and of people involved with the Black civil rights movement in the 1950s and early 1960s. It is part of a larger structural functional theory sometimes referred to as "value-added theory" (Stebbins 1987: 438, and Schaefer et al. 1996: 355), reflecting its early connections with economics, and sometimes as "structural-strain" (Teevan 1988: 388). In essence, Smelser outlined several steps (initially five, later six) leading to instances of "collective behavior" (e.g., mass panic selling of assets, voting for a protest party,[9] riots). The first of these steps was structural conduciveness. By itself, it is not really an explanation, more of a necessary but not sufficient structural state. This can be seen in Metta Spencer's discussion of Smelser's value-added theory, which she refers to as possessing six "ifs":

Structural conduciveness is the first "if." It is the most general condition for collective behavior. This simply means that certain situations must exist for collective behavior to be possible. For example, there can be no panic buying or selling on the stock market and no runs on banks in a society where there is no stock market and there are no banks. Similarly, race riots can happen only where there are two or more races in the same community.... All of these conditions are obvious. They refer to the kind of situation that makes collective behavior possible but by not means necessary. (Spencer 1979: 309)

Henslin and Nelson (1996) and Henslin et al. (2001) offer relative deprivation as an explanatory tool:

relative deprivation: in this context, the belief that people join social movements based on their evaluations of what they think they should have compared with what others have. (Henslin and Nelson 1996: 623; c.f., Henslin et al. 2001: 483)

The theory of relative deprivation has a long history in the discipline of sociology. It became popularized in sociological circles by structural functional theorist Robert K. Merton in one of his major works, *Social Theory and Social Structure*, first published in 1949. Merton used it as one of his "sociological theories of the middle range"(1968: 139) in his attempts to "study the sentiments and attitudes of American soldiers [particularly Black soldiers]—their attitudes toward induction, for example, or their appraisals of chances for promotion" (Merton 1968: 283). Judging from introductory textbooks, this theory did not find a home in sociology, but in social psychology, a sub-discipline that shares some theorists and theories with sociology. In my experience, the term is rarely seen in introductory sociology textbooks (Johnstone and Bauer 1998: 218), but is commonplace in their social psychology counterparts (e.g., Moghaddam 1998: 482–84;

Neal 1983: 362–63; Sampson 1971: 142–44, 371–72; Levin and Levin 1988: 106–08 and 210; and Feldman 1998: 89–90).

Henslin and his colleagues connect Oka with relative deprivation theory in the following ways:

> Don't the thousands of African Americans who participated in the civil rights movement of the 1950s, and the Mohawk warriors who, in 1990, asserted their land claims in the 78-day "Oka Crisis," offer ample evidence that his theory is valid? (Henslin and Nelson 1996: 623)

> A second explanation to account for why people join social movements is *deprivation theory*. According to this theory, people who are deprived of things deemed valuable in society—whether money, justice, status, or privilege—join social movements in the hope of redressing their grievances. This theory may seem so obvious as to need no evidence. Aren't the Mohawk warriors who occupied their land for 78 days in what became known across Canada as "The Oka Crisis" ample evidence that the theory is true? (Henslin et al. 2001: 442)

Disconnection by Isolating Oka

One major failing of these attempts at explanation is that they do not systematically link the Oka situation to a connected flow of events and initiatives that immediately preceded and followed the confrontation and that concern the systemic racism or colonialism in the Canadian justice system toward Aboriginal peoples. Isolating Oka in this way facilitates acceptance of the "causation-of-the-sociological-moment" and superficial explanations (as opposed to explanations that go deeper in time and wider into the systemic racist structure of justice).

Just before Oka was the Hickman Inquiry into the handling of the Donald Marshall case (see Appendix F). This inquiry, the results of which were released early in 1990, successfully brought to light the racism of the justice system in Nova Scotia. While the Donald Marshall case is mentioned in two textbooks, neither links the case with Oka. Similarly absent is reference to the cases of J.J. Harper (see Appendix G) and Helen Betty Osborne (see Appendix H), both of which led to the writing of briskly selling books by journalists and to the influential Manitoba Justice Inquiry, undertaken in 1988 and 1989.

To a large extent because of the Hickman Inquiry, the Manitoba Justice Inquiry, and the Oka confrontation, two major federal initiatives were launched. The first was the Royal Commission on Aboriginal People (RCAP), in 1991, but whose report was not completed until 1996. It was the most expensive royal commission in Canadian history, costing some $58 million. The 3,537-page report with its 440 specific recommendations is a necessary source for anyone writing about Aboriginal issues. Of the 14 textbooks, only Tepperman and Rosenberg (1998: 198–99) make brief mention of it. To their credit, they do make the connection between the RCAP and Oka. All the other books are silent on the subject.

The second federal initiative flowing from Oka that should have made sociological news was the First Nations Policing Policy of 1991, the goal of which was "to provide First Nations across Canada with access to police services that are professional, culturally appropriate, and accountable to the communities they serve" (as quoted in Steckley and Cummins 2001: 221). This has dramatically changed the face of policing in Aboriginal communities. By 2000, there were 49 First Nations Self-Administered Police Services, providing service to 184 of the more than 600 recognized First Nations bands in Canada. No mention of this development is made in any of the introductory sociology textbooks that make reference to Oka.

SUMMARY

In this chapter, I have looked mainly at how the 14 of 25 Canadian introductory sociology textbooks studied that mention Oka employ the "warrior frame" to portray that situation. I argued that this warrior frame is a sociological simulacrum that erases Aboriginal voice and the framing of Oka in any way that reflects Aboriginal knowledge production. In so doing, it renders inadequate any sociological attempt at explanation.

NOTES

1   This is the first, and, so far, most successful of four videos that Obomsawin has put together about Oka. The others are "My Name is Kahentiiosta" (1995), "Spudwrench: Kahnawake Man" (1997), and "Rocks at Whiskey Trench" (2001).

2   He states that "Much of this account is from K. Hughes, *The Summer of 1990*, Fifth Report of the Standing Committee on Aboriginal Affairs, 1991." The bias of this source can be seen in the fact that permission was granted from the Government of Canada, far from a neutral player in this matter.

3   The federal public relations budget for overseas consumption was rumoured at the time as being about $12 million.

4   It is hard to say exactly why they were excluded. It could be that they were not the "squeaky wheel" of violence the Mohawk Warriors were, or because they had not been represented at the barricade from the beginning, or because, with all the shifts in chiefs and council that had taken place prior to the confrontation, their leadership was suspect both in the community and outside of it.

5   As mentioned above, this aspect of the historiography of seventeenth-century New France was replicated recently in the CBC series, "Canada: A People's History."

6   My impression is that, as in the introductory sociology textbooks, the more anonymous the naming of the SQ, the more anti-Mohawk the presentation of the Oka confrontation.

7   The one exception to this that I have discovered is with use of David Stymeist's 1975 study (see Chapter One) and that merely presents Aboriginal peoples as no more than victims, possessing no agency, no capacity to deal with racism.

8   The website is www.turtleisland.org.

9   Structural conduciveness was part of Maurice Pinard's explanation of why in the 1962 federal election, 25.9 percent of the popular vote in Quebec went to the Social Credit Party (Pinard 1971).

Six Concluding Questions

CHAPTER EIGHT

I. How do you know that textbooks are wrong when they talk about Indians?

In October 1989, I went on a four-day lecture tour of rural Virginia, giving lectures at the sponsoring institution of Southwestern Virginia Community College and nearby primary, middle, and secondary schools. I was treated with a gracious kindness that was my first experience of the justly famed "southern hospitality." I must have surprised my hosts, then, when, in giving the first (and still the only) after-dinner speech of my life I was somewhat aggressive in my condemnation of the representation of Aboriginal history in the area. My first targets were the plaques headed by the line "Indian Outrage." I said that if I were to be seconded to the college there for a year (then being considered), I would put up homemade signs saying "White Man Outrage" beside each one of those plaques. I continued by saying there would be no great loss if early history textbooks were all mysteriously burned. After a series of comments of this type, I was asked, politely, a question for which I did not have a good answer at that time: "How do you know that textbooks are wrong when they talk about Indians?" This project is the first decent response I have given to that question.

2. HOW DID I LEARN TO DISTRUST TEXTBOOKS WHEN THEY TALK ABOUT ABORIGINAL PEOPLES?

It was easy for me to develop a healthy suspicion concerning traditional textbook teachings by Euroamericans concerning Aboriginal culture and history. Not long after I began my study of Aboriginal languages in 1973, I discovered that what was traditionally taught about Aboriginal-based place names was often wrong. My first lesson was my work on the name "Toronto." It comes from a Mohawk word (something like *tkaronto*) meaning "trees or poles in water," referring to a fish weir first constructed more than 4,000 years ago.[1] And yet, most tourism websites I checked on March 24, 2003, the federal Department of Indian Affairs website, and the Ontario Ministry of Education (according to the Grade 6 teachers to whom I have talked) still reproduce the incorrect statement that it comes from a Huron term meaning "meeting place." This is no more true than the romantic "Thunder of Waters" interpretation for the Neutral name "Niagara,"[2] or that words such as these are translated from "the Indian language."

This distrust of textbook traditions on Aboriginal peoples has been reinforced in many ways over the last 30 years. Two years prior to working on the thesis that became this book, I wrote a book of the biographies of five historical Aboriginal women I had long admired (Steckley 1999). One of the biographies was that of Thanadelthur, a young Chipewyan woman of the early eighteenth century who, more than any other person, was instrumental in connecting her people to the fur trade and achieving peace with the Cree in so doing. I wondered how a young woman of such a dynamic nature could have been raised in a culture that all of my early reading told me assigned to women a lowly status earning no respect.[3] Diamond Jenness, in his very influential *Indians of Canada*[4] stated that Chipewyan women "ranked lower than in any other tribe" (Jenness 1932: 386). Wendell H. Oswalt, in the long chapter on the Chipewyan in his popular work *This Land Was Theirs* wrote, "Females were subordinated to men in every way, and the men were oppressive. Women were treated cruelly and held in gross contempt by the men" (Oswalt 1966: 27).

The incorrect perception of Thanadelthur came from Simon Hearne's well-known published account of his travels through the far north from 1769 to 1772. Hearne was a good writer and a keen observer, but his main source of information about Chipewyan women was Matonabbee, a prominent Chipewyan trader who, along with his followers, accompanied Hearne on his travels. Matonabbee's often-quoted and misleading statement about women in his culture has done much damage in outsider perception of the historic role of those women:

> Women ... were made for labour, one of them can carry, or haul, as much as two men can do. They also pitch our tents, make and mend our clothing, keep us warm at night; and in fact, there is no such thing as travelling any considerable distance, or for any length of time, in this country, without their assistance. Women ... though they do everything, are maintained at a trifling expence [sic] for as they always stand cook, the very licking of their fingers in scarce times, is sufficient for their subsistence. (Hearne 1968:35)

Matonabbee was more a "trading-post Indian" than he was a man who reflected the teachings of his people. He was born and raised at a trading post and had earned the outsider-determined status of what the Hudson's Bay Company called the "leading Indian" of the Chipewyan, as he brought in through various means, both fair and foul, more furs in trade than any of his countrymen. He acquired seven wives, whom he ruthlessly exploited. His upbringing, standing, authority, and sense of self came primarily from the HBC, not from the Chipewyan. And yet, he is the single most influential source of (mis)information on traditional Chipewyan female gender roles.

3. CAN THIS STUDY BE REPLICATED WITH OTHER ISSUES?

The issues studied here were chosen because they stood most prominently at the crossroads of my particular paths of expertise and interests. All involved lessons I had taught (in two cases in part mistakenly) and in one case had written about. Other scholars with different backgrounds and interests can find other elements just as salient. Clearly, I have come nowhere close to exhausting the issues that may be chosen to illustrate my basic points.

Of course, an intersecting feminist/Aboriginal perspective may be applied as well. The introductory sociology textbooks are ripe for that. This is particularly true for the indigenous project that Tuhiwai Smith referred to as "gendering," which entails recognizing how colonial forces have negatively affected relationships between the genders. There is a definite opportunity for recognition of gendering of Aboriginal peoples in Canadian introductory sociology textbooks, but that opportunity is all but completely missed.

While I do not feel completely capable of developing a thorough intersecting feminist/Aboriginal approach, I can outline some of the elements it might contain. The Indian Act historically discriminated against Aboriginal women in several ways. Until 1951, they were not allowed to vote in band elections; this is in stark contrast to the role that women played in some cultures in signing treaties.[5] According to Section 12 (1) (b) of the Indian Act, set in place in 1876, a woman who had status as an "Indian" lost that status if she married a man who did not have status (even if he were of an Aboriginal background). Her children likewise would not have status. However, the children of White women who married status Indian men would have status. Similarly, upon marriage, a woman lost her band status and became a member of her husband's band (if it were different from hers). This was only changed in 1985, after a series of long, dragged-out court cases beginning in 1970 that divided fundamentally along gender faultlines a good number of Aboriginal communities.

This provision did not reflect traditional Aboriginal practices in Canada, where, it could easily be argued, there was greater equality of the sexes than was the case in the European countries from which the colonial governments came.[6]

Despite its significance to Aboriginal peoples, and for reasons both discussed and not mentioned here (such as the patriarchal perspective they reflect), the gendering effect of the Indian Act is not discussed in Canadian introductory sociology textbooks, even in those few instances in which the discriminatory provision is mentioned. For example, in an early textbook written by Forcese and Richer (two male sociologists), we read:

> We point out only that the prevailing opinion among status Indian spokesmen is that the patrilineal rule should remain in force, providing a simple way of controlling entry into group membership and a way of restricting that membership. Anthropologists have frequently pointed out the function of unilineal descent[7] (tracing through one line for social purposes) in sorting people out into discrete segments. (Forcese and Richer 1975: 196)

Significantly, the authors failed to identify the fact that, at that point in time, almost all "status Indian spokesmen" were just that: spokes*men*. They spoke for a male power that had been given an exaggerated strength by the patriarchal provisions of the Indian Act.

Of course there are other fruitful lines that may be pursued. I barely dealt with issues concerning the Métis experience in Canada and how that has been treated in Canadian introductory sociology textbooks. It would not take much work to develop at least one chapter on that subject. Likewise, I did not discuss residential schools or treaties, both potential sources for insightful chapters.

4. IS IT ONLY INTRODUCTORY SOCIOLOGY TEXT-BOOKS THAT CAN BE STUDIED IN THIS WAY?

The discipline of my first two degrees, anthropology, errs in similar ways to sociology, as was pointed out in earlier chapters of this book.[8] Perhaps, even, it is somewhat more sinister when these flaws appear in anthropology textbooks, as the discipline makes claim to the inclusion of the voice of the peoples studied. Traditional Canadian history textbooks may also be analysed in similar ways. The "Mi'kmaq Mercenary Myth," referred to in Chapter One (see also the first chapter in Steckley 1999), could be one aspect of this study. Introductory books in psychology and Canadian political science similarly are worth studying. One point of entry for the latter would be to ascertain the presence or absence of a discussion of the Great Law of Peace. My argument for its inclusion in a Canadian book is that the Peacemaker was a Canadian.

5. CAN A FORMULA BE TAKEN FROM THIS STUDY AND APPLIED ELSEWHERE?

I was asked in my thesis defence whether there was a formula that would come from this study that could be used outside the study of Aboriginal peoples. I hesitated, in part because of my distrust of such formulas and because of my love for detailed, highly specific work that reveals the flaws in traditional interpretations and illustrates that traditional interpretations presented in textbooks should be challenged before they are accepted. This latter love I had encouraged by reading similar writings in the tradition of the textbook history of biology in the work of the, sadly, recently deceased Stephen J. Gould, the Harvard-based evolutionary biologist and prolific and elegant popularizer of science.

Another significant reason why I balk at proposing such a formula is that I feel that I would be stepping beyond my "truth" in so doing. My 30 years of experience in Aboriginal studies are not as reliable in providing insights into Latino/Hispanic, African American, or feminist studies. My hesitancy here was generously described by an Aboriginal member of my committee as talking like an elder in restricting my truth to my own direct experience.

6. WHERE DO WE GO FROM HERE?

Where does this lead us? As we saw in the introduction and literature review, Sylvia Hale (1992) called for a greater variety of theory in introductory sociology textbooks than the three essentialized and canonized paradigms of functionalism, conflict theory, and symbolic interactionism, especially as the latter two seem to be operating to serve functionalism in their interpretation. Dorothy Smith rightfully made the case that sociology reflects a standpoint, so it must seek a broader set of standpoints. In her case, the argument was for a feminist standpoint (and not what Sylvia Hale cleverly terms "Girl Scout feminism"). Here, I am arguing that, for Canadian introductory sociology textbooks to present information about Aboriginal peoples in a way that is worthy of the best aims and works of the discipline, the writers must engage in what can be called "Aboriginal sociology."

What should this Aboriginal sociology entail? It begins with the recognition of the inadequacy of the traditional methods of knowledge production of sociology to speak about Aboriginal peoples. It continues with the perception that Canadian introductory sociology textbooks regularly reproduce simulacra and that these are, by their very nature, connected both with the source and methods of knowledge production and with a complicity with colonialist governmental practices past and present. Finally, if the writers of these textbooks continue to ignore Aboriginal voice in their knowledge production, they will continue to produce simulacra such as these and will continue to be complicit in the colonialist practices of governments in so doing. They are not being neutral, objective, or distanced. They are taking a side.

Aboriginal sociology also involves recognition of the validity and crucial importance of Indigenous research projects, as outlined by Tuhiwai Smith, especially those of celebrating survival, remembering, reading, reframing, and democratizing. Implied and involved with this is the realization that the non-Aboriginal cultural background of the writers of introductory sociology textbooks entails a limited standpoint, as Dorothy Smith (1990) informs us, that will miss core concepts that are intrinsically important to understanding Aboriginal peoples from an Aboriginal standpoint. As suggested in Chapter Three, the significance of elders is one of these core concepts, as they are involved with all the social institutions of Aboriginal life—education, justice, religion, and politics, for example. Anyone in any way involved with Aboriginal culture is aware of their significance; however, to people coming from other cultures where the elders' role is diminished, they could miss, and have missed, this important point.

Spirituality is another such core concept, one that has been erased in all four simulacra discussed in this thesis. The reserve is a spiritual centre, often (one can probably say usually) the location of a number of sacred sites of significance. As we have seen, part of the inadequacy of the simulacra of the potlatch is the inability of the sociological writers to report on the important spiritual aspects of the ceremony. Part of the blindness of the CDIES simulacrum is lack of recognition of the importance of the spiritual knowledge and wisdom of the Inuit elders. And the sociological representation of the Oka situation fails to involve a discussion of the Great Law, which is interwoven with spirituality and may be considered unimportant by sociological writers as it is "just a myth." As with the elders, spirituality is part of all the social institutions of Aboriginal life.

More generally, the development of an Aboriginal sociology entails recognizing that non-sociologists have authority in talking about Aboriginal life. There are very few Aboriginal sociologists, something that the discipline should note and rectify. For the Aboriginal standpoint to be represented, the knowledge production of Aboriginal journalists, educators, film-makers, elders, and literary writers should be respected. All of them have voices considered important in Aboriginal society. That alone should guarantee their inclusion in introductory sociology textbooks.

In my first year of university, sociology opened my eyes to a world of understanding that changed my perception forever. Every semester I teach introductory sociology, I tell my students that my goal in teaching them the course is to change how they think. I quote, with pride, a former sociology student of mine, a Brazilian nun, who said that my course had "ruined her" in terms of her previous perception of society. I am a believer in the discipline. I would not teach the subject if I weren't. But I strongly believe that it needs to change its textual presentation of Aboriginal peoples (and I suspect other non-mainstream groups) in ways as radical as how the discipline itself altered my viewpoint. Anything less is to allow Canadian introductory sociology textbooks to fail Aboriginal peoples and to fail the students who read them.

Notes

1   Steckley 1992b.
2   Steckley 1992a.
3   This insight is not, by any means, unique to me. Henry S. Sharp, an anthropologist who has studied and worked with the Chipewyan for many years, stated: "[A]fter more than twenty-five years of fieldwork, ... I have never been able to reconcile the harshness of the images of Chipewyan gender relations presented in the historical record with the nature of gender relations that I have observed among contemporary Chipewyan" (Sharp 1995: 61).
4   Although flawed when it was written in 1932, this book went through six more, unchanged, editions, the last in 1989.
5   When, for example, on May 22, 1784, the Mississauga signed away a large tract of land in southwestern Ontario, the signatories included the "Sachems" (peace chiefs), the "War Chiefs," and the "Principal Women" of that nation.
6   One small indicator of that is that of the approximately 56 Aboriginal societies in Canada today, 14 or one-quarter had a tradition of being matrilineal, determining kinship along the female side.
7   This is not a strictly appropriate invocation of this anthropological principle, as not all Aboriginal groups were unilineal, and as a good number were matrilineal (see the previous note).

8   In Chapter Four on culturally determined Inuit elder suicide, one example was given
     from Ferraro 1995: 24–25. In Chapter Five on the potlatch, reference was given to
     Spradley and McCurdy 1997: 165.

Appendices

Appendix A:
Canadian Introductory Sociology Textbooks Analysed in the Study

Anderson, Karen L. 1996. *Sociology: A Critical Introduction.* Scarborough, ON: Nelson.

Bailey, Gordon, and Noga Gayle. 1993. *Sociology: An Introduction; From the Classics to Contemporary Feminism.* Toronto, ON: Oxford University Press.

Blishen, Bernard, Frank E. Jones, Kaspar D. Naegele, and John Porter (Eds.). 1961, 1964, 1968, and 1971. *Canadian Society: Sociological Perspectives.* Toronto, ON: Macmillan of Canada.

Bolaria, B. Singh (Ed.). 1991. *Social Issues and Contradictions in Canadian Society.* Toronto, ON: Harcourt, Brace, Jovanovich.

Boydell, Craig, Carl F. Grindstaff, and Paul C. Whitehead (Eds.). 1971. *Critical Issues in Canadian Society.* Toronto, ON: Holt, Rinehart and Winston.

Brym, Robert. 2001. *New Society: Sociology for the 21st Century*, 3rd ed. Toronto, ON: Harcourt Canada.

Clark, S.D. 1976. *Canadian Society in Historical Perspective*. Toronto, ON: McGraw-Hill Ryerson.

Crysdale, Stewart, and Christopher Beattie. 1973 and 1977. *Sociology Canada: An Introductory Text*. Toronto, ON: Butterworth.

_____. (Eds.). 1974 and 1977. *Sociology Canada: Readings*. Toronto, ON: Butterworth and Company.

Curtis, James, and Lorne Tepperman (Eds.). 1990. *Images of Canada: The Sociological Tradition*. Scarborough, ON: Prentice Hall.

Forcese, Dennis, and Stephen Richer. 1975. *Issues in Canadian Society: An Introduction to Sociology*. Scarborough, ON: Prentice Hall.

_____. 1982 and 1988. *Social Issues: Sociological Views of Canada*. Scarborough, ON: Prentice Hall.

Fry, John A. (Ed.). 1984. *Contradictions in Canadian Society: Readings in Introductory Sociology*. Toronto, ON: John Wiley & Sons.

Gallagher, James E., and Ronald D. Lambert (Eds.). 1971. *Social Process and Institution: The Canadian Case*. Toronto, ON: Holt, Rinehart and Winston.

Grayson, J. Paul (Ed.). 1983. *Introduction to Sociology: An Alternate Approach*. Toronto, ON: Gage Publishing.

Hagedorn, Robert (Ed.). 1980, 1983a, and 1986. *Sociology*. Toronto, ON: Holt, Rinehart and Winston.

_____. 1983b. *Essentials of Sociology*. Toronto, ON: Holt, Rinehart and Winston.

Henslin, James, and Adie Nelson. 1996. *Sociology: Canadian Edition: A Down-to-Earth Approach*. Toronto, ON: Allyn and Bacon.

Henslin, James, Dan Glenday, Ann Duffy, and Norene Pupo. 2001. *Sociology: Canadian Edition: A Down-to-Earth Approach*, 2nd ed. Toronto, ON: Allyn and Bacon.

Hiller, Harry H. 1976. *Canadian Society: A Sociological Analysis*. Scarborough, ON: Prentice Hall.

Himelfarb, Alexander, and C. James Richardson. 1979. *People, Power and Process: Sociology for Canadians*. Toronto, ON: McGraw-Hill Ryerson.

_____. 1982 and 1991. *Sociology for Canadians: Images of Society.* Toronto, ON: McGraw-Hill Ryerson.

_____. 1984 and 1992. *Sociology for Canadians: A Reader.* Toronto, ON: McGraw-Hill Ryerson.

Holmes, Richard (Ed.). 1988. *Fundamentals of Sociology.* Toronto, ON: Holt, Rinehart and Winston.

Ishwaran, K. (Ed.). 1986. *Sociology: An Introduction.* Toronto, ON: Addison-Wesley.

Johnstone, Geoffrey, and Kathryn Bauer. 1998. *Sociology and Canadian Society.* Toronto, ON: Emond Montgomery.

Kendall, Diana, Rick Linden, and Jane Lothian Murray. 1998 and 2000. *Sociology in Our Times: The Essentials,* Canadian ed. Scarborough, ON: Nelson.

Knuttila, Murray. 1993. *Sociology Revisited: Basic Concepts and Perspectives.* Toronto, ON: McClelland & Stewart.

Laskin, Richard. 1964. *Social Problems: A Canadian Profile.* Toronto, ON: McGraw-Hill Ryerson.

Lundy, Katherina, and Barbara Warme. 1986 and 1990. *Sociology: A Window on the World.* Toronto, ON: Methuen.

Macionis, John, Juanne Nancarrow Clarke, and Linda Gerber. 1994. *Sociology: Canadian Edition.* Scarborough, ON: Prentice Hall.

Macionis, John, and Linda Gerber. 1999 and 2002. *Sociology: Canadian Edition.* Scarborough, ON: Prentice Hall.

Macionis, John, S. Mikael Jansson, and Celia M. Benoit. 2002. *Sociology: The Basics.* Scarborough, ON: Prentice Hall.

Mann, W.E. (Ed.). 1968. *Canada: A Sociological Profile.* Toronto, ON: Copp Clark.

Mann, W.E., and Les Wheatcroft. (Eds.). 1976. *Canada: A Sociological Profile.* 3rd ed. Toronto, ON: Copp Clark.

Mansfield, Nick. 1982. *Introductory Sociology: Canadian Perspectives.* Don Mills, ON: Collier Macmillan.

Ramu, G.N., and Stuart M. Johnson. 1976. *Introduction to Canadian Society: Sociological Analysis.* Toronto, ON: Macmillan.

Richardson, R.J., and Lorne Tepperman (Eds.). 1987. *An Introduction to the Social World.* Toronto, ON: McGraw-Hill Ryerson.

Rosenberg, M. Michael, William Shaffir, Allan Turowetz, and Morton Weinfeld. 1983. *An Introduction to Sociology*. Toronto, ON: Methuen.

Rossides, Daniel W. 1968. *Society as a Functional Process: An Introduction to Sociology*. Toronto, ON: McGraw-Hill Ryerson.

Schaefer, Richard T., Robert P. Lamm, Penny Biles, and Susannah J. Wilson. 1996. *Sociology: An Introduction: First Canadian Edition*. Toronto, ON: McGraw-Hill Ryerson.

Spencer, Metta. 1976, 1979, 1981, 1982, 1985, 1990, 1993, and 1996. *Foundations of Modern Sociology*, Canadian edition. Scarborough, ON: Prentice Hall.

Stebbins, Robert A. 1987. *Sociology: The Study of Society*. New York, NY: Harper and Row.

Teevan, James. 1982a, 1987, 1989, and 1995. *Basic Sociology: A Canadian Introduction*. Scarborough, ON: Prentice Hall.

_____.1982b, 1986, 1988, and 1992. *Introduction to Sociology: A Canadian Focus*. Scarborough, ON: Prentice Hall.

Tepperman, Lorne, and James Curtis (Eds.). 1987. *Readings in Sociology: An Introduction*. Toronto, ON: McGraw-Hill Ryerson.

Tepperman, Lorne, and M. Rosenberg. 1991, 1995, and 1998. *Macro/Micro: A Brief Introduction to Sociology*. Scarborough, ON: Prentice Hall.

Warme, Barbara, Elinor Malus, and Katherina Lundy. 1994. *Sociology: A Window on the World*. Toronto, ON: Methuen.

Westhues, Kenneth. 1982. *First Sociology*. Toronto, ON: McGraw-Hill Ryerson.

Zeitlin, Irving M., with Robert J. Brym. 1991. *The Social Condition of Humanity: Canadian Edition*. Toronto, ON: Oxford University Press.

APPENDIX B:
The Chilcotin War

The atmosphere in British Columbia surrounding the move toward banning the potlatch is not easily expressed in only a few words. It can be illustrated through telling a story of what came to be known in the history books as "The Chilcotin War." The name itself tells a story. The Chilcotin are an Athabaskan-speaking First Nation that today numbers somewhat less than 2,000 people, slightly less than their estimated population at first contact. The Chilcotin had been fundamentally untouched by European contact until 1862, when the Gold Rush and small pox hit them hard.

Their land was being encroached upon, although the Chief Commissioner of Lands and Works in British Columbia did not feel that the colony needed to purchase the land through treaty, as would be done from 1850 to 1921 in Ontario, Manitoba, Saskatchewan, and Alberta.

Any feelings that the Chilcotin had that they were being pushed off their land with no compensation were exacerbated in 1863 when Alfred Waddington began to construct a road through the heart of their territory. The road crew hired Chilcotin to work for them and treated them poorly. Promissory notes were issued instead of pay, and the people had little access to food.

In the spring of 1864, a road crew foreman named Brewster accused half-starved Chilcotin workers of stealing flour. He took down their names and issued a prediction that they would die of smallpox. To the Chilcotin, that probably sounded like a threat that he would deliberately spread the disease. On April 29, three Chilcotin went to the man who operated a ferry, asking him to share food with them. In their culture, if someone had food, it would be shared with those who had not. The ferry man apparently refused. He was killed, and the food was taken.

The three Chilcotin went to the road crew that night to talk to 16 Chilcotin who worked with 12 White men. They were persuaded to attack the White men, their food situation and the White incursion onto their land probably being the main factors in their decision. They killed nine of the road crew; three escaped. Further down the road was the hated Brewster and three others. They were soon killed also.

The Chilcotin met up with a respected older leader of their people, Telloot, and their numbers grew to about 30. They later killed a White settler who, like Brewster, had apparently threatened them with smallpox and had earlier driven them off a traditional campsite, claiming it as his own.

When the newspaper editors in Victoria found out what was going on, their reports were predictably one-sided, calling for vengeance. The editor of the *British Colonist* said that White colonists should not rest until "every member of that rascally murderous tribe is suspended from the trees of their own forest." Governor Seymour organized two parties to go to Chilcotin country, one under a man named Cox that included about 50 men, mostly Americans in the area looking to find gold. A Chilcotin leader, known as Chief Alexis, who had not been involved with the action, was sent to Seymour to bring a message from the two leaders of the "uprising," Telloot and Klatsassin. They offered to cease hostilities and give themselves up. According to the Chilcotin, Cox said that he would guarantee the Chilcotin safety if they came peacefully to a meeting arranged for August 11. Telloot, Klatsassin, and six others accompanied Chief Alexis in good faith. Cox apparently broke his word, surrounding them with his men, and commanding them to lay down their weapons and surrender. Telloot is reputed to have smashed his rifle against a tree, declaring "King George men [i.e., the British] are all great liars."

Two Chilcotin were freed with no charges laid, and one escaped. Five were convicted— Telloot, Klatsassin, his 18-year-old son, and two others. In September, they were hanged in front of an audience of about 200. All told, 20 White men had been killed, but the death toll for the Chilcotin was not written down.

If it had been, then in the record might be included those Chilcotin who died of starvation in the winter of 1864–65, driven out of their homeland by the disruption of the events.

In 1993, the BC Attorney-General Colin Gabermann apologized to the Chilcotin for the execution of the five, rightly calling the hangings a tragedy.

Appendix C:
The Sundance

The Okan (in Blackfoot, "ceremonial pole") or Sundance was the main ceremony of the people of the Prairies. It was initiated, sponsored, and presided over by a woman of significance:

> The decision to hold a Sun Dance was made by a pure woman—i.e., a virgin or faithful wife—who had a male relative in danger of losing his life. A husband might be ill or a son may not have returned from a raid. The woman made a public vow that if the person's life was spared, she would sponsor a Sun Dance. Then, if her prayer was answered, she began preparations for the summer festival. (Dempsey 1995: 392)

Sometimes, as a spiritual offering, young men inserted leather thongs through their chest or back muscles, the other end of the thong attached either to a pole or to a buffalo skull. They would dance until the thongs ripped free. This was one reason given by the federal government of Canada when it banned the Sundance in 1895. The following is a response by an anonymous Blackfoot:

> We know that there is nothing injurious to our people in the Sun-dance.... It has been our custom, during many years, to assemble once every summer for this festival.... We fast and pray, that we may be able to lead good lives and to act more kindly towards each other.
>
> I do not understand why the white men desire to put an end to our religious ceremonials. What harm can they do our people? If they deprive us of our religion, we will have nothing left, for we know of no other that can take its place. (Nabokov 1991: 225)

(Adapted from Steckley and Cummins 2001: 93)

APPENDIX D:
The Pass System

The pass system, introduced by General Middleton in 1885 during the second Riel resistance, forbade Aboriginal peoples in the Prairies from leaving their reserves without first obtaining a pass that would permit them to do so. Its purpose was to control Aboriginal peoples, particularly the Plains Cree and the Blackfoot, so that they would not join the Métis in their fight. In 1886, books of passes were issued. In order for Aboriginal peoples to obtain a pass, they had to get permission from their farming instructor. The police enforced this rule, even though in 1892 government lawyers made it known that the system was illegal. Neither the Indian Act nor any other legislation allowed the Department of Indian Affairs to institute such a system. The North-West Mounted Police (NWMP) temporarily stopped trying to enforce it, but there were howls of public protest and statements of outrage from non-Aboriginals. During the period of non-enforcement, the restriction of food rations was the sole means of forcing people to stay on the reserves.

The NWMP returned to applying the rule, even though they, as well as some Aboriginal peoples, were aware of its illegality. As Aboriginal peoples were not permitted at that time to become lawyers, they could not fight it in the courts. The system continued until the 1930s.

(Adapted from Steckley and Cummins 2001: 218–19)

APPENDIX E:
Wampum 81 of the Great Law

When the men of the Five Nations, now called forth to become warriors, are ready for battle with an obstinate opposing nation that has refused to accept the Great Peace, then one of the five War Chiefs shall be chosen by the warriors of the Five Nations to lead the army into battle. It shall be the duty of the War Chief so chosen to come before his warriors and address them. His aim shall be to impress upon them the necessity of good behavior and strict obedience to all the commands of the War Chiefs. He shall deliver an oration exhorting them with great zeal to be brave and courageous and never to be guilty of cowardice. At the conclusion of his oration he shall march forward and commence the War Song and he shall sing:

> Now I am greatly surprised
> And, therefore I shall use it—
> The power of my War Song.
> I am of the Five Nations
> And I shall make supplication
> To the Almighty Creator.
> He had furnished this army.
> My warriors shall be mighty
> In the strength of the Creator.
> Between him and my song they are
> For it was he who gave the song
> This war song that I sing!

(From www.constitution.org/cons/iroquois)

Appendix F:
The Donald Marshall Case

On May 28, 1971, 17-year-old Donald Marshall, Jr., a Mi'kmaq (and son of a chief), along with a friend of his, Sandy Seale, were walking through a park in Sydney, Nova Scotia. They spotted two White men in the park and decided to ask them for some money. This led to a scuffle in which Seale was stabbed to death by one of the men, Roy Ebsary, who was carrying a large knife. There were no witnesses to the murder, other than the three who had been directly involved.

Marshall was quickly named the prime suspect. Three teenagers who had been in the area, but who had not witnessed the stabbing, gave their testimony to the police concerning the little they knew. Gradually, they were coerced by Detective Sergeant John MacIntyre into implicating Marshall with stories that became the same tall tale. One of the teenagers, a 14-year-old, eventually testified that he had been threatened with a jail sentence if he did not tell the story MacIntyre wanted to hear. In the trial that followed that November, the prosecutor, violating the ethics but not the letter of the law of his profession, refused to let the defence see the original versions of the teenagers' testimony. Marshall was convicted of murder by a jury of 12 White men. The judge sentenced him to life. MacIntyre became Chief of Police of the Sydney force in 1976.

Ten days later, Jimmy MacNeill, who had been Ebsary's companion on the night of the stabbing, went to the Sydney police to tell them that Ebsary had committed the act. His description of the killer matched that which Marshall had given during the trial. The police questioned Ebsary (who had been charged less than a year before with the possession of an offensive weapon—a knife), but accepted his denials as a comfortable truth.

Eleven years later, a man came forward to say that when he had lived in Ebsary's house, he had heard the man brag of killing someone in 1971. He knew Marshall, so he visited him in prison. They contacted Marshall's lawyer, and the RCMP reopened the case in 1982, assigning Harry Wheaton, the plain-clothes coordinator of the RCMP in Sydney, to the investigation. Wheaton, and his investigative partner, Corporal Jim Carroll, had to be especially diligent in pursuing this case, as the file the Sydney police gave them initially did not contain all the items it should have (e.g., Jimmy MacNeill's statement of Ebsary's guilt). Their diligence was rewarded as they eventually spoke to the three key witnesses, who admitted that they had lied in their coached official statements to the Sydney police.

The case went to the Nova Scotia Court of Appeal in the spring of 1982. While the Crown prosecutor acknowledged that the Mi'kmaq man should be acquitted, he also asked the five judges involved to exonerate the criminal justice system of any blame on the grounds that its reputation must be upheld: "It seems reasonable to assume that the public will suspect that there is something wrong with the system if a man can be convicted of a murder he did not commit" (York 1990: 161–62). The judges accepted this position, and despite the fact that they acquitted Marshall in 1983, they blamed him more than the system for the lack of justice he received. They felt that he had initiated the series of actions that led to his conviction and that in the trial he had been "evasive" in his answers. A later report (the Hickman Report, see below) condemned the actions and words of the Nova Scotia Court of Appeal as amounting to "a defence of the criminal justice system at Marshall's expense, notwithstanding overwhelming evidence to the contrary" (as quoted in Harris 1990: 408–09).

RCMP investigator Wheaton was appalled by the cavalier attitude of senior officials of the Nova Scotia justice system during and immediately after the successful appeal, as can be seen in his reaction to a speech by the most senior such official at the time:

> The Attorney General of Nova Scotia came to our annual
> officers' mess dinner and said that he didn't understand

why the press was making all the fuss over the Marshall case. I had to be restrained from leaving the room in the middle of his speech. The man simply didn't realize the suffering and heartache involved in this thing, nor the immense social issues that are still at play. I just couldn't stomach the trivializing of a case that changed so many people's lives and my whole outlook as a policeman. (Harris 1990: 402–03)

Fortunately, the matter did not end with the appeal. A two-year Royal Commission (the Hickman Commission) followed. It revealed the deep anti-Mi'kmaq prejudice embedded in every aspect of the justice system in Nova Scotia. It was learned, for example, that Sydney police officers often referred to Mi'kmaq as "broken arrows" and "wagon burners." No Mi'kmaq to that point had ever been a police officer or even a member of a jury in Sydney. In the words of the three non-Nova Scotian (one from Quebec, one from Ontario and one from Newfoundland) senior justice officials who released their seven-volume report on January 26, 1990:

> The criminal justice system failed Donald Marshall, Jr. at virtually every turn from his arrest and wrongful conviction for murder in 1971 up to, and even beyond, his acquittal by the Court of Appeal in 1983. The tragedy of the failure is compounded by evidence that this miscarriage of justice could—and should—have been prevented, or at least corrected quickly, if those had carried out their duties in a professional and/or competent manner. That they did not is due, in part, to the fact that Donald Marshall, Jr. is a Native (as quoted in Harris 1990: 407).

Shortly after the release of the Hickman Report, Nova Scotia's Attorney General apologized to Marshall and his family, saying, "The justice system failed Donald Marshall, Jr. and I accept that one of the reasons he was wrongfully convicted and imprisoned was that he is a Native" (Harris 1990: 410).

(Adapted from Cummins and Steckley 2002)

APPENDIX G:
The J.J. Harper Case

In 1988, there were between 40,000 and 50,000 Aboriginal peoples living in the city of Winnipeg (Frideres 1998: 241). The 1,140-member police force had nine Aboriginal constables at that time.

At roughly 2:30 a.m. on March 9, 1988, John Joseph Harper was walking home in downtown Winnipeg after having a few coffee-and-whiskeys at a local tavern. He was Cree, 36, the father of three, a leader in the Indian Lake Tribal Council, and a well-respected man in local Aboriginal circles.

Meanwhile, elsewhere, two young Aboriginal men had stolen a car and had been apprehended. The police were still in the area.

A police officer walked toward J.J. Harper, who ignored him as he had committed no crime. The constable asked Harper to show identification. Harper refused. The constable asked him again, and Harper just walked away. The officer grabbed him by the arm and turned him around. Within a few minutes Harper was dead, shot to death by the policeman's gun.

The investigation was minimal. The scene of the killing was hosed down before morning light, possibly washing clean clues that could have revealed what happened. The officer claimed in court that Harper, whom the officer felt looked like one of the suspects, pushed him down and tried to grab his gun. He claimed that, in the ensuing struggle, his finger found its way to the trigger and the gun accidentally went off. Yet, the gun was not dusted for fingerprints to corroborate the story.

Within 36 hours of Harper's death, the police chief said his officer was innocent of any wrongdoing, and the mayor of Winnipeg agreed with him. Later investigation revealed much that is questionable about the way the case was handled. The officer in charge of the initial investigation committed suicide.

(Adapted from Steckley and Cummins 2001: 220)

APPENDIX H:
The Helen Betty Osborne Case

On November 12, 1971, in The Pas, Manitoba, four young White men, who were drinking heavily, went cruising for Aboriginal girls, a common practice in the area. They saw a 19-year-old Cree woman, Helen Betty Osborne, out walking. They tried to coax her into the car, but she refused. They grabbed her, forced her into the car, and drove out of town. They tore her clothes off, and at least one of the men sexually assaulted her. She was stabbed with a screwdriver 56 times and died.

The identity of the guilty parties soon became public knowledge. One of the four men, Lee Colgan, described the slaying to friends, acquaintances, people he met in bars, even a local sheriff, and a civilian employee of the RCMP. At a party in 1972, Dwayne Johnston, then around 17, described how he killed the Cree woman, boasting about the act. Yet nothing was done about it, even though there were physical clues linking the men to the scene of the crime.

The non-Aboriginal community protected the young men. A friend threatened someone who wanted to tell. A local lawyer counselled the men to remain quiet.

It took 14 years before anything substantive was done about the crime. In 1985, the police put an ad about the case in the local newspaper and got a response from a woman who had heard the story in 1972. Colgan made a deal with the prosecution, agreeing to testify if all charges against him related to the killing were dropped. Johnston and Jim Houghton (who along with Johnston had been outside the car with the victim) were arrested in 1986. The fourth man was not charged with anything as he claimed to have been too drunk at the time to remember any details.

One hundred and four prospective jurors were considered. Twenty of them were Aboriginal, but they were rejected by the lawyers. The jury let Jim Houghton go free, but convicted Dwayne Johnston. He served a 10-year sentence and was released on full parole in October 1997, to considerable protest from Aboriginal peoples across Canada.

(Adapted from Steckley and Cummins 2001: 232)

References

Books and Articles

Acoose, Janice. 1995. *Iskwewak–Kah' Ki Yaw Ni Wahkomakanak: Neither Indian Princess nor Easy Squaws*. Toronto, ON: Women's Press.

Adams, Howard. 1975. *Prison of Grass: Canada From the Native Point of View*. Toronto, ON: New Press.

_____. 1989. *Prison of Grass: Canada from the Native Point of View*. Saskatoon, SK: Fifth House Publishers.

_____. 1993. "Cultural Decolonization." In Don Fiddler (Ed.), *Gatherings: The Eno'wkin Journal of First North American Peoples* (pp. 251–66). Penticton, BC: Theytus Books.

_____. 1995. *A Tortured People: The Politics of Colonization*. Penticton, BC: Theytus Books.

_____. 1999. *A Tortured People: The Politics of Colonization*, 2nd ed. Penticton, BC: Theytus Books.

Agger, Ben. 1989. "Do Books Write Authors? A Study of Disciplinary Hegemony." *Teaching Sociology* (July): 356–59.

Alfred, Gerald R. 1995. *Heeding the Voices of Our Ancestors: Kahnawake Mohawk Politics and the Rise of Native Nationalism*. Toronto, ON: Oxford University Press.

_____. 1999. *Peace, Power, Righteousness: An Indian Manifesto*. Toronto, ON: Oxford University Press.

Anderson, Karen L. 1996. *Sociology: A Critical Introduction*. Scarborough, ON: Nelson.

Apple, Michael W., and Linda K. Christian–Smith. 1991. "The Politics of the Textbook." In *The Politics of the Textbook* (pp. 1–21). New York, NY: Routledge.

Armstrong, Jeannette. 1982. *Enwhisteetkwa: Walk on Water*. Penticton, BC: Okanagan Tribal Council.

_____. 1984. *Neekna and Chemai*. Penticton, BC: Theytus Books.

_____. 1985. *Slash*. Penticton, BC: Theytus Books.

_____. 1991. *Breath Tracks*. Penticton, BC: Theytus Books.

_____. 1993. *Looking at the Words of Our People: First Nations Analysis of Literature*. Penticton, BC: Theytus Books.

_____. 1998. "Unclean Tides: An Essay on Salmon and Relations." In Judith Roche and Meg McHutchison (Eds.), *First Fish, First People: Salmon Tales of the North Pacific Rim* (pp. 180–93). Vancouver, BC: University of British Columbia Press.

Armstrong, Jeannette, and Lally Grauer (Eds.). 2001. *Native Poets in Canada: A Contemporary Anthology*. Peterborough, ON: Broadview Press.

Assu, Harry, with Joy Inglis. 1989. *Assu of Cape Mudge: Recollections of a Coastal Indian Chief*. Vancouver, BC: University of British Columbia Press.

_____. 1996. "Renewal of the Potlatch at Cape Mudge." In K.S. Coates and R. Fisher (Eds.), *Out of the Background: Readings on Canadian Native History* (pp. 353–66). Toronto, ON: Copp Clark.

Augustine, Noah. 2000. "Indian Reserve a Haven from Racism." *Toronto Star* OP–Ed (April 18: A21).

Bailey, Gordon, and Noga Gayle. 1993. *Sociology: An Introduction; From the Classics to Contemporary Feminism*. Toronto, ON: Oxford University Press.

Balikci, Asen. 1961. "Suicidal Behavior among the Netsilik Eskimos." In Bernard Blishen, Frank E. Jones, Kaspar Naegele, and John Porter (Eds.), *Canadian Society: Sociological Perspectives*. Toronto, ON: Macmillan.

Barnouw, Victor. 1987. *An Introduction to Anthropology: Ethnology*, vol. 2, 5th ed. Chicago, IL: The Dorsey Press.

Baudrillard, Jean. 1983. *Simulations*. Paul Foss, Paul Patton, and Philip Beitchman (Trans.). New York, NY: Semiotext[e].

Banting, Frederick G. 1927. "Private and Confidential Report to Mr. O. S. Finnie." Dept of the Interior, Northwest Territories and Yukon Branch, Nov. 8, 1927, National Archives of Canada, RG85, vol. 2081, file 1012-4 pt3A, p. 2.

Beare, Margaret. 1996. "Organized Crime and Money Laundering." In Robert A. Silverman, James J. Teevan, and Vincent F. Sacco (Eds.), *Crime in Canadian Society*, 5th ed. (pp. 187–245). Toronto, ON: Harcourt Brace.

Beattie, Christopher, and Stewart Crysdale. 1974 and 1977. *Sociology Canada: Readings*. Toronto, ON: Butterworth.

Benedict, Ruth. 1934. *Patterns of Culture*. New York, NY: Mentor Books.

_____. 1940. *Race: Science or Politics?* New York, NY: Modern Age.

_____. 1959. *Patterns of Culture*. Preface by Margaret Mead. Boston, MA: Houghton Mifflin.

Birket–Smith, Kaj. 1929. *The Caribou Eskimos*. Report of the Fifth Thule Expedition, vol. 5. Copenhagen.

Blishen, Bernard, and Frank E. Jones, Kaspar D. Naegele, and John Porter. (Eds.). 1961, 1964, 1968, and 1971. *Canadian Society: Sociological Perspectives*. Toronto, ON: Macmillan.

Boas, Franz. 1888. *The Central Eskimos*. Sixth Annual Report of the Bureau of American Ethnology. (pp. 388–669). Washington, DC: Smithsonian Institute.

_____. 1897. "The Social Organization and the Secret Societies of the Kwakiutl Indians." Reprint. *Report of the United States National Museum for 1895*. (pp. 311–738). Washington, DC: Government Printing Office.

_____. 1909. *The Kwakiutl of Vancouver Island*, vol. 5: 2. (pp. 301–522). New York, NY: Jesup North Pacific Expedition.

_____. 1921. *Ethnology of the Kwakiutl*. 35th Annual Report, 1 and 2. Washington, DC: Bureau of American Ethnology.

_____. 1925. "Contributions to the Ethnology of the Kwakiutl." *Columbia University Contributions to Anthropology* 3. New York, NY: Columbia University Press.

_____. 1930. "Religion of the Kwakiutl." *Columbia University Contributions to Anthropology* 10: 1 and 2. New York, NY: Columbia University Press.

_____. 1935. *Kwakiutl Culture as Reflected in Mythology*. New York, NY: Memoirs of the American Folk–Lore Society 28.

_____. 1943. "Kwakiutl Tales." *Columbia University Contributions to Anthropology* 26: 2. New York, NY: Columbia University Press.

_____. 1964 (1888). *The Central Eskimos*. Lincoln, NB: University of Nebraska Press.

_____. 1966. *Kwakiutl Ethnography*. Helen Codere (Ed.). Chicago, IL: University of Chicago Press.

Bohannan, Paul. 1992. *We, the Alien: An Introduction to Cultural Anthropology*. Prospect Heights, IL: Waveland Press.

Bolaria, B. Singh. (Ed.). 1991. *Social Issues and Contradictions in Canadian Society*. Toronto, ON: Harcourt, Brace, Jovanovich.

Bonaparte, Darren. 2002a. "A Line on a Map: A Mohawk Perspective on the International Border at Akwesasne."

_____. 2002b. "Saiowisakeron: The Jake Ice Story." www.wampumchronicles.com/saiowisakeron.html.

_____. 2002c. "What You Don't Know and Why You Don't Know It: The Hidden History of the Seven Nations of Canada." www.wampumchronicles.com/hiddenhistory.htm.

Boyd, N. 1988. "Canadian Punishment of Illegal Drug Use: Theory and Practice." In J.C. Blackwell and P.G. Erickson (Eds.), *Illicit Drugs in Canada: A Risky Business*. Scarborough, ON: Nelson.

Boydell, Craig, Carl F. Grindstaff, and Paul C. Whitehead (Eds.). 1971. *Critical Issues in Canadian Society*. Toronto, ON: Holt, Rinehart and Winston.

Boyer, R., R. Dufour, M. Préville, and L. Bujold-Rown. 1994. "State of Mental Health." *A Health Profile of the Inuit: Report of the Santé Québec Health Survey among the Inuit of Nunavik, 1992*, vol. 2. (pp. 117–44). Montréal, QC: Ministère de la santé et des services sociaux, Governement du Québec.

Bracken, Christopher. 1997. *The Potlatch Papers: A Colonial Case History*. Chicago, IL: University of Chicago Press.

Braroe, N. 1975. *Indian and White: Self-image and Interaction in a Canadian Plains Community*. Stanford, CT: Stanford University Press.

Brody, Hugh. 1991 (1975). *The People's Land: Eskimos and Whites in the Eastern Arctic*. Middlesex, UK: Penguin.

Brym, Robert. 2001. *New Society: Sociology for the 21st Century*, 3rd ed. Toronto, ON: Harcourt Canada.

Burke, Dan, Barry Came, Ann McLaughlin, and Bruce Wallace. 1990. "The Fury of Oka." *Maclean's* September 10: pp. 16–18, 19.

Burke, James. 1976. *Paper Tomahawks: From Red Tape to Red Power*. Winnipeg, MB: Queenston House.

Calliou, Sharilyn. 1998. "Us/Them, Me/You: Who? (Re)thinking the Binary of First Nations and Non–First Nations." *Canadian Journal of Native Education* July.

Campbell, Maria. 1973. *Halfbreed*. New York, NY: Saturday Review Press

Cardinal, Harold. 1969. *The Unjust Society: The Tragedy of Canada's Indians*. Edmonton, Alberta: New Press Publishers.

_____. 1977. *The Rebirth of Canada's Indians*. Toronto, ON: New Press Publishers

Cavan, Ruth. 1965 (1928). *Suicide*. New York, NY: Russell and Russell.

_____. 1968. *Delinquency and Crime: Cross Cultural Perspectives*. Philadelphia, PA: Lippincott.

Clark, S.D. 1976. *Canadian Society in Historical Perspective*. Toronto, ON: McGraw–Hill Ryerson.

CBC. 2000. "Adventurers and Mystics." Directors Claude Lortie and Serge Turbide. Canada: A People's History, 2nd episode (first aired, October 28, 2000).

Clinard, Marshall B., and Robert F. Meier. 1985 (1963). *The Sociology of Deviant Behavior*, 6th ed. New York, NY: Holt, Rinehart and Winston.

Clutesi, George. 1969. *Potlatch*. Victoria, BC: The Morriss Printing Company.

Codere, Helen. 1950. *Fighting with Property*. Monographs of the American Ethnological Society 18. New York, NY: J.J. Augustin.

_____. 1956. "The Amiable Side of Kwakiutl Life: The Potlatch and the Play-Potlatch." *American Anthropologist* 58: pp. 334–51.

Crantz, David. 1820 (1767). *The History of Greenland: Including an Account of the Mission Carried on by the United Brethren in That Country*, 2 vols. London: Longman, Hurst, Rees, Orr, and Bram.

Cronk, Lee. 1997 (1989). "Reciprocity and the Power of Giving." In James P. Spradley and David McCurdy (Eds.), *Conformity and Conflict: Readings in Cultural Anthropology*, 9th ed. (pp. 157–63). New York, NY: HarperCollins.

Cross, Ronald, and Hélène Sévigny. 1994. *Lasagna: The Man behind the Mask*. Vancouver, BC: Talonbooks.

Crysdale, Stewart, and Christopher Beattie. 1973 and 1977. *Sociology Canada: An Introductory Text*. Toronto, ON: Butterworth.

Curtis, James, and Lorne Tepperman (Eds.). 1990. *Images of Canada: The Sociological Tradition*. Scarborough, ON: Prentice Hall.

David, Dan. 1992. "Razorwire Dreams." In Linda Jaine and Drew Hayden Taylor (Eds.), *Voices: Being Native in Canada* (pp. 20–31). Saskatoon, SK: University of Saskatchewan Extension Division.

Dawson, Carl A. 1961. "Foreword." In Bernard Blishen, Frank E. Jones, Kaspar D. Naegele, and John Porter (Eds.), *Canadian Society: Sociological Perspectives*. Toronto, ON: Macmillan.

Dawson, Carl A., and Warren E. Getty. 1948. *An Introduction to Sociology*, 3rd ed. New York, NY: The Ronald Press Company.

Dei, George, Irma James, L. Karumanchery, S. James–Wilson, and J. Zine. 2000. *Aboriginal Margins: The Challenges and Possibilities of Inclusive Schooling*. Toronto, ON: Canadian Scholars' Press.

Delisle, Andrew. 1984. "How We Regained Control over Our Lives and Territories: The Kahnawake Story." In Leroy Little Bear, Menno Boldt, and J. Anthony Long (Eds.), *Pathways to Self–Determination: Canadian Indians and the Canadian State* (pp. 141–47). Toronto, ON: University of Toronto Press.

Deloria, Vine Jr. 1969. *Custer Died for Your Sins: An Indian Manifesto*. New York, NY: Macmillan.

Derrida, Jacques. 1992. "Donner la mort." In Jean-Michael Rabaté and Michael Wetzel (Eds.), *L'ethique de don: Jacques Derrida et la pensée du don* (pp. 11–108). Paris: Métaillé–Transition.

Dickason, Olive. 1997. *Canada's First Nations: A History of Founding Peoples from Earliest Times*, 2nd ed. Toronto, ON: McClelland & Stewart.

_____. 2002. *Canada's First Nations: A History of Founding Peoples from Earliest Times*, 3rd ed. Toronto, ON: McClelland & Stewart.

Dosman, Edgar J. 1972. *Indians: An Urban Dilemma*. Toronto, ON: McClelland & Stewart.

Drucker, Philip, and Robert F. Heizer. 1967. *To Make My Name Good: A Reexamination of the Southern Kwakiutl Potlatch*. Berkeley and Los Angeles, CA: University of California Press.

Dumont, James. 1981. "Reflections of the Directions of Native Studies Departments in Canadian Universities." *Canadian Journal of Native Studies* 1: pp. 179–83.

Durkheim, Émile. 1938 (1895). *Rules of the Sociological Method*. Chicago, IL: University of Chicago Press.

_____. 1966 (French, 1897 and English, 1951). *Suicide: A Study in Sociology*. John A. Spaulding (Trans.). George Simpson (Ed. and intro.). New York, NY: Free Press.

Elliott, Jean. 1971. *Minority Canadians: Native Peoples*. Scarborough, ON: Prentice Hall.

Ember, Carol R., and Melvin Ember. 1999. *Cultural Anthropology*, 9th ed. Upper Saddle River, NJ: Prentice Hall.

Fee, Margery. 1990. "Upsetting Fake Ideas: Jeannette Armstrong's Slash and Beatrice Culleton's April Raintree" *Canadian Literature* 124–5: pp. 168–80.

Feldman, Robert S. 1998. *Social Psychology*, 2nd ed. Upper Saddle River, NJ: Prentice Hall.

Ferguson, Jack. 1970. "Social Change in the Western Arctic." In W.E. Mann (Ed.), *Social and Cultural Change in Canada* (pp. 27–50). Toronto, ON: Copp Clark.

Ferraro, Gary. 1995. *Cultural Anthropology: An Applied Perspective*. Minneapolis/St. Paul, MN: West Publishing Company.

Feyerabend, Paul. 1970. "How to be a Good Empiricist: A Plea for Tolerance in Matters Epistemological." In B.A. Brody (Ed.), *Readings in the Philosophy of Science* (pp. 319–39). Englewood Cliffs, NJ: Prentice Hall.

_____.1975. *Against Method: Outline of an Anarchistic Theory of Knowledge.* London, UK: Verso.

Fleras, Augie, and Jean Elliott. 1992. *The Nations Within.* Toronto, ON: Oxford University Press.

_____.1999. *Unequal Relations: An Introduction to Race, Ethnic, and Aboriginal Dynamics in Canada,* 3rd ed. Scarborough, ON: Prentice Hall, Allyn and Bacon.

Forcese, Dennis, and Stephen Richer. 1975. *Issues in Canadian Society: An Introduction to Sociology.* Scarborough, ON: Prentice Hall.

_____. 1982 and 1988. *Social Issues: Sociological Views of Canada.* Scarborough, ON: Prentice Hall.

Foucault, Michel. 1978. *The History of Sexuality,* vol. 1: *An Introduction.* New York, NY: Pantheon Books.

_____. 1980. "Two Lectures." In Colin Gordon (Ed.), *Power/Knowledge* (pp. 78–108). New York, NY: Pantheon Books.

_____. 1994 (1972). *The Archaeology of Knowledge.* London, UK: Routledge. Trans. from *L'Archéologie du savoir* 1969.

Freeman, Minnie Aodia. 1978. *Life among the Qallunaat.* Edmonton, AB: Hurtig Publishers.

Frideres, James S. 1974. *Canada's Indians: Contemporary Conflicts.* Scarborough, ON: Prentice Hall.

_____. 1983. *Native People in Canada: Contemporary Conflicts,* 2nd ed. Scarborough, ON: Prentice Hall.

_____. 1988. *Native People in Canada: Contemporary Conflicts,* 3rd ed. Scarborough, ON: Prentice Hall.

Frideres, James S., with Lilianne Ernestine Korsenbrink–Gelissen. 1993. *Native Peoples in Canada: Contemporary Conflicts,* 4th ed. Scarborough, ON: Prentice Hall.

_____. 1998. *Aboriginal Peoples in Canada: Contemporary Conflicts,* 5th ed. Scarborough, ON: Prentice Hall.

Frideres, James S., and René Gadacz. 2001. *Aboriginal Peoples in Canada: Contemporary Conflicts,* 6th ed. Toronto, ON: Prentice Hall.

Friedl, John, and John Pfeiffer. 1977. *Anthropology: The Study of People.* New York, NY: Harper & Row.

Fry, John A. (Ed.). 1984. *Contradictions in Canadian Society: Readings in Introductory Sociology*. Toronto, ON: John Wiley & Sons.

Gallagher, James E., and Ronald D. Lambert. (Eds.). 1971. *Social Process and Institution: The Canadian Case*. Toronto, ON: Holt, Rinehart and Winston.

Garte, Edna. 1981. "Where the Partridge Drums." *Journal of American Indian Education* 21, 1 (October). http://jaie.asu.edu/v21/V21S1whe.html.

George (Kanentiio), Doug. 2000. "For Some a Heroic Time." NatNews@egroups.com.

Gerber, Linda. 1976. "Minority Survival: Community Characteristics and Out-Migration from Indian Communities across Canada." Dissertation. University of Toronto.

———. 1977. "Community Characteristics and Out–migration from Indian Communities: Regional Trends." Paper presented at Department of Indian Affairs and Northern Development, Ottawa, November 9.

———. 1979. "The Development of Canadian Indian Communities: A Two-Dimensional Typology Reflecting Strategies of Adaptation to the Modern World." *Canadian Review of Sociology and Anthropology* 16, 4: pp. 404–21.

———. 1984. "Community Characteristics and Outmigration from Canadian Indian Reserves: Path Analyses." *Canadian Review of Sociology and Anthropology* 21: pp. 145–65.

———. 1990. "Multiple Jeopardy: A Social–Economic Comparison of Men and Women among the Indian, Metis and Inuit Peoples of Canada." *Canadian Ethnic Studies* XXII, 3: pp. 69–84.

———. 1995. "Indian, Métis, and Inuit Women and Men: Multiple Jeopardy in Canadian Context." In E.D. Nelson and B.W. Robinson (Eds.), *Gender in the 1990s: Images, Realities, and Issues* (pp. 466–77). Scarborough, ON: Nelson.

Giroux, Henry. 1997. "Border Pedagogy in the Age of Postmodernism." *Pedagogy and the Politics of Hope: Theory, Culture and Schooling*. Boulder, CO: Westview Press.

Glascock, A.P., and S.L. Feinman. 1981. "Social Asset or Social Burden: Treatment of the Aged in Non–Industrial Societies." In C.L. Fry (Ed.), *Dimension: Aging, Culture and Health*. New York, NY: Praeger.

Goldman, Irving. 1975. *The Mouth of Heaven: An Introduction to Kwakiutl Religious Thought*. New York, NY: John Wiley & Sons.

Gomme, Ian McDermid. 1993. *The Shadow Line: Deviance and Crime in Canada*. Toronto, ON: Harcourt, Brace, Jovanovich.

Grand Council Treaty Number Nine. 1977. "Building Our Future." *Bulletin* 18, 2: pp. 21–4. Ottawa, ON: Canadian Association in Support of Native Peoples.

Grayson, J. Paul (Ed.). 1983. *Introduction to Sociology: An Alternate Approach*. Toronto, ON: Gage.

Guemple, Lee. 1969. "Human Resources Management: the Dilemma of the Aging Eskimo." *Sociological Symposium* 2 (Spring).

_____. 1974. "The Dilemma of the Aging Eskimo." In Christopher Beattie and Stewart Crysdale (Eds.), *Sociology Canada: Readings* (pp. 203–14). Toronto, ON: Butterworth. Revised and Abridged. From *Sociological Symposium* 2 (Spring 1969): 59–74.

_____. 1980. "Growing Old in Inuit Society." In Victor W. Marshall (Ed.), *Aging in Canada*. Toronto, ON: Fitzhenry and Whiteside.

Haas, Jack, and William Shaffir. 1978. *Shaping Identity in Canadian Society*. Toronto, ON: Prentice Hall.

Hagedorn, Robert (Ed.). 1980, 1983a, and 1986. *Sociology*. Toronto, ON: Holt, Rinehart and Winston.

_____. 1983b. *Essentials of Sociology*. Toronto, ON: Holt, Rinehart and Winston.

Hale, Sylvia. 1992. "Facticity and Dogma in Introductory Sociology Texts: The Need for Alternative Methods." In William K. Carroll, Linda Christiansen–Ruffman, Raymond F. Currie, and Deborah Harrison (Eds.), *Fragile Truths: 25 Years of Sociology and Anthropology in Canada* (pp. 135–53). Ottawa, ON: Carleton University Press.

Hall, Captain Charles Francis. 1970 (1864, 1865). *Life with the Esquimaux: A Narrative of Arctic Experience in Search of Search of Survivors of Sir John Franklin's Expedition*. London: Sampson Low and Son.

Hall, Louis. nd. *The Warriors Handbook*.

Hanbury, David T. 1904. *Sport and Travel in the Northland of Canada*. London, UK: Edward Arnold.

Harris, Michael. 1990. *Justice Denied: The Law versus Donald Marshall*, 2nd ed. Toronto, ON: HarperCollins.

Hartnagel, Tim. 1992. "Correlates of Criminal Behaviour." In Rick Lindonn (Ed.), *Criminology: A Canadian Perspective*, 2nd ed. Toronto, ON: Holt, Rinehart and Winston.

Hawkes, Ernest W. 1970 (1916). *The Labrador Eskimo*. Geological Survey of Canada, Memoir 91, Anthropological Series 14. Ottawa, ON: Department of Mines. Reprint. 1970, Johnson Reprint Company.

Health Canada. 1995. *Suicide in Canada: Update of the Report of the Task Force on Suicide in Canada*. Ottawa: Mental Health Division, Health Services Directorate, Health Programs and Services Branch.

Hearne, Simon. 1968. *A Journey from Prince of Wales's Fort in Hudson's Bay to the Northern Ocean : 1769, 1770, 1771, 1772*. Toronto, ON: Macmillan.

Heartfield, Kate. 1998. "Aboriginal Elder Visits U of O Campus." *Fulcrum Online* 59–09, (October).

Henslin, James, and Adie Nelson. 1996. *Sociology: Canadian Edition: A Down–to–Earth Approach*. Toronto, ON: Allyn and Bacon.

Henslin, James, Dan Glenday, Ann Duffy, and Norene Pupo. (Eds.). 2001. *Sociology: Canadian Edition: A Down–to–Earth Approach*, 2nd ed. Toronto, ON: Allyn and Bacon.

Hiller, Harry H. 1976. *Canadian Society: A Sociological Analysis*. Scarborough, ON: Prentice Hall.

Himelfarb, Alexander, and C. James Richardson. 1979. *People, Power and Process: Sociology for Canadians*. Toronto, ON: McGraw–Hill Ryerson.

_____. 1982 and 1991. *Sociology for Canadians: Images of Society*. Toronto, ON: McGraw–Hill Ryerson.

_____. 1984 and 1992. *Sociology for Canadians: A Reader*. Toronto, ON: McGraw–Hill Ryerson.

Hoebel, E. Adamson. 1941. "Law–ways of Primitive Eskimos." *Journal of Criminal Law and Criminology* 341: pp. 663–683.

_____. 1965 (1954). *The Law of Primitive Man, A Study in Comparative Legal Dynamics*. Cambridge, MA: Harvard University Press.

Hofley, John R. 1992. "Canadianization: A Journey Completed?" In William K. Carroll et al. (Eds.), *Fragile Truths: 25 Years of Sociology and Anthropology in Canada* (pp. 102–22). Ottawa, ON: Carleton University Press.

Holm, Gustav F. 1914. "Ethnological Sketch of the Angmagssalik Eskimos." *Meddelelser Om Grønland* 34.

Holmes, Ellen Rhoads, and D. Lowell. 1995. *Other Cultures, Elder Years*, 2nd ed. Thousand Oaks, CA: Sage Publications.

Holmes, Richard. (Ed.). 1988. *Fundamentals of Sociology*. Toronto, ON: Holt, Rinehart and Winston of Canada.

Hornung, Rick. 1991. *One Nation under the Gun: Inside the Mohawk Civil War*. Toronto, ON: Stoddart.

Horton, Paul B. 1965. *Sociology and the Health Sciences*. New York, NY: McGraw-Hill.

Horton, Paul B., and Chester L. Hunt. 1976. *Sociology*, 4th ed. New York, NY: McGraw-Hill.

Howard, Michael. 1986. *Contemporary Cultural Anthropology*. Boston, MA and Toronto, ON: Little, Brown and Company.

Howley, James P. 1974 (1915). *The Beothuck or Red Indians*. Toronto, ON: Coles Publishing.

Hoxie, Frederick (Ed.). 1996. *Encyclopedia of North American Indians*. New York, NY: Houghton Mifflin.

Hughes, Charles. 1965. "Under Four Flags: Recent Culture Change among the Eskimos." *Current Anthropology* 6, 1 (February): pp. 3–69.

Hutchison, George, and Dick Wallace. 1977. *Grassy Narrows*. Toronto, ON: Van Nostrand Reinhold.

Hutton, Dr. Samuel King. 1912. *Among the Eskimos of Labrador: A Record of Five Years' Close Intercourse with the Eskimo Tribes of Labrador*. London, UK: Seeley, Service and Co. Ltd.

Isaacs, Sandy, Susan Keogh, Cathy Menard, and Jamie Hockin. 1998. "Suicide in the Northwest Territories: A Descriptive Review." *Chronic Diseases in Canada* 19, 4. Health Canada, www.hc-sc.gc.ca/hpb/ldc/publicat/cdic194/cd194c_e.html.

Jack, Jennie. 1991. "Witness to Oka." *New Directions* 6, 1 (February). http://nativenet.uthscsa.edu/archive/nl/01a/0133.html.

Jaine, Linda, and Drew Hayden Taylor (Eds.). 1992. *Voices: Being Native in Canada*. Saskatoon, SK: University of Saskatchewan Extension Division.

Jenness, Diamond. 1922. *The Life of the Copper Eskimo: Report of the Canadian Arctic Expedition, 1913–1918*. Vol. 12, Pt. A. Ottawa, ON: Department of Naval Service, King's Printer.

_____. 1932. *Indians of Canada*. Department of Mines, National Museum of Canada, Bulletin 65. Ottawa, ON: Acland.

Johnstone, Geoffrey, and Kathryn Bauer. 1998. *Sociology and Canadian Society*. Toronto, ON: Emond Montgomery.

Kaplan, E. Ann. 1987. *Rocking Around the Clock: Music Television, Postmodernism and Consumer Culture*. New York, NY: Routledge.

Kendall, Diana, Rick Linden, and Jane Lothian Murray. 1998 and 2000. *Sociology in Our Times: The Essentials*, Canadian ed. Scarborough, ON: Nelson.

Kershaw, Ann, and Mary Lasovich. 1991. *Rock–A–Bye Baby: A Death Behind Bars*. Toronto, ON: McClelland & Stewart.

King, Thomas. 1990. *All My Relations: An Anthology of Contemporary Canadian Native Prose*. Toronto, ON: McClelland & Stewart.

Kirmayer, Lawrence, Christopher Fletcher, and Lucy Boothroyd. 1998. "Suicide among the Inuit of Canada." In Antoon Leenaars, Susanne Wenckstern, Isaac Sakinofsky, Ronald Dyck, Michael Kral, and Roger Bland (Eds.), *Suicide in Canada* (pp. 189–211). Toronto, ON: University of Toronto Press.

Knuttila, Murray. 1993. *Sociology Revisited: Basic Concepts and Perspectives*. Toronto, ON: McClelland & Stewart.

Krause, Elliot. 1980. *Why Study Sociology?* New York: Random House.

Kulchyski, Peter, Don McCaskill, and David Newhouse (Eds.). 1999. *In the Words of Elders: Aboriginal Cultures in Transition*. Toronto, ON: University of Toronto Press.

Laroque, Emma. 1975. *Defeathering the Indian*. Agincourt, ON: The Book Society of Canada Ltd.

_____. 1988. "On the Ethics of Publishing Historical Documents." In Jennifer Brown and Robert Brightman (Eds.), *"The Orders of the*

Dreamed:" George Nelson on Cree and Ojibwa Religion and Myth, 1823. Winnipeg, MN: University of Manitoba Press.

_____. 1990. "Preface or Here Are Our Voices—Who Will Hear?" In Jeanne Perreault and Sylvia Vance (Eds.), *Writing the Circle: Native Women of Western Canada*. Edmonton, AB: NeWest Press.

_____. 1996. "The Colonization of a Native Woman Scholar." In Christine Miller and Patricia Churchryk (Eds.), *Women of the First Nations: Power, Wisdom and Strength* (pp. 11–18) Winnipeg, MN: University of Manitoba Press.

Laskin, Richard. 1964. *Social Problems: A Canadian Profile*. Toronto, ON: McGraw-Hill Ryerson.

Leighton, Alexander H., and Charles C. Hughes. 1955. "Notes on Eskimo Patterns of Suicide." *Southwestern Journal of Anthropology* 11, 4: pp. 327–38.

Levin, Jack, and William C. Levin. 1988. *The Human Puzzle: An Introduction to Social Psychology*. Belmont, CA: Wadsworth.

Lorimer, Rowland, and Jean McNulty. 1991. *Mass Communication in Canada*, 2nd ed. Toronto, ON: McClelland & Stewart.

Lundy, Katherina, and Barbara Warme. 1986 and 1990. *Sociology: A Window on the World*. Toronto, ON: Methuen.

Lyon, George. 1824. *The Private Journal of Captain G. F. Lyon of H.M.S. Hecla, During the Recent Voyage of Discovery under Captain Parry*. London, UK: John Murray.

Macionis, John, Juanne Nancarrow Clarke, and Linda Gerber. 1994. *Sociology: Canadian Edition*. Scarborough, ON: Prentice Hall.

Macionis, John, and Linda Gerber. 1999 and 2002. *Sociology: Canadian Edition*. Scarborough, ON: Prentice Hall.

Macionis, John, S. Mikael Jansson, and Celia M. Benoit. 2002. *Sociology: The Basics*. Scarborough, ON: Prentice Hall.

Mann, W.E. (Ed.). 1968a. *Canada: A Sociological Profile*. Toronto, ON: Copp Clark.

_____. 1968b. "Suicide." *Deviant Behaviour in Canada*. Toronto, ON: Social Science Publishers.

Mann, W.E., and Les Wheatcroft (Eds.). 1976. *Canada: A Sociological Profile*, 3rd ed. Toronto, ON: Copp Clark.

Mansfield, Nick. 1982. *Introductory Sociology: Canadian Perspectives*. Don Mills, ON: Collier Macmillan.

Manuel, George, and Michael Posluns. 1974. *The Fourth World: An Indian Reality*. Don Mills, ON: Collier Macmillan.

Maracle, Brian. 1996. *Back on the Rez: Finding the Way Home*. Toronto, ON: Viking Penguin.

Maracle, Lee. 1992. *Sundogs*. Penticton, BC: Theytus Books.

_____. 1996. *I Am Woman: A Native Perspective on Sociology and Feminism*. Vancouver, BC: Press Gang Publishers.

Marshall, Ingeborg. 1996. *A History and Ethnography of the Beothuk*. Montreal, QC and Kingston, ON: McGill–Queen's University Press.

Marshall, Victor W. (Ed.). 1980 and 1987. *Aging in Canada: Social Perspectives*. Markham, ON: Fitzhenry and Whiteside.

Mathiassen, Therkel. 1928. *Material Culture of the Iglulik Eskimos*. Report of the Fifth Thule *Expedition* VI, 1 (1921–24).

Mauss, Marcel. 1969. "Don, contrat, echange." *Oeuvres* 3: pp. 29–57; Paris: Éditions de Minuit.

_____. 1990. *The Gift: The Form and Reason for Exchange in Archaic Societies*. W.D. Hall (Trans.). London: Routledge. Published in French 1950 as "Essai sur le don," *Sociologie et Anthropologie*, Paris: Presses Universitaires de France. pp. 143–279.

McGahan, Peter. 1995. *Urban Sociology in Canada*. Toronto, ON: Butterworth.

McGillivray, Anne, and Brenda Comasky. 1999. *Black Eyes All of the Time: Intimate Violence, Aboriginal Women and the Justice System*. Toronto, ON: University of Toronto Press.

McNickle, D'arcy. 1972. "American Indians Who Never Were." *The American Indian Reader: Anthropology*. San Francisco, CA: Indian Historian Press.

Medicine, Beatrice. 1987. "My Elders Tell Me." In J. Barman, Y. Hébert, and D. McCaskill (Eds.), *Indian Education in Canada*, vol. 2: *The Challenge* (pp. 142–52). Vancouver, BC: University of British Columbia Press.

Mercer, Blaine E. 1958. *An Introduction to the Study of Society*. New York, NY: Harcourt, Brace and Company.

Mercredi, Ovide, and Mary Ellen Turpel. 1993. *In the Rapids: Navigating the Future of First Nations,* Toronto, ON: Viking Books.

Merton, Robert K. 1968 (1949). *Social Theory and Social Structure.* New York, NY: The Free Press.

Michelson, David Rubin. 1982. *From Ethnography to Ethnology: A Study of the Conflict of Interpretation of the Southern Kwakiutl Potlatch.* 1979 dissertation. Ann Arbor, MI: University Microfilms International.

Miller, Barbara D., Penny Van Esterik, and John Van Esterik. 2001. *Cultural Anthropology: Canadian Edition.* Toronto, ON: Allyn and Bacon.

Miller, Elmer S., and Charles A. Weitz. 1979. *Introduction to Anthropology.* Englewood Cliffs, NJ: Prentice Hall.

Ministry of Education, Ontario. 1999. *The Ontario Curriculum Grades 9 and 10—Native Studies.* Toronto: Ministry of Education.

_____. 1999. *The Ontario Curriculum Grades 11 and 12—Native Studies.* Toronto: Ministry of Education.

Minor, K. 1992. *Issumatuq: Learning from the Traditional Healing Wisdom of the Canadian Inuit.* Halifax, NS: Fernwood Publishing.

Mitchell, Michael. 1989. "Akwesasne: An Unbroken Assertion of Sovereignty." In Boyce Richardson, Assembly of First Nations (Ed.), *Drumbeat: Anger and Renewal in Indian Country* (pp. 105–36). Toronto, ON: Summerhill Press.

_____. 2000. "Cigarette Tax Increase Will Increase Smuggling, Risk Lives, and Threaten Public Safety, Akwesasne Grand Chief Warns Prime Minister." www.newswire.ca/releases/June2000/19/c6365.html.

Moghaddam, Fathali M. 1998. *Social Psychology: Exploring Universals across Cultures.* New York, NY: W.H. Freeman and Company.

Monture–Angus, Patricia. 1995. *Thunder in My Soul: A Mohawk Woman Speaks.* Halifax, NS: Fernwood.

Moore, Riley D. 1923. "Social Life of the Eskimo of St. Lawrence Island." *American Anthropologist* 25: pp. 339–75.

Mowat, Farley. 1968 (1951). *People of the Deer.* Toronto, ON: McClelland & Stewart.

_____. 1975. "The Snow Walker." *The Snow Walker* (pp. 131–42). Toronto, ON: McClelland & Stewart.

_____. 1975 (1959). *The Desperate People*. Toronto, ON: McClelland & Stewart.

Nabokov, Peter (Ed.). 1991. *Native American Testimony: A Chronicle of Indian–White Relations from Prophecy to the Present, 1492–1992*. Toronto, ON: Penguin.

Nagler, Mark. 1970. *Indians in the City*. Ottawa, ON: St. Paul's University, Canadian Research Centre for Anthropology.

Nanda, Serena. 1994. *Cultural Anthropology,* 5th ed. Belmont, CA: Wadsworth Publishing Company.

Nansen, Fridtjof. 1929 (1893). *Eskimo Life*. London, UK: Longman's.

Nash, Dennison. 1999. *A Little Anthropology,* 3rd ed. Upper Saddle River, NJ: Prentice Hall.

Neal, Arthur G. 1983. *Social Psychology: A Sociological Perspective*. Don Mills, ON: Addison–Wesley.

Nett, Emily M. 1993. *Canadian Families: Past and Present,* 2nd ed. Toronto, ON: Butterworth.

Novak, Mark. 1988, 1997, and 2001. *Aging and Society: A Canadian Perspective*. Toronto, ON: Nelson.

Nowell, Charles James. 1968 (1941). Clellan S. Ford (Ed.), *Smoke from Their Fires: The Life of a Kwakiutl Chief*. Hampden, CT: Archon Books.

Obomsawin, Alanis. 1993. *Kanehsatake: 270 Years of Resistance*. Montreal, QC: National Film Board of Canada.

_____. 1995. "My Name Is Kahentioosta." Montreal, QC: National Film Board of Canada.

_____. 1997. "Spudwrench: Kahnawake Man." Montreal, QC: National Film Board of Canada.

_____. 2000. "Rockets at Whiskey Trench." Montreal, QC: National Film Board of Canada.

Ogburn, William, and Meyer Nimkoff. 1964 (1947). *A Handbook of Sociology*. London: Routledge and Kegan Paul.

Okpik, Abraham. 1964. "What Does It Mean to Be an Eskimo?" In R. Laskin (Ed.), *Social Problems: A Canadian Profile* (pp. 129–31). Toronto, ON: McGraw-Hill.

Oswalt, Wendall. 1966. *This Land Was Theirs: A Study of the North American Indian*. New York, NY: Wiley & Sons.

Park, Michael Alan. 2000. *Introducing Anthropology: An Integrated Approach*. Toronto, ON: Mayfield Publishing Company.

Parry, W.E. 1824. *Journal of a Second Voyage for the Discovery of a Northwest Passage from the Atlantic to the Pacific; Performed in the Years 1821–22–23 in His Majesty's Ships Fury and Hecla*. London, UK: John Murray.

Pelletier, Wilfred. 1971. *For Every North American Indian That Begins to Disappear, I Also Begin to Disappear*. Toronto, ON: Neewin Publishing.

_____. 1974 "For Every North American Indian That Begins to Disappear, I Also Begin to Disappear." In J. Frideres (Ed.), *Canada's Indians: Contemporary Conflicts* (pp. 101–10). Scarborough, ON: Prentice Hall.

Pinard, Maurice. 1971. *The Rise of a Third Party*. Englewood Cliffs, NJ: Prentice Hall.

Ponting, J. Rick, and Roger Gibbins. 1980. *Out of Irrelevance: A Socio-political Introduction to Indian Affairs in Canada*. Toronto, ON: Butterworths.

Pratt, David. 1971. *How to Find and Measure Bias in Textbooks*. Englewood Cliffs, NJ: Educational Technology Press.

_____. 1984. "The Social Role of Sociology Textbooks in Canada." In J.R. Mallea and J.C. Young (Eds.), *Cultural Diversity and Canadian Education* (pp. 290–312). Ottawa, ON: Carleton University Press.

Pratt, David, and G.L. McDiarmid. 1971. *Teaching Prejudice: A Content Analysis of Social Science Textbooks*. Toronto, ON: Ontario Institute for Studies in Education.

Qitsualik, Rachel Attituq. 2001. "Suicide Is Price Inuit Paid for Tradition of Competency." www.indiancountry.com (January 22).

Ramu, G.N., and Stuart M. Johnson. 1976. *Introduction to Canadian Society: Sociological Analysis*. Toronto, ON: Macmillan.

Rasing, W.C.E. 1994. *Too Many People: Order and Non–Conformity in Igluliugmuit Social Process*. Nijmegen: Katholieke Universiteti Faculteit der Rechts geleendheid.

Rasmussen, Knud. 1927. *Across Arctic America: Intellectual Culture of the Iglulik Eskimos*. New York, NY: G.P. Putnam's Sons.

_____. 1929. "Intellectual Culture of the Iglulik Eskimos." *Report of the Fifth Thule Expedition, 1921–24*, vol. VII, 1. Copenhagen, Denmark: Gyldensalske Boghandel, Nordisk Forlag.

_____. 1931. "The Netsilik Eskimos." *Report of the Fifth Thule Expedition, 1921–24*, vol. 8. Copenhagen, Denmark: Gyldensalske Boghandel, Nordisk Forlag. 1–542.

Ray, P.H. 1885. *Report of the International Polar Expedition to Point Barrow, Alaska*. Washington, DC: Government Printing Office.

Reid, Gerald. 1999. "Kahnawake's Council of Chiefs, 1840 to 1889." *The Eastern Door* 7, 49 (January 15). www.easterndoor.com/Archives/7-48/7-48-C.htm.

Richardson, R.J., and Lorne Tepperman (Eds.). 1987. *An Introduction to the Social World*. Toronto, ON: McGraw-Hill Ryerson.

Robinson, Eric, and Henty Bird Quinney. 1985. *The Infested Blanket: Canada's Constitution—Genocide of Indian Nations*. Winnipeg, MB: Queenston House Publishing.

Rogers, Edward, and Jean Rogers. 1960. *The Individual in Mistassini Society*. Bulletin 1990. Ottawa, ON: National Museum of Canada.

Rosenberg, M. Michael, William Shaffir, Allan Turowetz, and Morton Weinfeld. 1983. *An Introduction to Sociology*. Toronto, ON: Methuen.

Rossides, Daniel W. 1968. *Society as a Functional Process: An Introduction to Sociology*. Toronto, ON: McGraw–Hill Ryerson.

Ryan, J. 1978. *Wall of Words: The Betrayal of the Urban Indian*. Toronto, ON: Peter Martin Associates.

Said, Edward. 1978. *Orientalism*, New York, NY: Pantheon.

Sampson, Edward E. 1971. *Social Psychology and Contemporary Society*. New York, NY: John Wiley & Sons.

Sanderson, Stephen K. 1988. *Macrosociology: An Introduction to Human Societies*. New York, NY: Harper and Row.

Satzewich, Vic, and Terry Wotherspoon. 1993. *First Nations: Race, Class and Gender Relations*. Toronto, ON: Nelson.

Schaefer, Richard T., Robert P. Lamm, Penny Biles, and Susannah J. Wilson. 1996. *Sociology: An Introduction: First Canadian Edition.* Toronto, ON: McGraw–Hill Ryerson.

Schmidt, John T. 1964. "Lo, the Poor, Irresponsible, Lazy Indian" (orig. *Saturday Night,* Nov. 21, 1955). In R. Laskin (Ed.), *Social Problems: A Canadian Profile.* Toronto, ON: McGraw–Hill.

Seeley, John, R.A. Sim, and E.W. Loosely. 1963. *Crestwood Heights: A Study of the Culture of Suburban Life.* New York, NY: Wiley & Sons.

Sharp, Henry S. 1995. "Asymmetric Equals: Women and Men among the Chipewyan." In Laura Klein and Lillian Ackerman (Eds.), *Women and Power in Native North America.* Norman, OK: University of Oklahoma Press.

Shkilnyk, Anastasia. 1985. *A Poison Stronger Than Love: The Destruction of an Ojibwa Community,* New Haven, CN: Yale University Press.

Sioui, Georges E. 1992. *For an Amerindian Autohistory: An Essay on the Foundations of a Social Ethic.* Montreal, QC and Kingston, ON: McGill–Queen's University Press.

Smelser, Neil J. 1962. *Theory of Collective Behavior.* New York, NY: Free Press of Glencoe.

Smith, Donald B. 1974. *Le Sauvage, The Native People in Quebec: Historical Writing on the Heroic Period (1534–1663) of New France.* Ottawa, ON: National Museums of Canada.

Smith, Dorothy. 1990. *The Conceptual Practices of Power: A Feminist Sociology of Knowledge.* Toronto, ON: University of Toronto Press.

Smith, Ronald, and Frederich W. Preston. 1977. *Sociology: An Introduction.* New York, NY: St. Martin's Press.

Spencer, Metta. 1976, 1979, 1981, 1982, 1985, 1990, 1993, and 1996. *Foundations of Modern Sociology,* Canadian ed. Scarborough, ON: Prentice Hall.

Spencer, Robert F. 1959. *The North Alaskan Eskimo: A Study in Ecology and Society.* Bulletin 171. Washington, DC: Smithsonian Institute Bureau of American Ethnology.

Spittal, William G. (Ed.). 1990. *Iroquois Women: An Anthology.* Ohsweken, ON: Irocrafts.

Spradley, James. 1969. *Guests Never Leave Hungry: The Autobiography of James Sewid, a Kwakiutl Indian.* New Haven, CT: Yale University Press.

Spradley, James W. and D.W. McCurdy. 1997. *Conformity and Conflict: Readings in Cultural Anthropology*, 9th ed. Boston: Little, Brown and Company.

Stark, Rodney. 1987. *Sociology.* Belmont, CA: Wadsworth.

Stebbins, Robert A. 1987. *Sociology: The Study of Society.* New York, NY: Harper and Row.

Steckley, John L. 1992. "Niagara: An Interpretation." *Arch Notes* 4: pp. 17–22.

_____. 1992. "Toronto: What Does It Mean?" *Arch Notes* 3: pp. 23–32.

_____. 1999. *Beyond Their Years: Five Native Women's Stories.* Toronto, ON: Canadian Scholars' Press.

Steckley, John, and Bryan Cummins. 2001. *Full Circle: Canada's First Nations.* Toronto, ON: Prentice Hall.

Steinmetz, S.R. 1964 (1894). "Suicide among Primitive Peoples." *American Anthropologist* 7 (January): (pp. 53–60). New York, NY: Klaus Reprint Company.

Stenning, Philip. 1996. *Police Governance in First Nations in Ontario.* Toronto, ON: Centre of Criminology, University of Toronto.

Stymeist, David. 1975. *Ethnics and Indians: Social Relations in a Northwestern Ontario Town.* Toronto, ON: Peter Martin Associates.

Such, Peter. 1973. *Riverrun*, Toronto, ON: Clarke Irwin.

Sumner, William Graham. 1934 (1906). *Folkways: A Study of the Sociological Importance of Usages, Manners, Customs, Mores and Morals.* Boston, MA: Ginn.

Teevan, James. 1982a, 1987, 1989, and 1995. *Basic Sociology: A Canadian Introduction.* Scarborough, ON: Prentice Hall.

_____. 1982b, 1986, 1988, and 1992. *Introduction to Sociology: A Canadian Focus.* Scarborough, ON: Prentice Hall.

Tepperman, Lorne, and James Curtis (Eds.). 1987. *Readings in Sociology: An Introduction.* Toronto, ON: McGraw-Hill Ryerson.

Tepperman, Lorne, and M. Rosenberg (Eds.). 1991, 1995 and 1998. *Macro/Micro: A Brief Introduction to Sociology*. Scarborough, ON: Prentice Hall.

Tester, F.J., and Peter Kulchyski. 1994. *Tammarniit (Mistakes): Inuit Relocation in the Eastern Arctic 1939–1963*. Vancouver, BC: University of British Columbia Press.

Thalbitzer, William. 1941. *The Amassalik Eskimo, Contributions to the Ethnology of the East Greenland Natives*, 2nd Part. Copenhagen, Denmark: C.A. Reitzels Forlag.

Tierney, William. 1994. "Cultural Citizenship and Educational Democracy." In W. Tierney (Ed.), *Building Communities of Difference: Higher Education in the Twenty First Century*. Westport, MA: Bergin and Garvey.

Tuhiwai Smith, Linda. 1999. *Decolonizing Methodologies: Research and Indigenous Peoples*. Dunedin, NZ: University of Otago Press.

Turner, Lucien. 1894. *Ethnology of the Ungava District, Hudson Bay Territory*. 11th Annual

Report, 1889–90. Washington, DC: Bureau of American Ethnology.

Valaskakis, Gail Guthrie. 2000. "Telling Our Stories: The Role, Development, and Future of Aboriginal Communications." In Marlene Brant Castellano, Lynne Davis, and Louise Lahache (Eds.), *Aboriginal Education: Fulfilling the Promise*. Vancouver, BC: University of British Columbia Press.

Vallee, Frank G. 1962. *Kabloona and Eskimo in the Central Keewatin*. Ottawa, ON: Northern Coordination and Research Centre, Department of Northern Affairs and National Resources.

Vanderburgh, Rosamond M. 1987. "Modernization and Aging in the Anicinabe Context." In V.W. Marshal (Ed.), *Aging in Canada: Social Perspectives*, 2nd ed. (pp. 100–10). Markham, ON: Fitzhenry and Whiteside.

Veblen, Thorstein. 1912 (1899). *The Theory of the Leisure Class*. New York, NY: Macmillan.

Wagamese, Richard. 1996. *The Terrible Summer*. Toronto, ON: Warwick Publishing.

_____. 1998. "Reconstructing Aboriginal History." *Windspeaker* (July). www.ammsa.com/windspeaker.

Ward, Margaret. 2002. *The Family Dynamic: A Canadian Perspective*, 3rd ed. Toronto, ON: Nelson Thomson Learning.

Warme, Barbara, Elinor Malus, and Katherina Lundy. 1994. *Sociology: A Window on the World*. Toronto, ON: Methuen.

Webster, Gloria. 1993. [Video 3]. "Potlatch." *First Nations: The Circle Unbroken*. Montreal, QC: National Film Board.

Webster, Gloria Cranmer. 1996. "Kwakiutl." In Frederick Hoxie (Ed.), *Encyclopedia of North American Indians* (pp. 320–22). New York, NY: Houghton Mifflin.

Webster's Third New International Dictionary of the English Language. 1981. Philip Gove (Ed.). Springfield, MA: Merriam-Webster.

Welch, Sharon. 1990. A Feminist Ethic of Risk. Minneapolis, MN, Fortress Press.

Westhues, Kenneth. 1982. *First Sociology*. Toronto, ON: McGraw-Hill Ryerson.

Weyer, Edward M. 1962 (1932). *The Eskimos: Their Environment and Folkways*. Hamden, CT: Archon Books.

Wilson, Stand, and Peggy Wilson. 1998. "Relational Accountability to All Our Relations." *Canadian Journal of Native Education* (July).

Woodbury, Hanni, Reg Henry, and Harry Webster. 1992. *Concerning the League: The Iroquois League Tradition as Dictated in Onondaga by John Arthur Gibson*. Memoir 9. Winnipeg, MB: Algonquian and Iroquoian Linguistics.

Wuttunee, William. 1971. *Ruffled Feathers: Indians in Canadian Society*. Calgary, AB: Bell Books.

York, Geoffrey, and Loreen Pindera. 1991. *People of the Pines: The Warriors and the Legacy of Oka*. Toronto, ON: Little Brown and Company.

Zeitlin, Irving M., with Robert J. Brym. 1991. *The Social Condition of Humanity: Canadian Edition*. Toronto, ON: Oxford University Press.

Selected Websites

www.ammsa.com/windspeaker
www.constitution.org/cons/iroquois/txt
www.easterndoor.com/Archives
www.envirowatch.org/gndvst.htm
www.indiancountry.com
www.kahnawake.com/peacekeepers/past.htm
www.schoolnet.ca/aboriginal/umista2/potlatch-e.html
www.wampumchronicles.com/bordercrossing.html

Index of
Aboriginal Voices

Index of Canadian Introductory Sociology Textbooks
(by Author/Editor names)

General Index